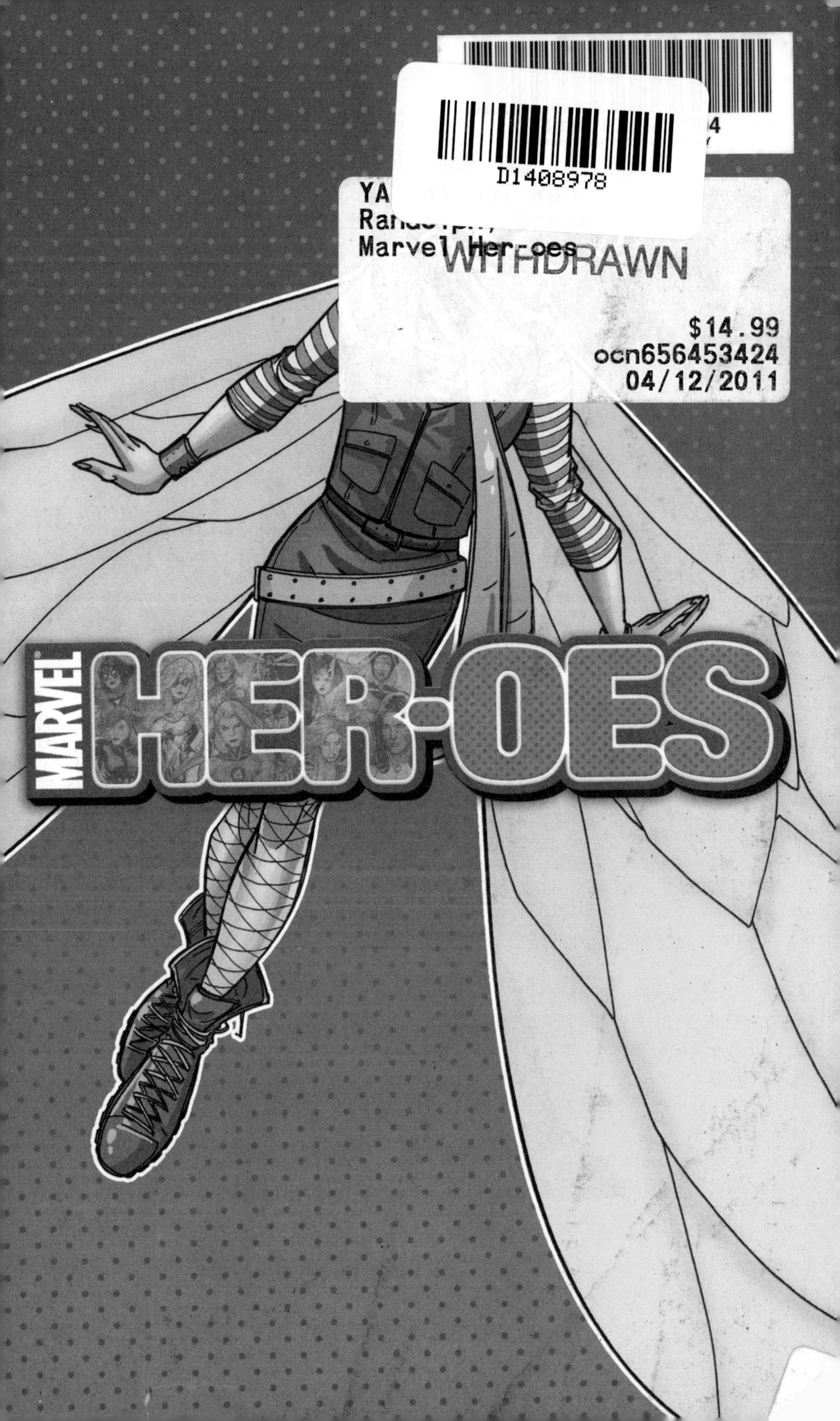
MARVEL
HER-OES

WRITER: GRACE RANDOLPH
ARTIST: CRAIG ROUSSEAU

COLORIST: VERONICA GANDINI

LETTERER: FISHBRAIN

COVERS: CRAIG ROUSSEAU & GURIHIRU (ISSUE #1) AND SARA PICHELLI & VERONICA GANDINI (ISSUES #2-4)

SUPERVISING EDITOR: NATHAN COSBY

EDITOR: SANA AMANAT

SAVAGE SHE-HULK #1

WRITER: STAN LEE

PENCILER: JOHN BUSCEMA

INKER: CHIC STONE

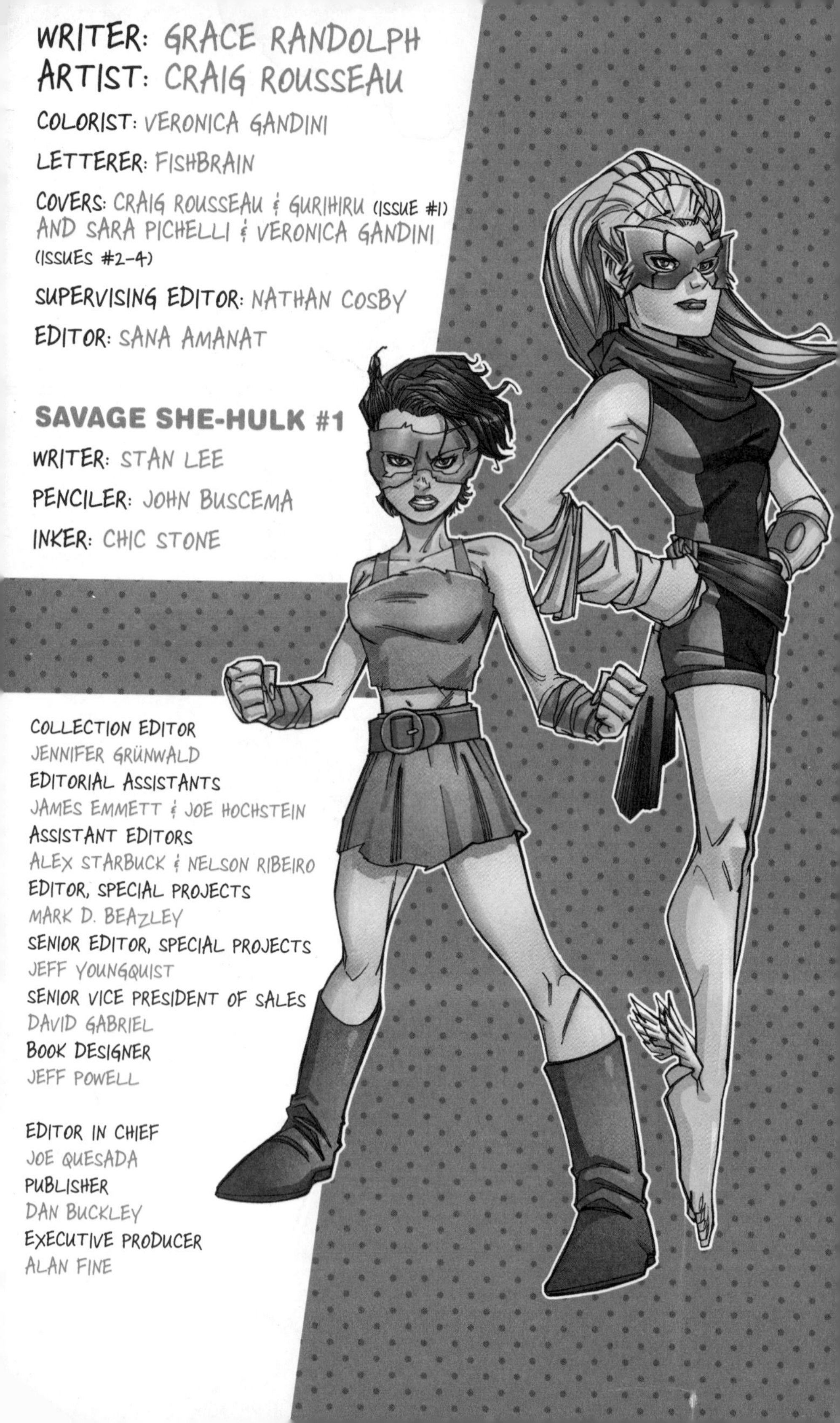

COLLECTION EDITOR
JENNIFER GRÜNWALD
EDITORIAL ASSISTANTS
JAMES EMMETT & JOE HOCHSTEIN
ASSISTANT EDITORS
ALEX STARBUCK & NELSON RIBEIRO
EDITOR, SPECIAL PROJECTS
MARK D. BEAZLEY
SENIOR EDITOR, SPECIAL PROJECTS
JEFF YOUNGQUIST
SENIOR VICE PRESIDENT OF SALES
DAVID GABRIEL
BOOK DESIGNER
JEFF POWELL

EDITOR IN CHIEF
JOE QUESADA
PUBLISHER
DAN BUCKLEY
EXECUTIVE PRODUCER
ALAN FINE

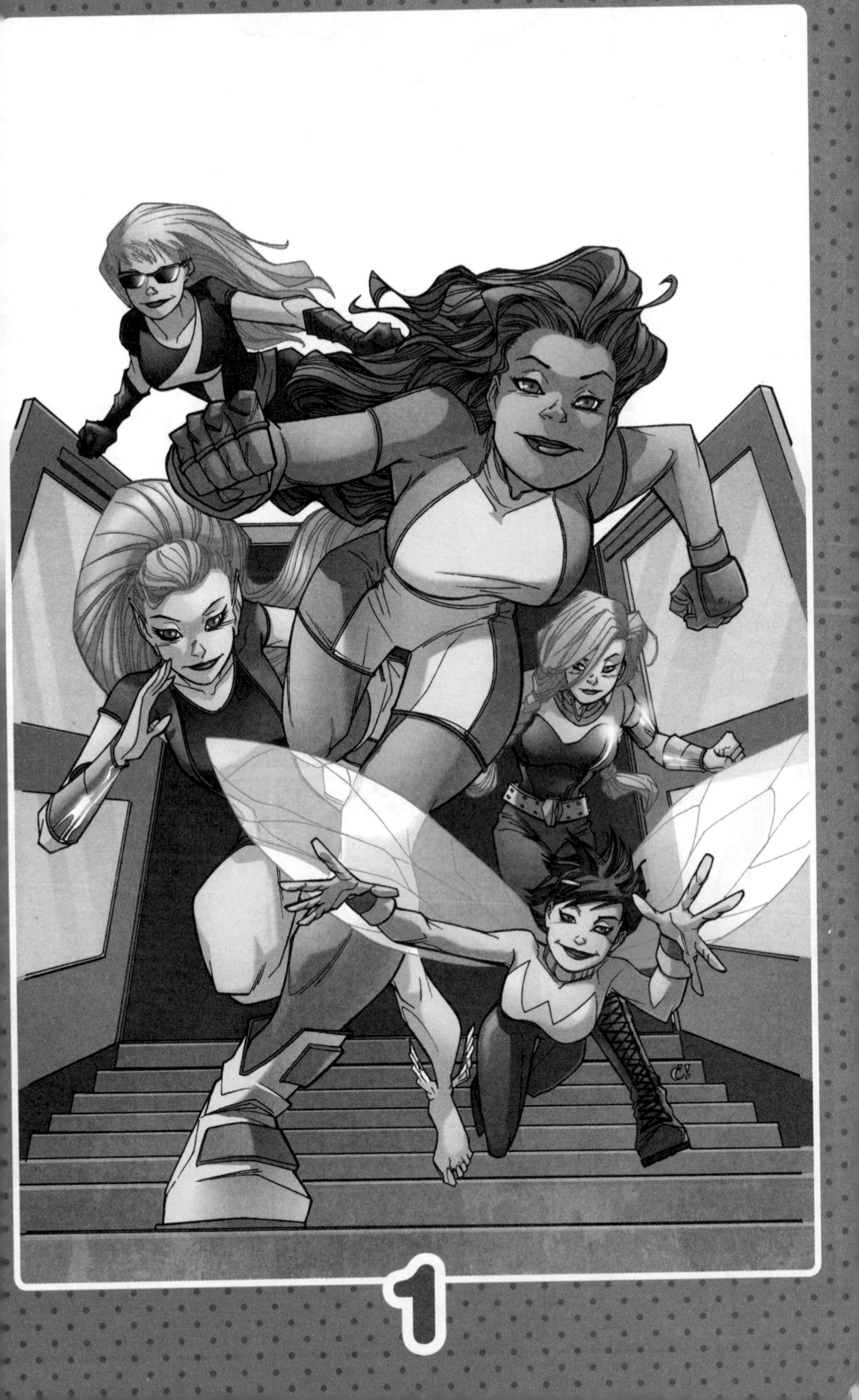

1

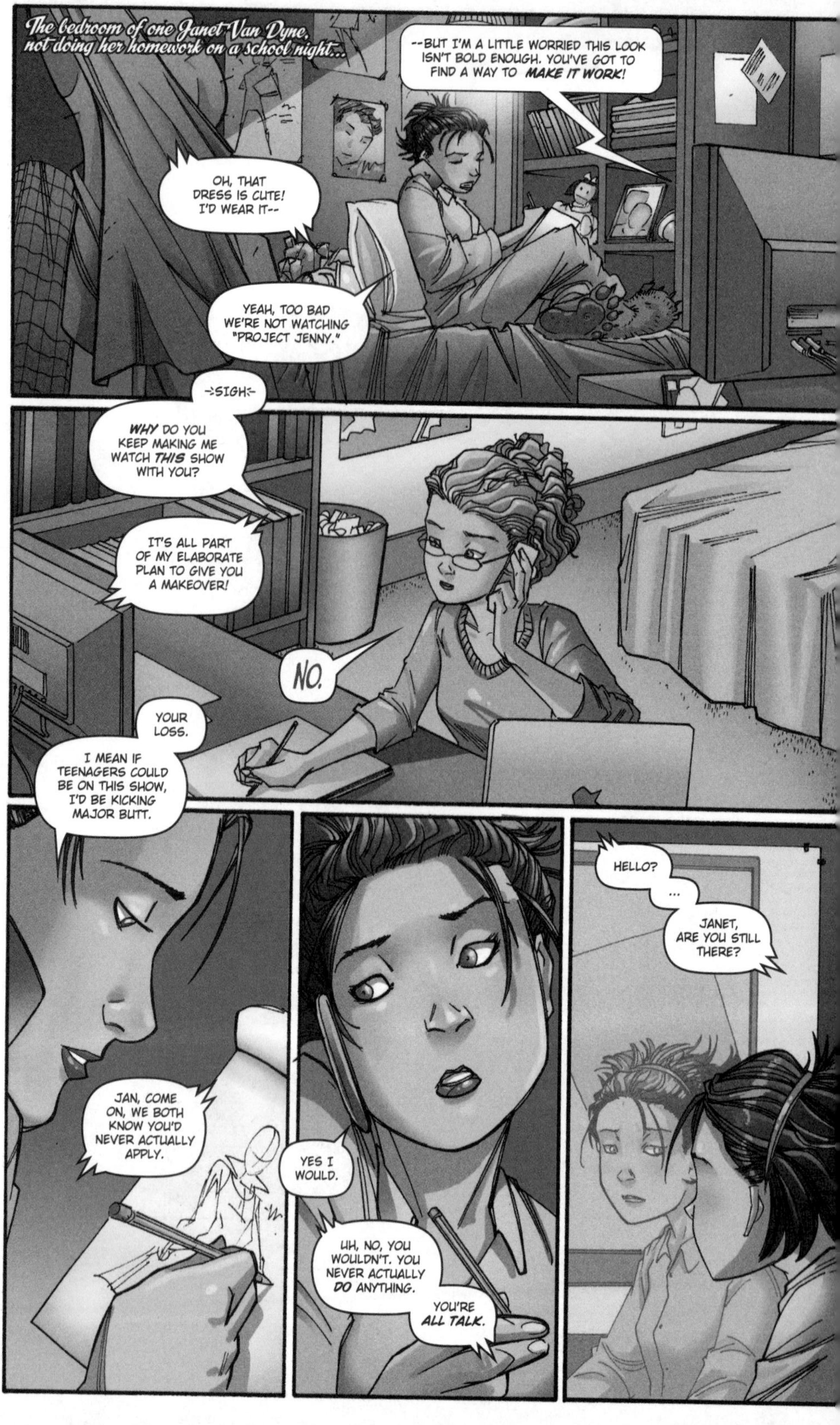
The bedroom of one Janet Van Dyne, not doing her homework on a school night...
--BUT I'M A LITTLE WORRIED THIS LOOK ISN'T BOLD ENOUGH. YOU'VE GOT TO FIND A WAY TO MAKE IT WORK!
OH, THAT DRESS IS CUTE! I'D WEAR IT--
YEAH, TOO BAD WE'RE NOT WATCHING "PROJECT JENNY."
-SIGH-
WHY DO YOU KEEP MAKING ME WATCH THIS SHOW WITH YOU?
IT'S ALL PART OF MY ELABORATE PLAN TO GIVE YOU A MAKEOVER!
NO.
YOUR LOSS.
I MEAN IF TEENAGERS COULD BE ON THIS SHOW, I'D BE KICKING MAJOR BUTT.
JAN, COME ON, WE BOTH KNOW YOU'D NEVER ACTUALLY APPLY.
YES I WOULD.
UH, NO, YOU WOULDN'T. YOU NEVER ACTUALLY DO ANYTHING.
YOU'RE ALL TALK.
HELLO?
...
JANET, ARE YOU STILL THERE?

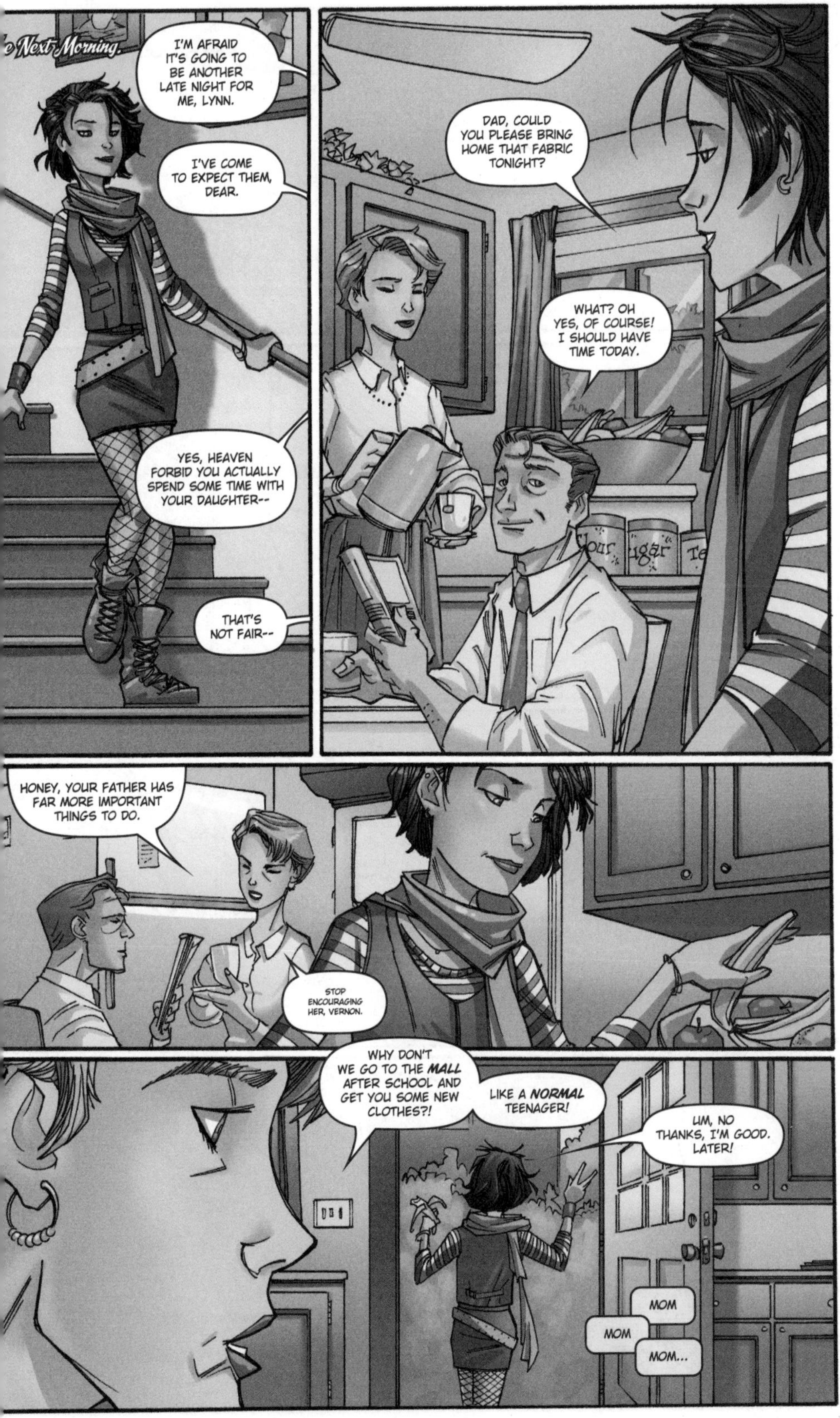
e Next Morning.
I'M AFRAID IT'S GOING TO BE ANOTHER LATE NIGHT FOR ME, LYNN.
I'VE COME TO EXPECT THEM, DEAR.
YES, HEAVEN FORBID YOU ACTUALLY SPEND SOME TIME WITH YOUR DAUGHTER--
THAT'S NOT FAIR--
DAD, COULD YOU PLEASE BRING HOME THAT FABRIC TONIGHT?
WHAT? OH YES, OF COURSE! I SHOULD HAVE TIME TODAY.
Flour
Sugar
Te
HONEY, YOUR FATHER HAS FAR MORE IMPORTANT THINGS TO DO.
STOP ENCOURAGING HER, VERNON.
WHY DON'T WE GO TO THE ***MALL*** AFTER SCHOOL AND GET YOU SOME NEW CLOTHES?!
LIKE A ***NORMAL*** TEENAGER!
UM, NO THANKS, I'M GOOD. LATER!
MOM
MOM
MOM...

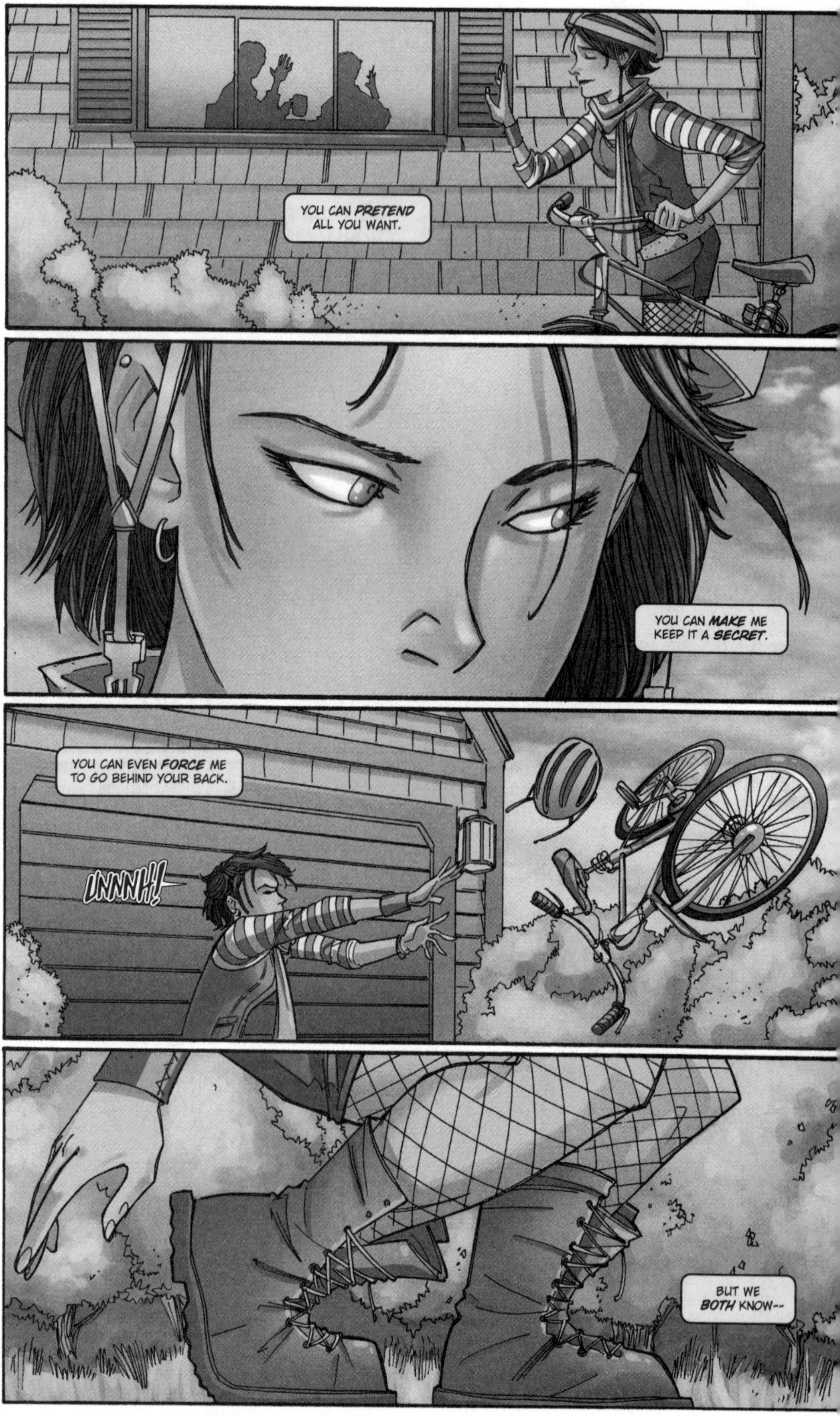
YOU CAN PRETEND ALL YOU WANT.
YOU CAN MAKE ME KEEP IT A SECRET.
YOU CAN EVEN FORCE ME TO GO BEHIND YOUR BACK.
UNNNH!
BUT WE BOTH KNOW--

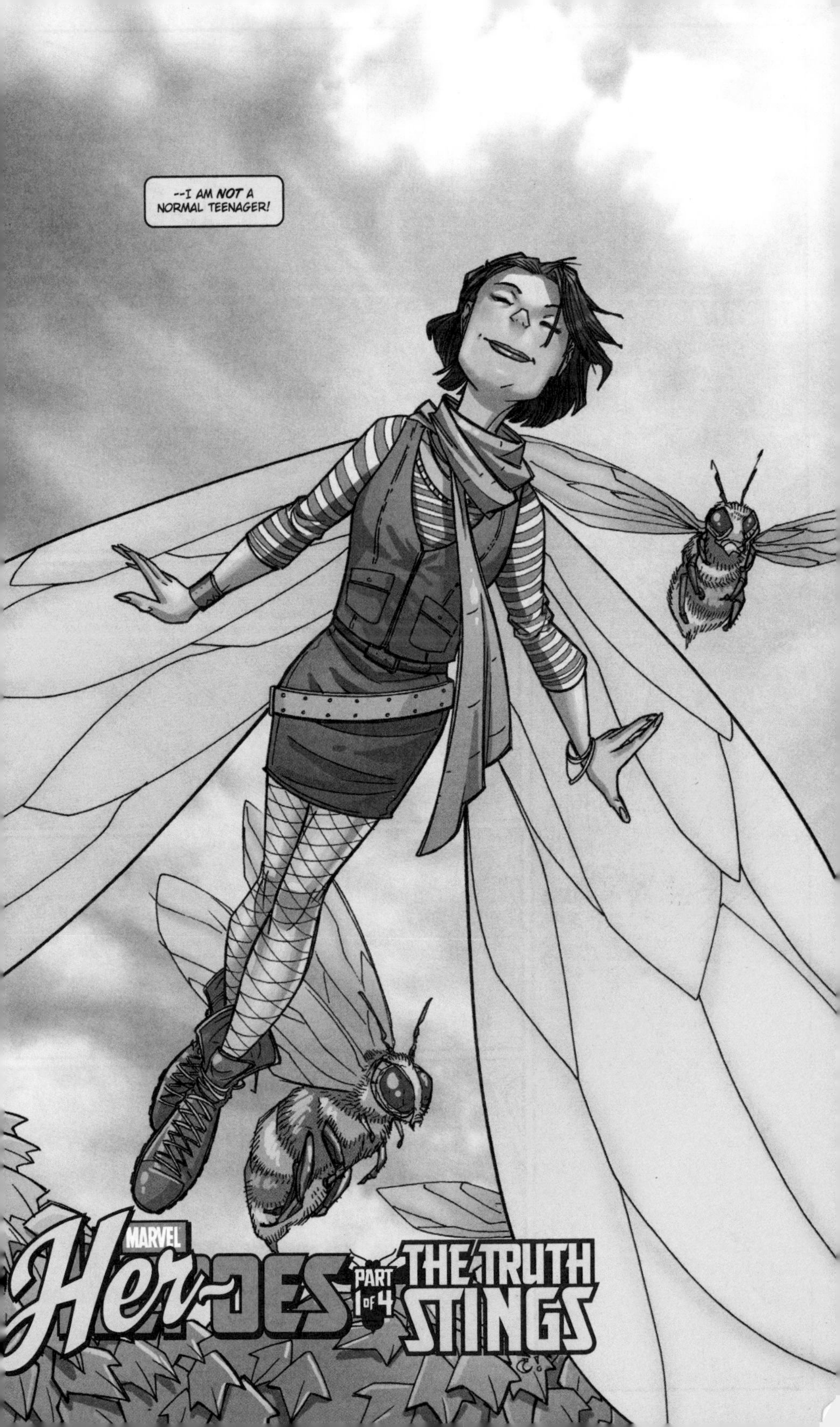
--I AM NOT A NORMAL TEENAGER!
MARVEL
Her-OES
PART 1 OF 4
THE TRUTH STINGS

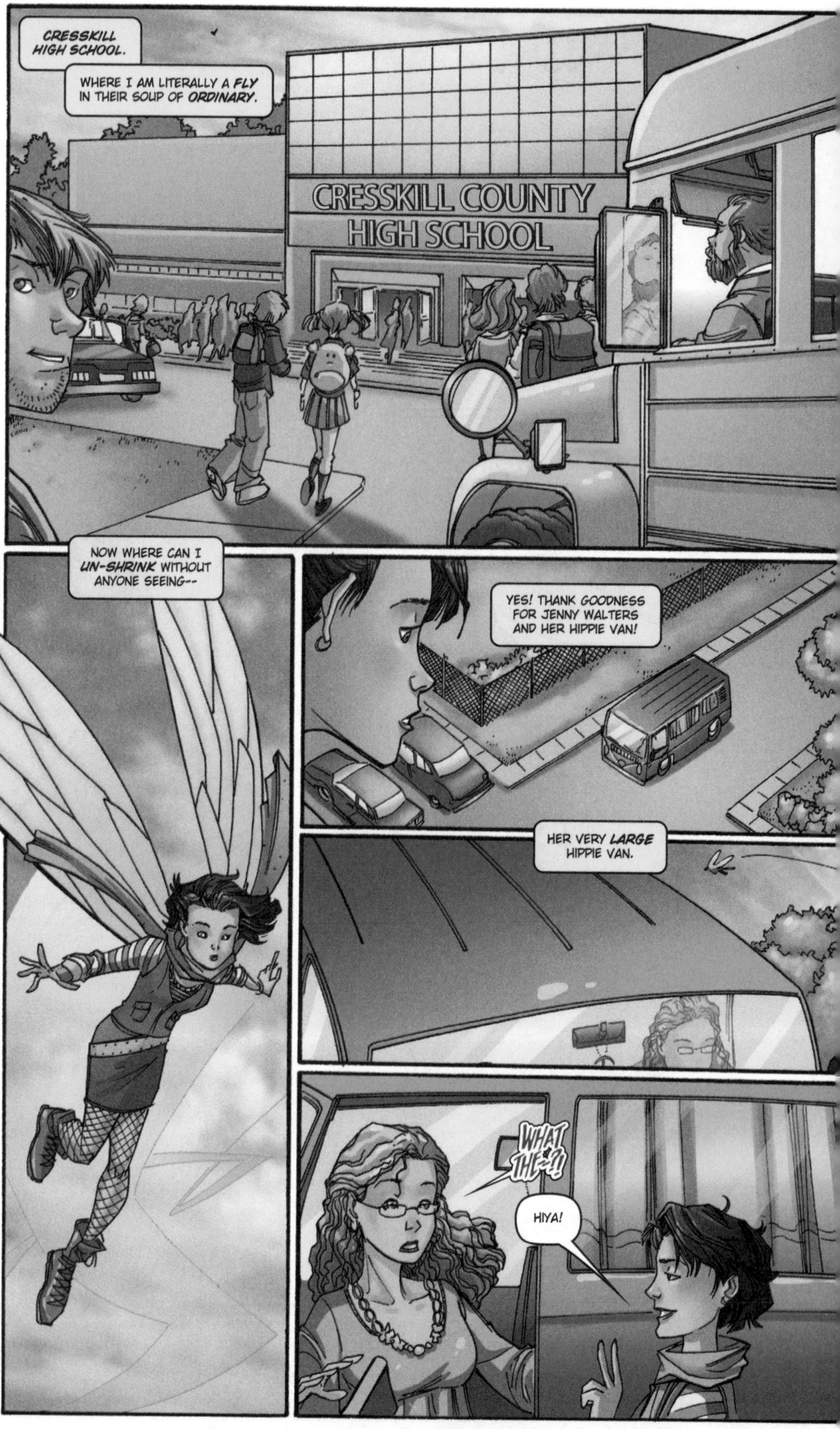
CRESSKILL HIGH SCHOOL.
WHERE I AM LITERALLY A FLY IN THEIR SOUP OF ORDINARY.
CRESSKILL COUNTY HIGH SCHOOL
NOW WHERE CAN I UN-SHRINK WITHOUT ANYONE SEEING--
YES! THANK GOODNESS FOR JENNY WALTERS AND HER HIPPIE VAN!
HER VERY LARGE HIPPIE VAN.
WHAT THE--?!
HIYA!

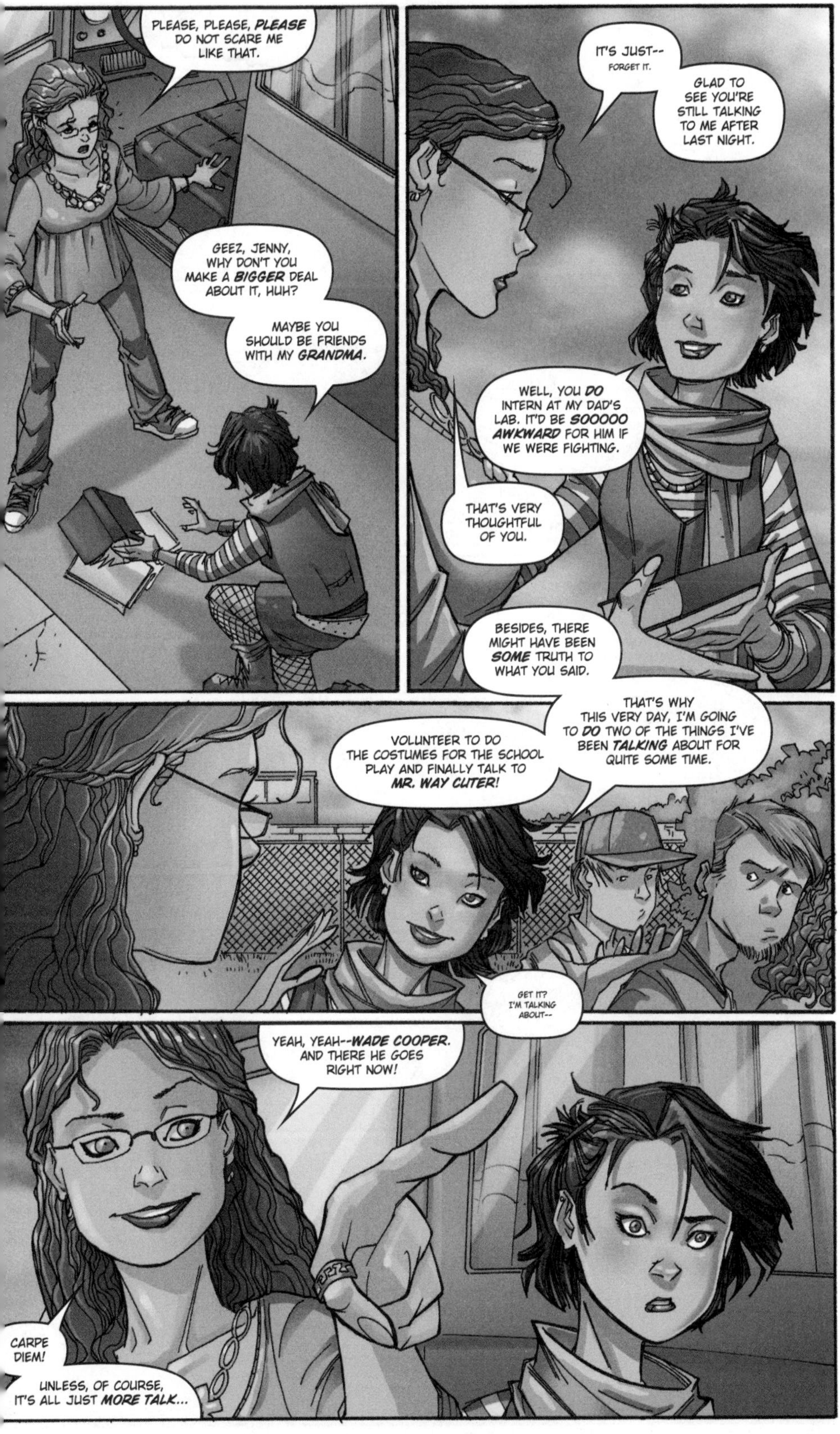
PLEASE, PLEASE, PLEASE DO NOT SCARE ME LIKE THAT.
GEEZ, JENNY, WHY DON'T YOU MAKE A BIGGER DEAL ABOUT IT, HUH?
MAYBE YOU SHOULD BE FRIENDS WITH MY GRANDMA.
IT'S JUST-- FORGET IT.
GLAD TO SEE YOU'RE STILL TALKING TO ME AFTER LAST NIGHT.
WELL, YOU DO INTERN AT MY DAD'S LAB. IT'D BE SOOOOO AWKWARD FOR HIM IF WE WERE FIGHTING.
THAT'S VERY THOUGHTFUL OF YOU.
BESIDES, THERE MIGHT HAVE BEEN SOME TRUTH TO WHAT YOU SAID.
THAT'S WHY THIS VERY DAY, I'M GOING TO DO TWO OF THE THINGS I'VE BEEN TALKING ABOUT FOR QUITE SOME TIME.
VOLUNTEER TO DO THE COSTUMES FOR THE SCHOOL PLAY AND FINALLY TALK TO MR. WAY CUTER!
GET IT? I'M TALKING ABOUT--
YEAH, YEAH--WADE COOPER. AND THERE HE GOES RIGHT NOW!
CARPE DIEM!
UNLESS, OF COURSE, IT'S ALL JUST MORE TALK...

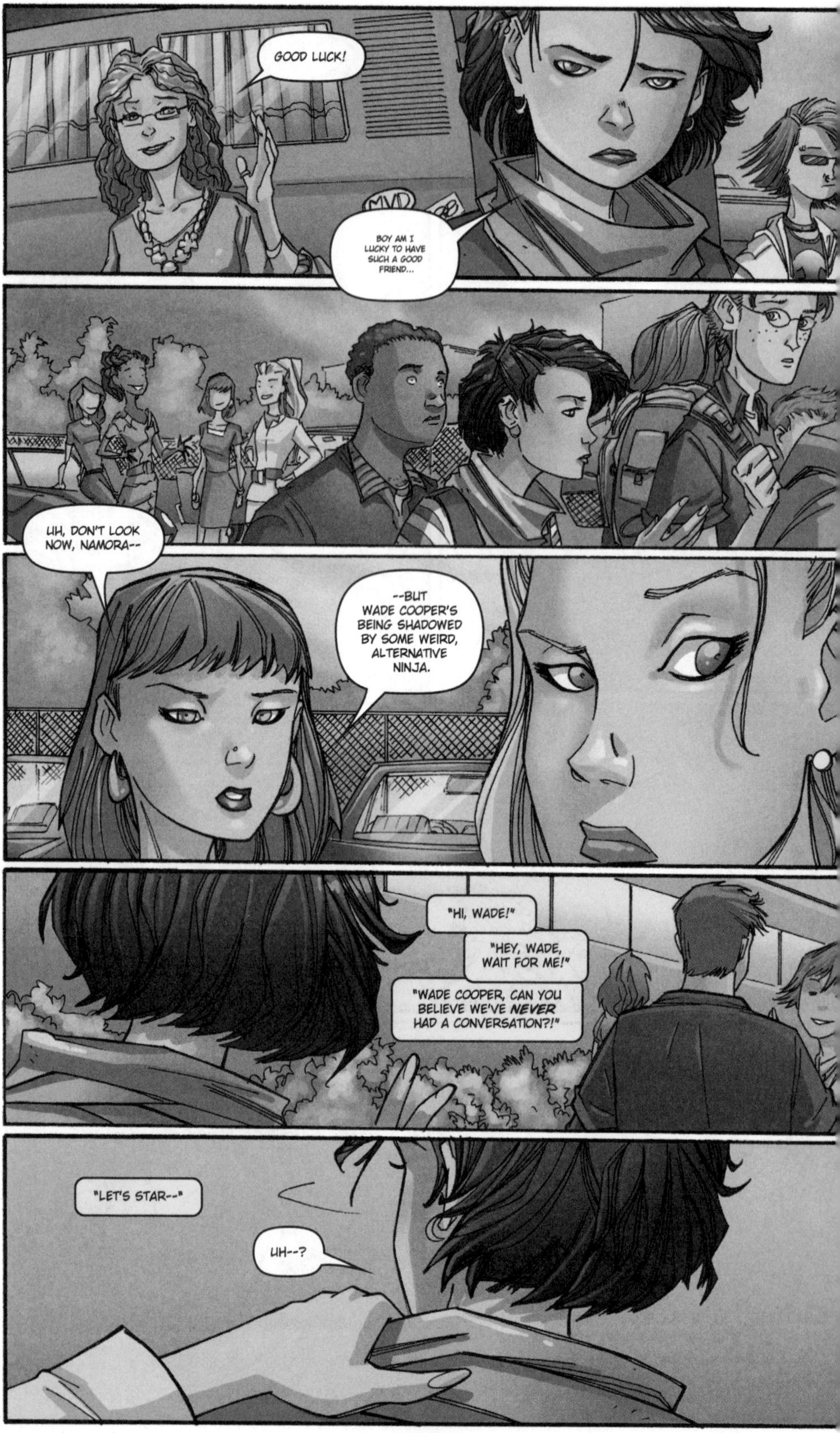
GOOD LUCK!
BOY AM I LUCKY TO HAVE SUCH A GOOD FRIEND...
UH, DON'T LOOK NOW, NAMORA--
--BUT WADE COOPER'S BEING SHADOWED BY SOME WEIRD, ALTERNATIVE NINJA.
"HI, WADE!"
"HEY, WADE, WAIT FOR ME!"
"WADE COOPER, CAN YOU BELIEVE WE'VE *NEVER* HAD A CONVERSATION?!"
"LET'S STAR--"
UH--?

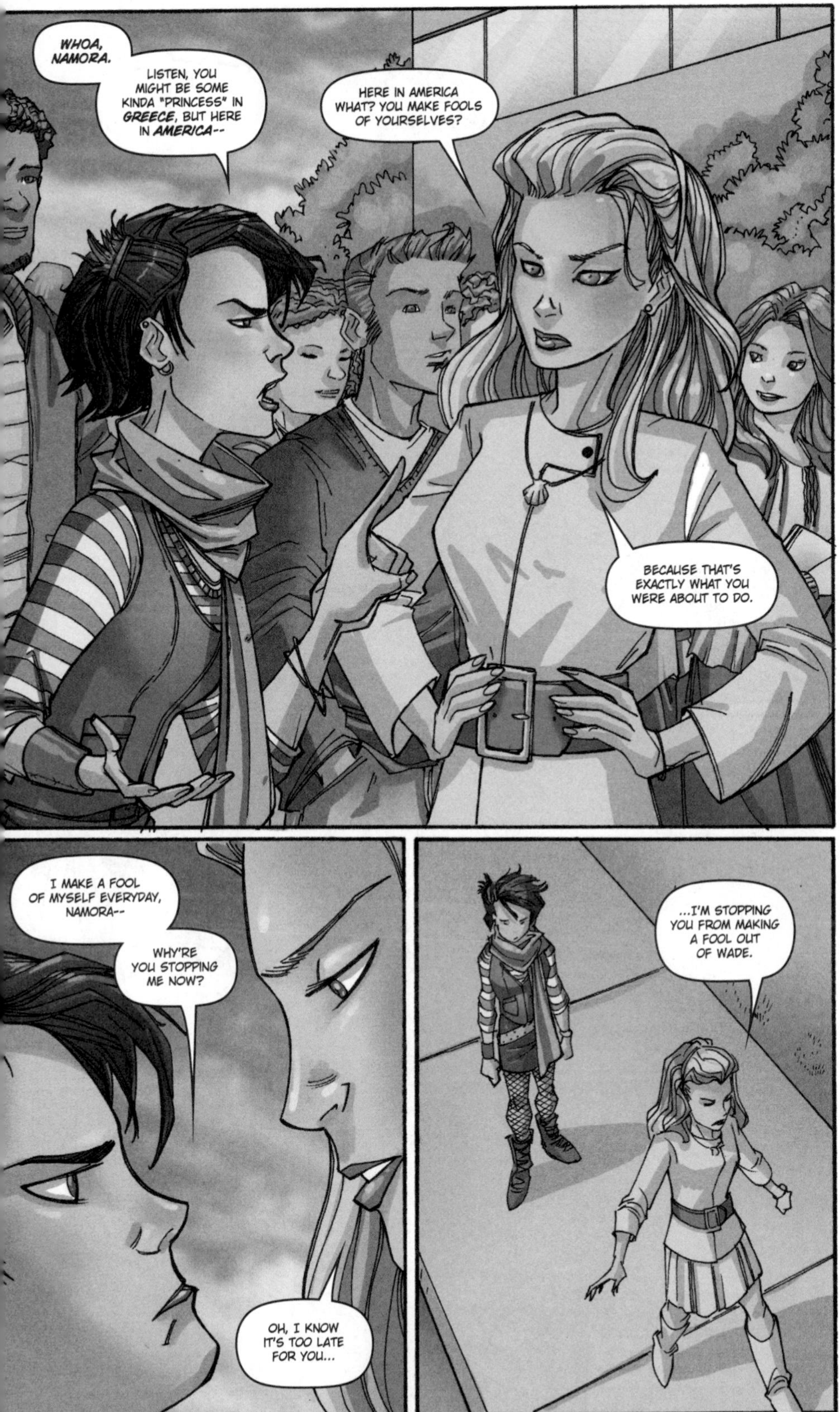

WHOA, NAMORA.
LISTEN, YOU MIGHT BE SOME KINDA "PRINCESS" IN GREECE, BUT HERE IN AMERICA--
HERE IN AMERICA WHAT? YOU MAKE FOOLS OF YOURSELVES?
BECAUSE THAT'S EXACTLY WHAT YOU WERE ABOUT TO DO.
I MAKE A FOOL OF MYSELF EVERYDAY, NAMORA--
WHY'RE YOU STOPPING ME NOW?
OH, I KNOW IT'S TOO LATE FOR YOU...
...I'M STOPPING YOU FROM MAKING A FOOL OUT OF WADE.

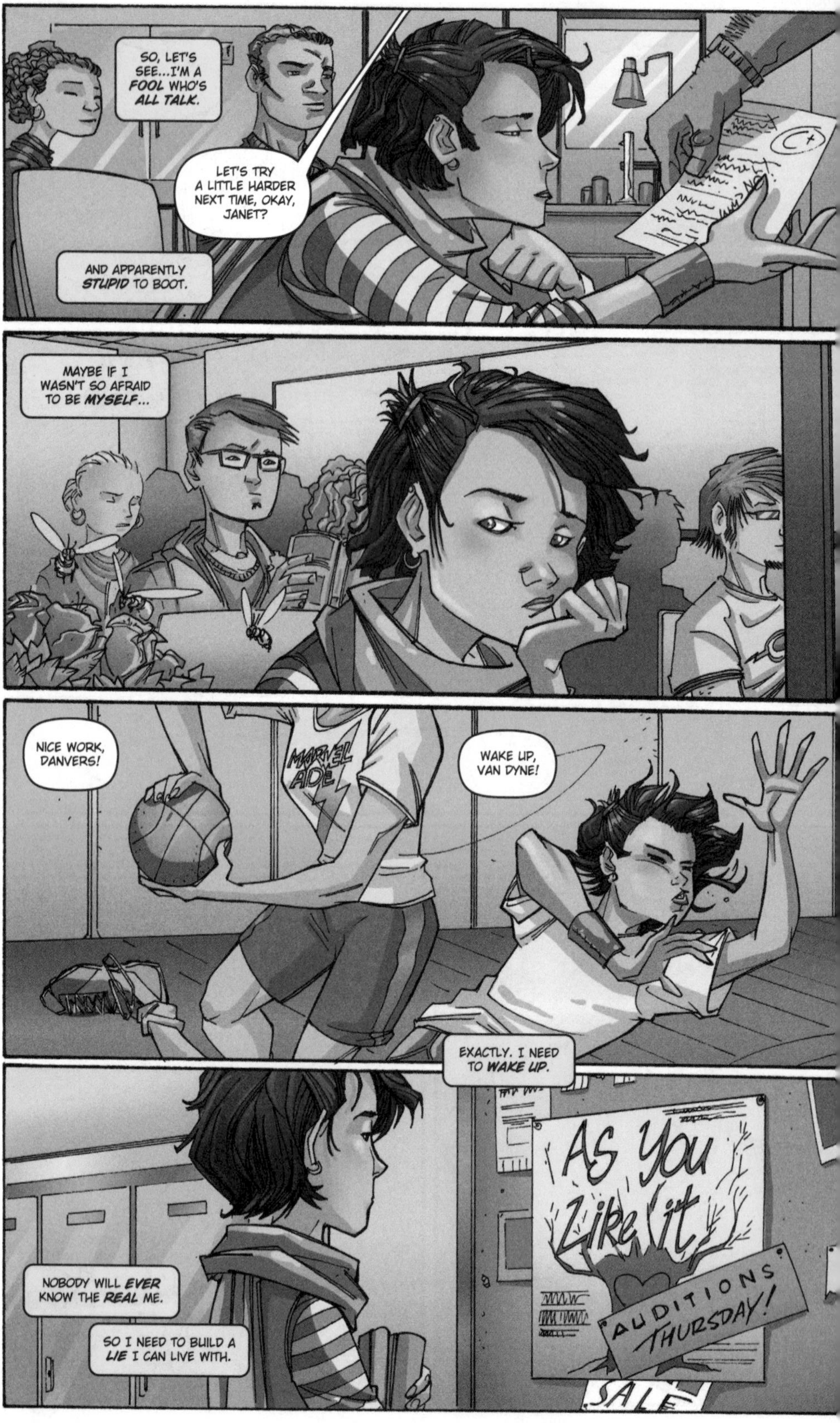
SO, LET'S SEE...I'M A FOOL WHO'S ALL TALK.
LET'S TRY A LITTLE HARDER NEXT TIME, OKAY, JANET?
AND APPARENTLY STUPID TO BOOT.
MAYBE IF I WASN'T SO AFRAID TO BE MYSELF...
NICE WORK, DANVERS!
MARVEL ADE
WAKE UP, VAN DYNE!
EXACTLY. I NEED TO WAKE UP.
As You Like it
AUDITIONS THURSDAY!
NOBODY WILL EVER KNOW THE REAL ME.
SO I NEED TO BUILD A LIE I CAN LIVE WITH.
SALE

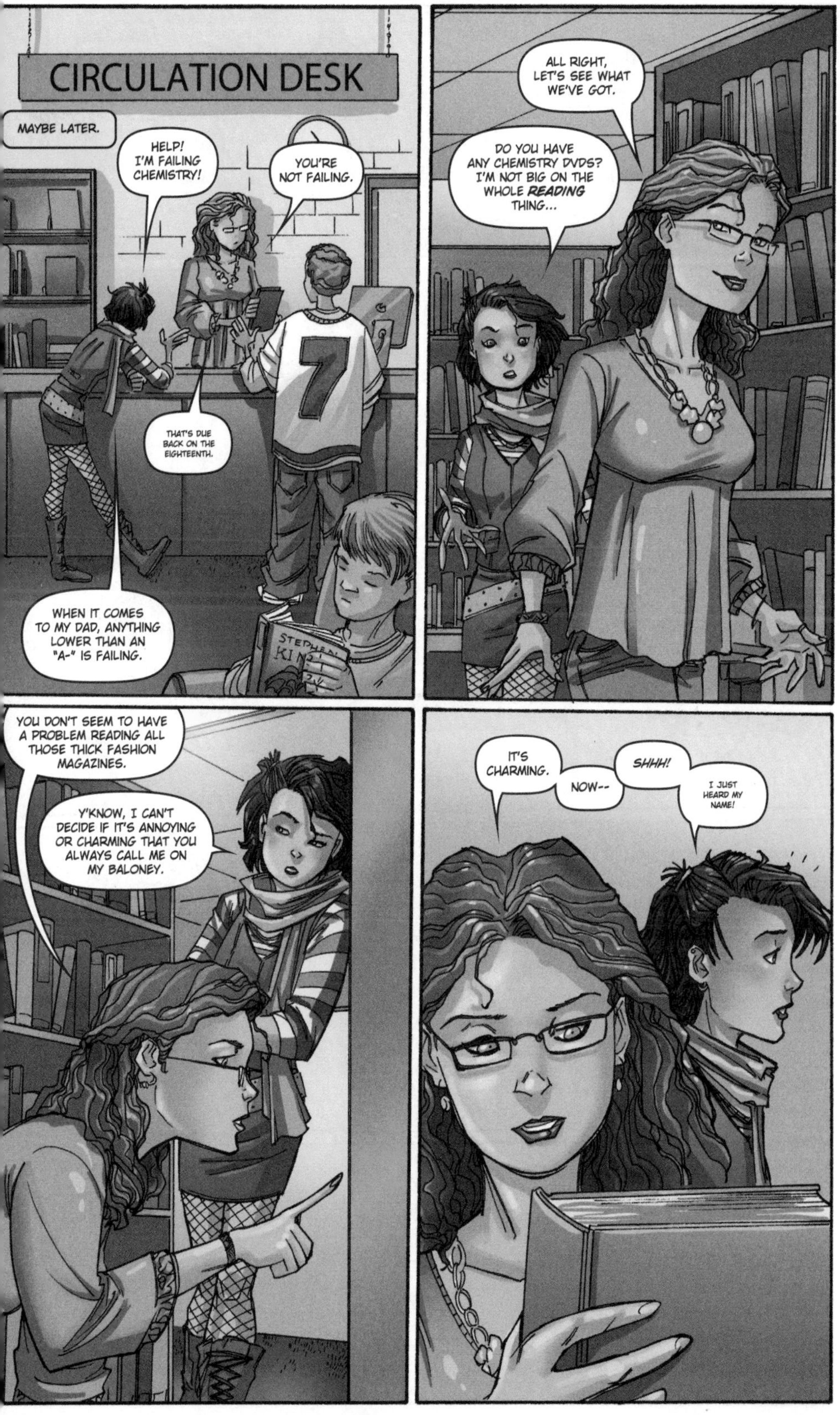
CIRCULATION DESK
MAYBE LATER.
HELP! I'M FAILING CHEMISTRY!
YOU'RE NOT FAILING.
THAT'S DUE BACK ON THE EIGHTEENTH.
WHEN IT COMES TO MY DAD, ANYTHING LOWER THAN AN "A-" IS FAILING.
ALL RIGHT, LET'S SEE WHAT WE'VE GOT.
DO YOU HAVE ANY CHEMISTRY DVDS? I'M NOT BIG ON THE WHOLE *READING* THING...
YOU DON'T SEEM TO HAVE A PROBLEM READING ALL THOSE THICK FASHION MAGAZINES.
Y'KNOW, I CAN'T DECIDE IF IT'S ANNOYING OR CHARMING THAT YOU ALWAYS CALL ME ON MY BALONEY.
IT'S CHARMING.
NOW--
SHHH!
I JUST HEARD MY NAME!

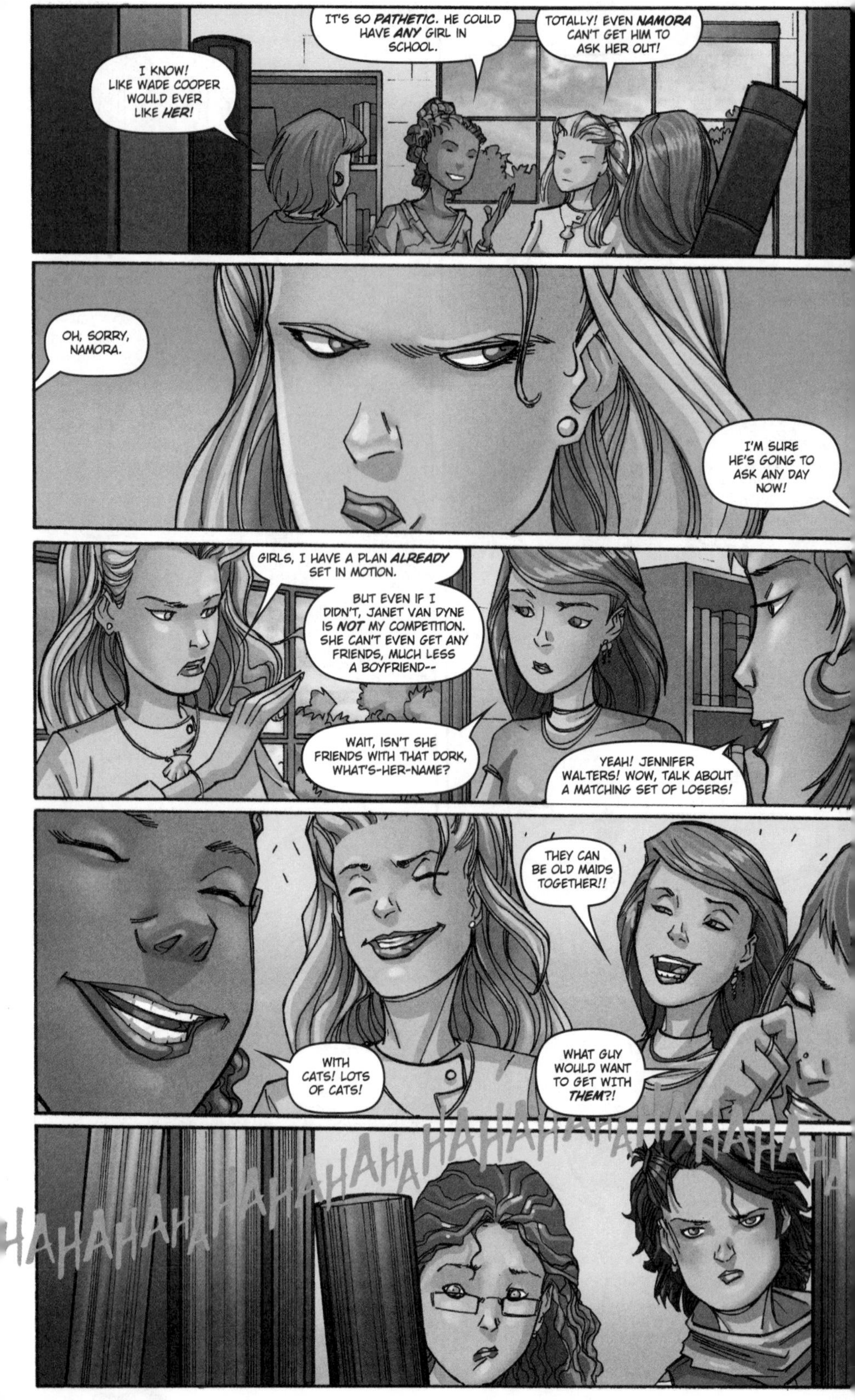
I KNOW! LIKE WADE COOPER WOULD EVER LIKE *HER*!
IT'S SO *PATHETIC*. HE COULD HAVE *ANY* GIRL IN SCHOOL.
TOTALLY! EVEN *NAMORA* CAN'T GET HIM TO ASK HER OUT!
OH, SORRY, NAMORA.
I'M SURE HE'S GOING TO ASK ANY DAY NOW!
GIRLS, I HAVE A PLAN *ALREADY* SET IN MOTION.
BUT EVEN IF I DIDN'T, JANET VAN DYNE IS *NOT* MY COMPETITION. SHE CAN'T EVEN GET ANY FRIENDS, MUCH LESS A BOYFRIEND--
WAIT, ISN'T SHE FRIENDS WITH THAT DORK, WHAT'S-HER-NAME?
YEAH! JENNIFER WALTERS! WOW, TALK ABOUT A MATCHING SET OF LOSERS!
THEY CAN BE OLD MAIDS TOGETHER!!
WITH CATS! LOTS OF CATS!
WHAT GUY WOULD WANT TO GET WITH *THEM*?!
HAHAHAHAHAHAHAHAHAHAHAHAHAHAHAHAHA

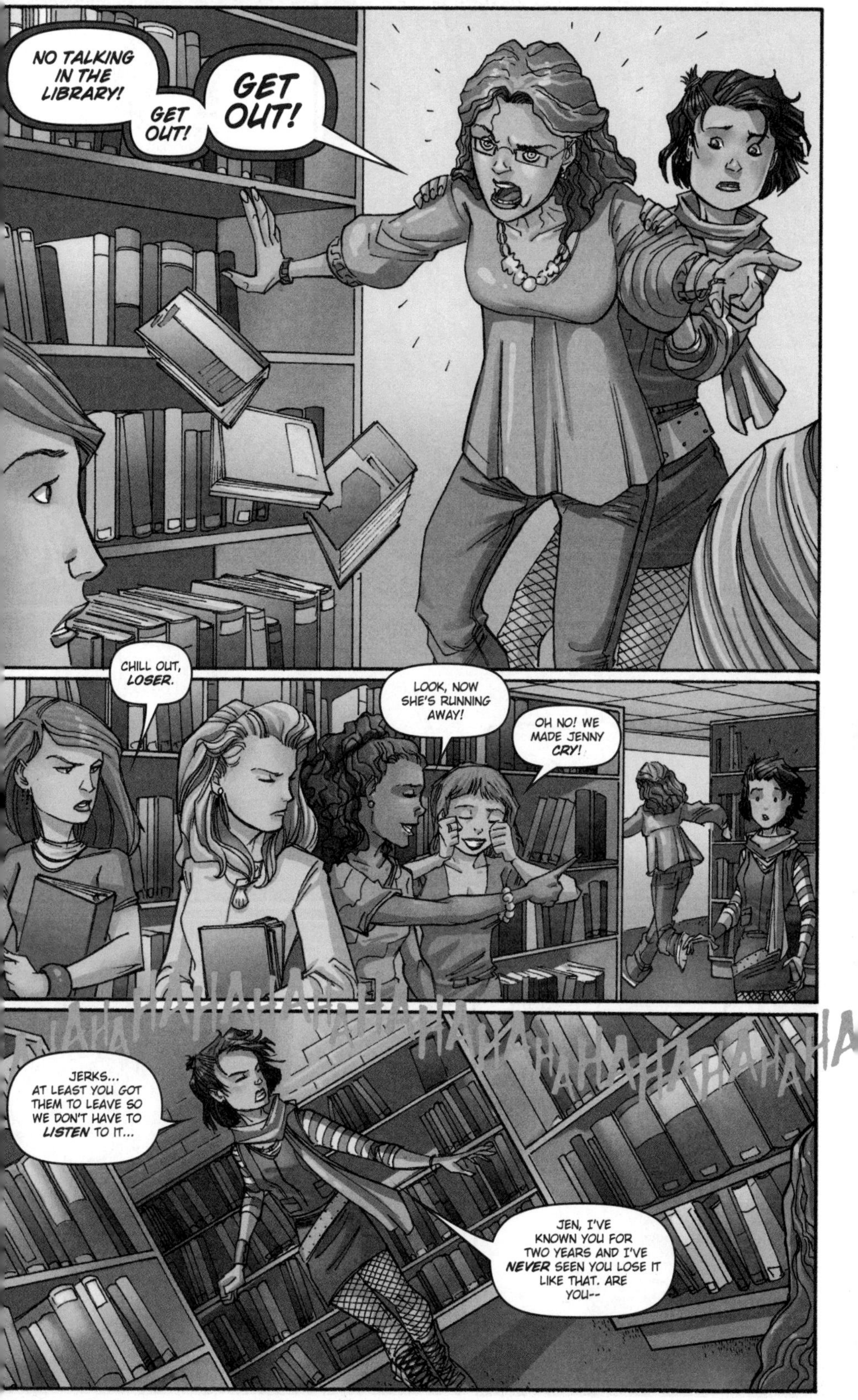
NO TALKING IN THE LIBRARY!
GET OUT!
GET OUT!
CHILL OUT, LOSER.
LOOK, NOW SHE'S RUNNING AWAY!
OH NO! WE MADE JENNY CRY!
HAHAHAHAHAHAHAHAHAHAHAHAHAHAHA
JERKS... AT LEAST YOU GOT THEM TO LEAVE SO WE DON'T HAVE TO LISTEN TO IT...
JEN, I'VE KNOWN YOU FOR TWO YEARS AND I'VE NEVER SEEN YOU LOSE IT LIKE THAT. ARE YOU--

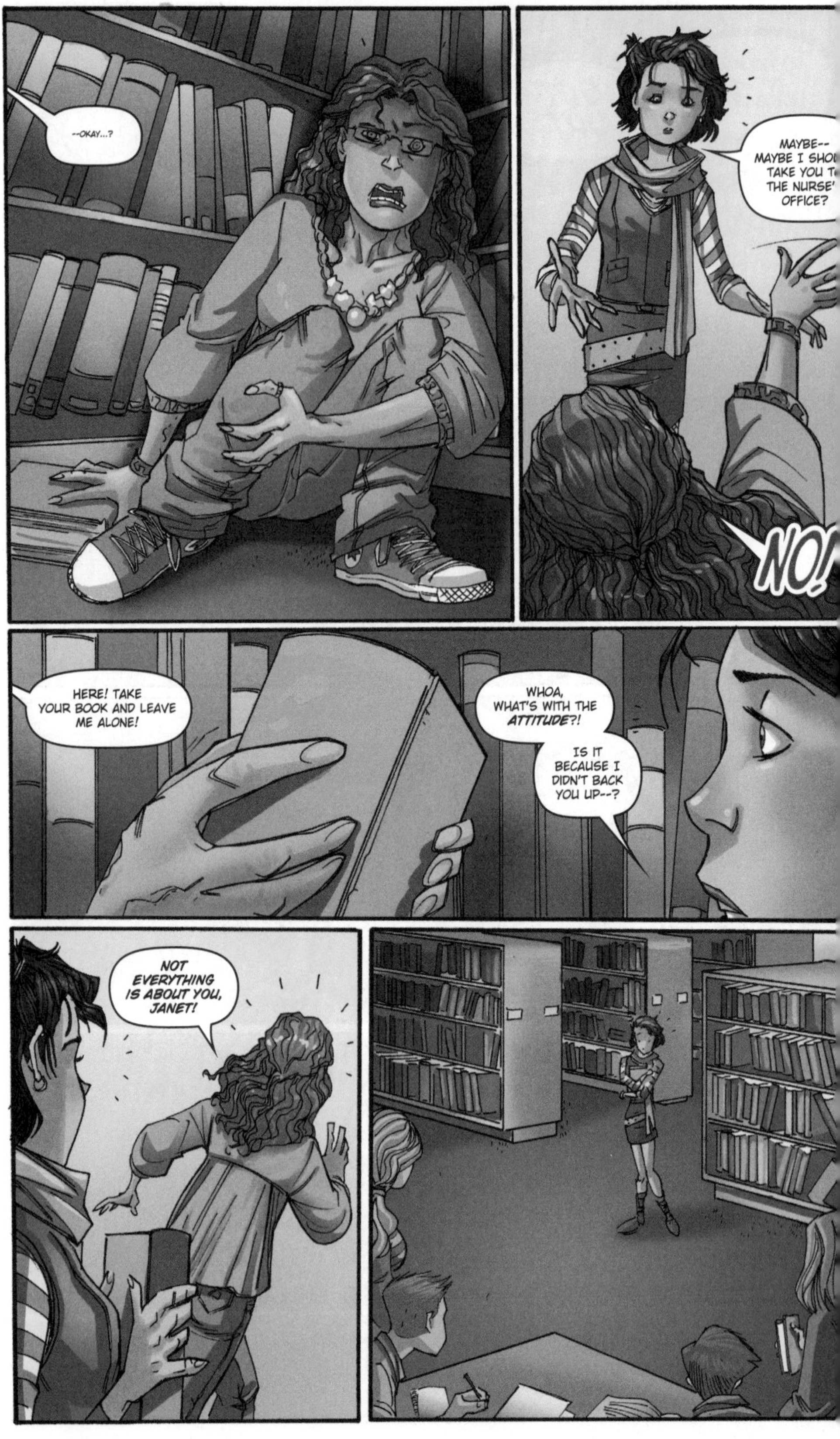
--OKAY...?
MAYBE--
MAYBE I SHO
TAKE YOU T
THE NURSE'
OFFICE?
NO!
HERE! TAKE
YOUR BOOK AND LEAVE
ME ALONE!
WHOA,
WHAT'S WITH THE
ATTITUDE?!
IS IT
BECAUSE I
DIDN'T BACK
YOU UP--?
NOT
EVERYTHING
IS ABOUT YOU,
JANET!

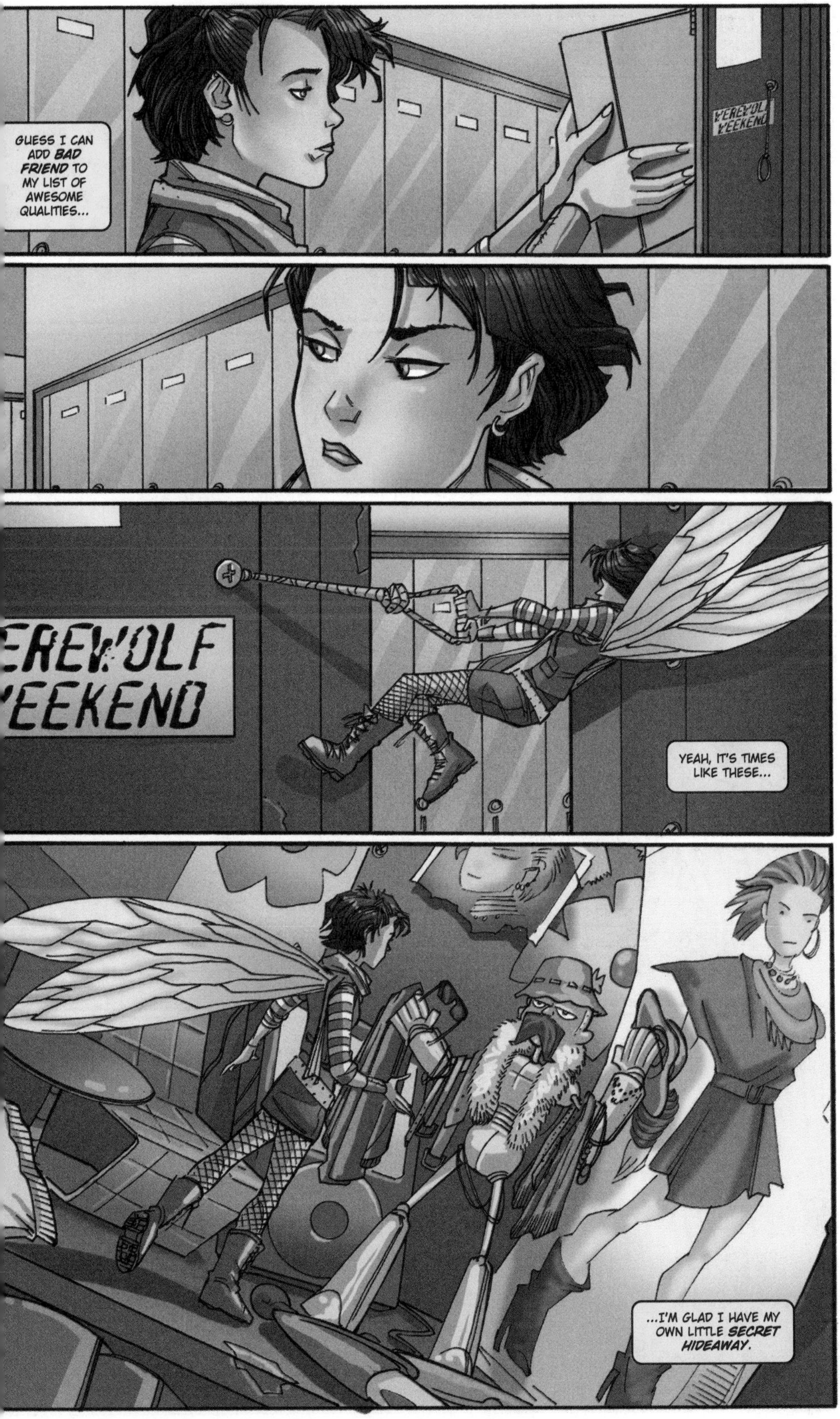
GUESS I CAN ADD BAD FRIEND TO MY LIST OF AWESOME QUALITIES...
WEREWOLF WEEKEND
EREWOLF WEEKEND
YEAH, IT'S TIMES LIKE THESE...
...I'M GLAD I HAVE MY OWN LITTLE SECRET HIDEAWAY.

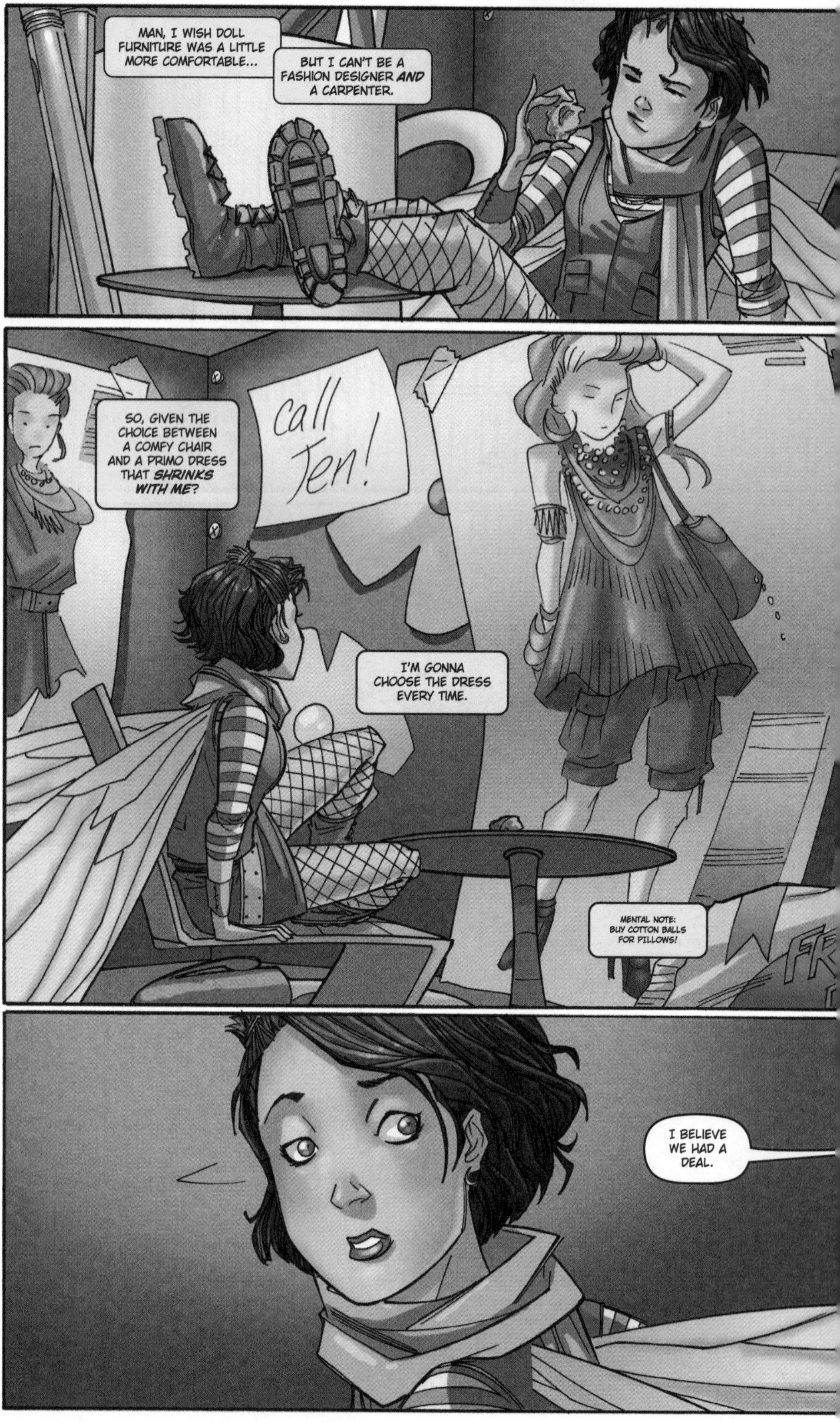
MAN, I WISH DOLL FURNITURE WAS A LITTLE MORE COMFORTABLE...
BUT I CAN'T BE A FASHION DESIGNER AND A CARPENTER.
SO, GIVEN THE CHOICE BETWEEN A COMFY CHAIR AND A PRIMO DRESS THAT SHRINKS WITH ME?
Call Jen!
I'M GONNA CHOOSE THE DRESS EVERY TIME.
MENTAL NOTE: BUY COTTON BALLS FOR PILLOWS!
I BELIEVE WE HAD A DEAL.

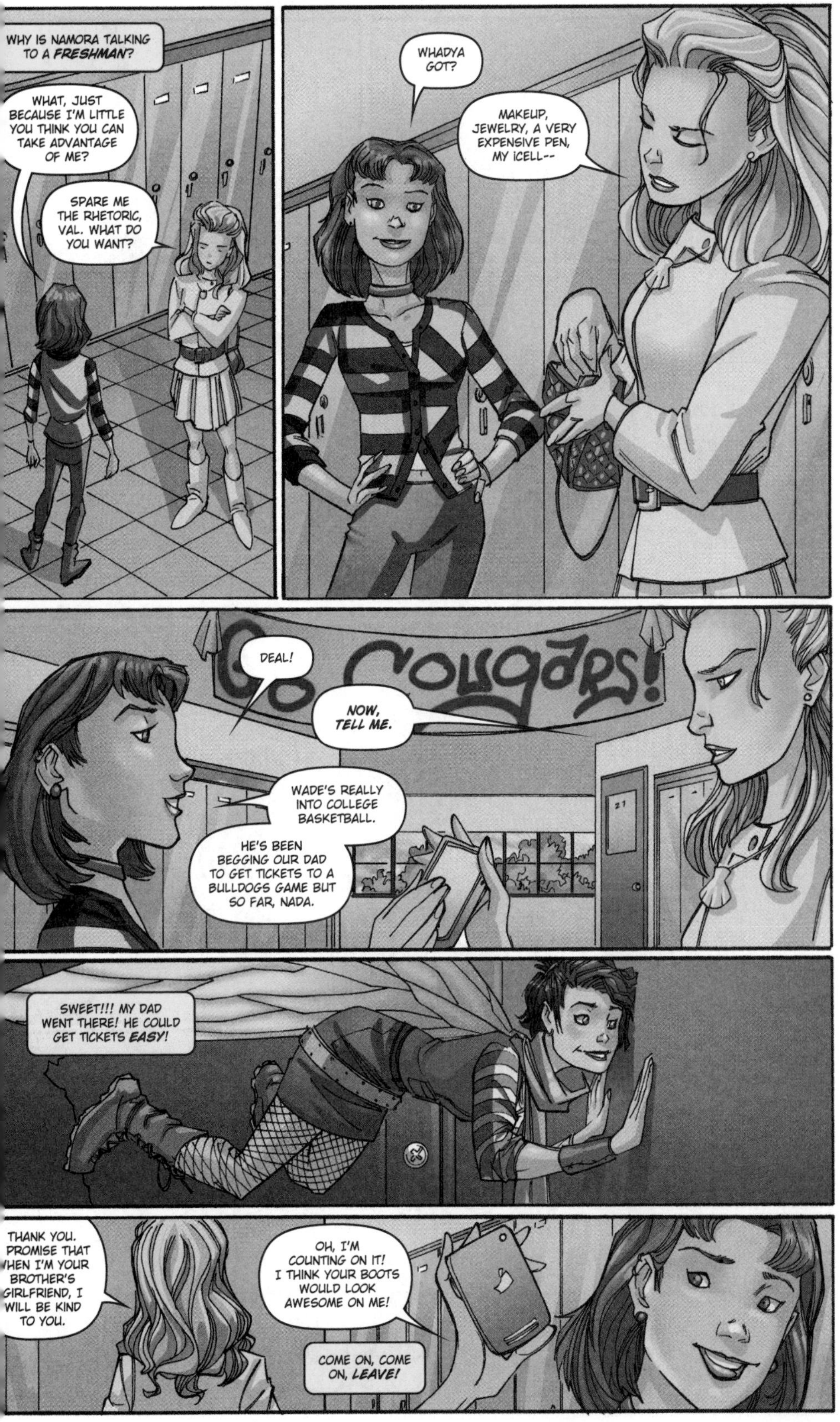

WHY IS NAMORA TALKING TO A ***FRESHMAN***?
WHAT, JUST BECAUSE I'M LITTLE YOU THINK YOU CAN TAKE ADVANTAGE OF ME?
SPARE ME THE RHETORIC, VAL. WHAT DO YOU WANT?
WHADYA GOT?
MAKEUP, JEWELRY, A VERY EXPENSIVE PEN, MY iCELL--
DEAL!
NOW, TELL ME.
WADE'S REALLY INTO COLLEGE BASKETBALL.
HE'S BEEN BEGGING OUR DAD TO GET TICKETS TO A BULLDOGS GAME BUT SO FAR, NADA.
SWEET!!! MY DAD WENT THERE! HE COULD GET TICKETS ***EASY***!
THANK YOU. PROMISE THAT WHEN I'M YOUR BROTHER'S GIRLFRIEND, I WILL BE KIND TO YOU.
OH, I'M COUNTING ON IT! I THINK YOUR BOOTS WOULD LOOK AWESOME ON ME!
COME ON, COME ON, ***LEAVE!***

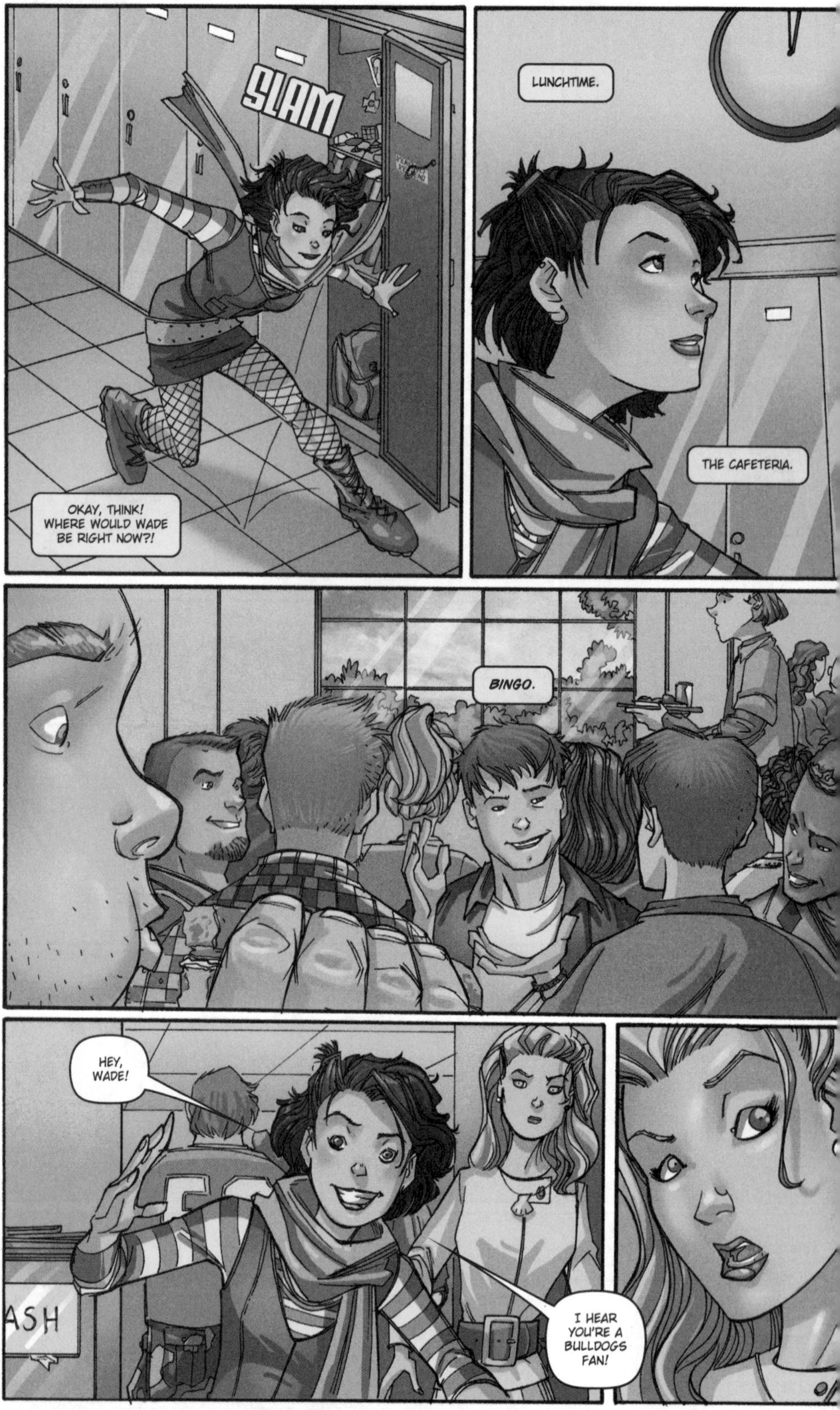
SLAM
OKAY, THINK! WHERE WOULD WADE BE RIGHT NOW?!
LUNCHTIME.
THE CAFETERIA.
BINGO.
HEY, WADE!
I HEAR YOU'RE A BULLDOGS FAN!
ASH

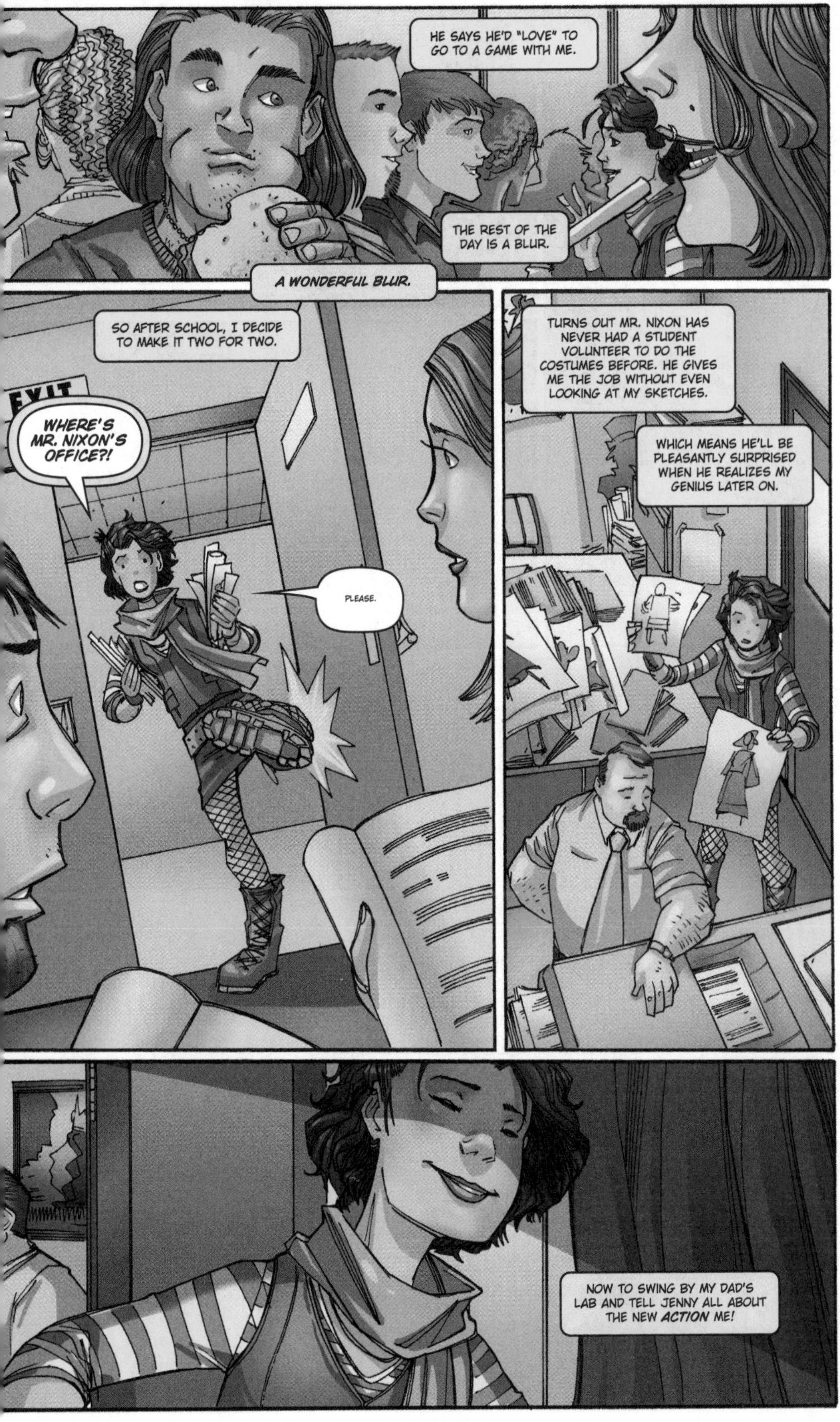
HE SAYS HE'D "LOVE" TO GO TO A GAME WITH ME.
THE REST OF THE DAY IS A BLUR.
A WONDERFUL BLUR.
SO AFTER SCHOOL, I DECIDE TO MAKE IT TWO FOR TWO.
EXIT
WHERE'S MR. NIXON'S OFFICE?!
PLEASE.
TURNS OUT MR. NIXON HAS NEVER HAD A STUDENT VOLUNTEER TO DO THE COSTUMES BEFORE. HE GIVES ME THE JOB WITHOUT EVEN LOOKING AT MY SKETCHES.
WHICH MEANS HE'LL BE PLEASANTLY SURPRISED WHEN HE REALIZES MY GENIUS LATER ON.
NOW TO SWING BY MY DAD'S LAB AND TELL JENNY ALL ABOUT THE NEW *ACTION* ME!

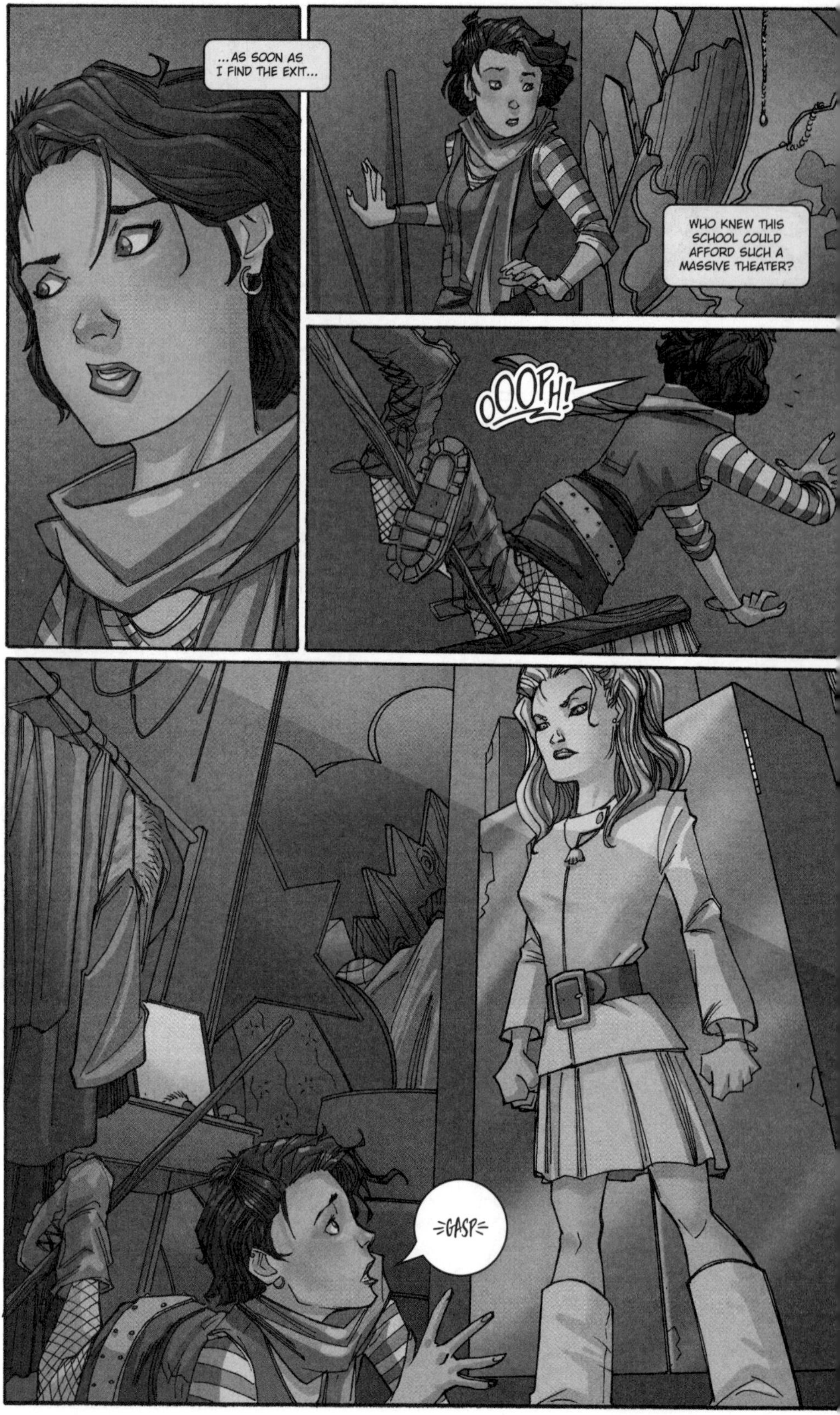
...AS SOON AS I FIND THE EXIT...
WHO KNEW THIS SCHOOL COULD AFFORD SUCH A MASSIVE THEATER?
OOOPH!
GASP

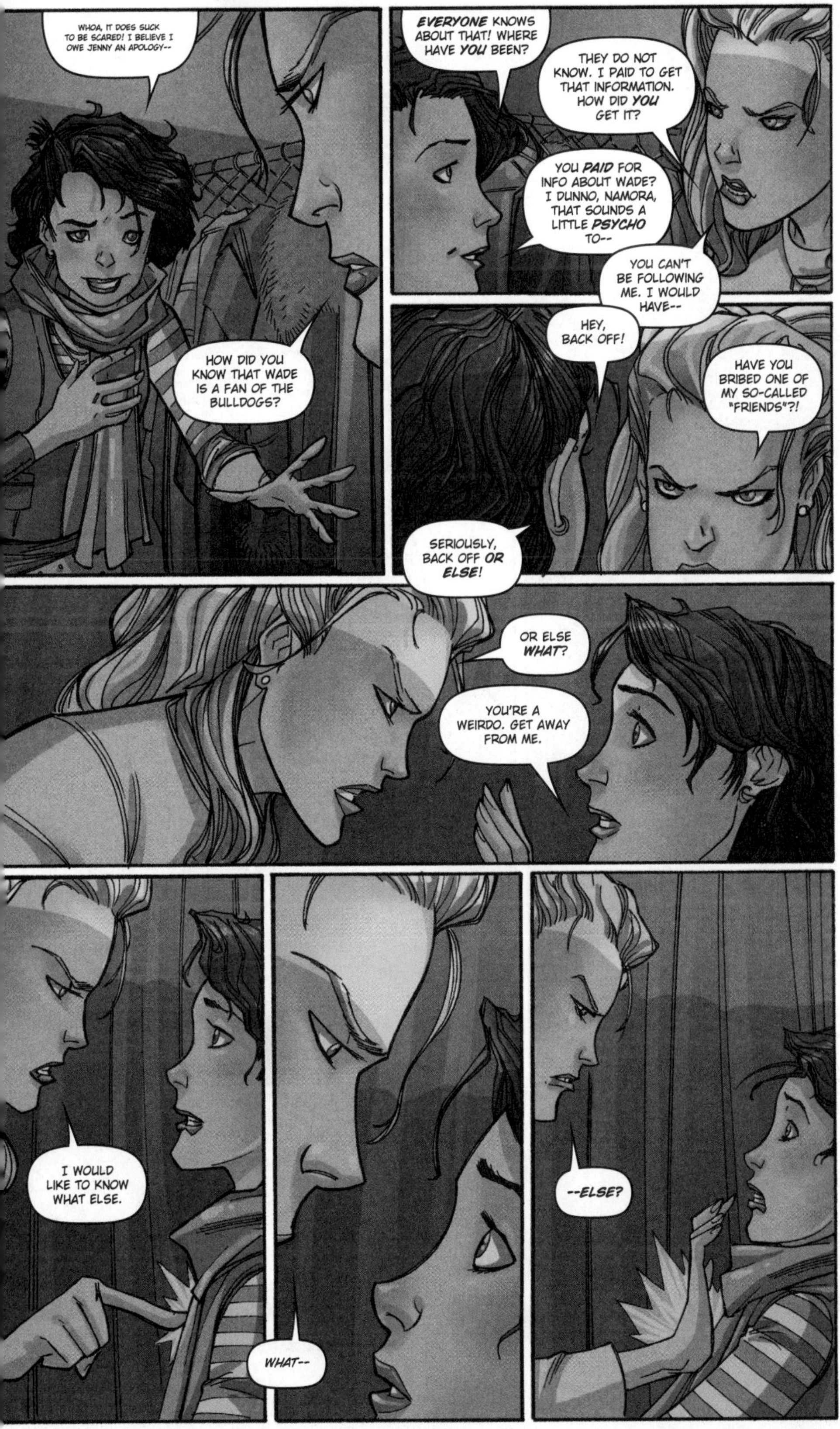
WHOA, IT DOES SUCK TO BE SCARED! I BELIEVE I OWE JENNY AN APOLOGY--
HOW DID YOU KNOW THAT WADE IS A FAN OF THE BULLDOGS?
EVERYONE KNOWS ABOUT THAT! WHERE HAVE YOU BEEN?
THEY DO NOT KNOW. I PAID TO GET THAT INFORMATION. HOW DID YOU GET IT?
YOU PAID FOR INFO ABOUT WADE? I DUNNO, NAMORA, THAT SOUNDS A LITTLE PSYCHO TO--
YOU CAN'T BE FOLLOWING ME. I WOULD HAVE--
HEY, BACK OFF!
HAVE YOU BRIBED ONE OF MY SO-CALLED "FRIENDS"?!
SERIOUSLY, BACK OFF OR ELSE!
OR ELSE WHAT?
YOU'RE A WEIRDO. GET AWAY FROM ME.
I WOULD LIKE TO KNOW WHAT ELSE.
WHAT--
--ELSE?

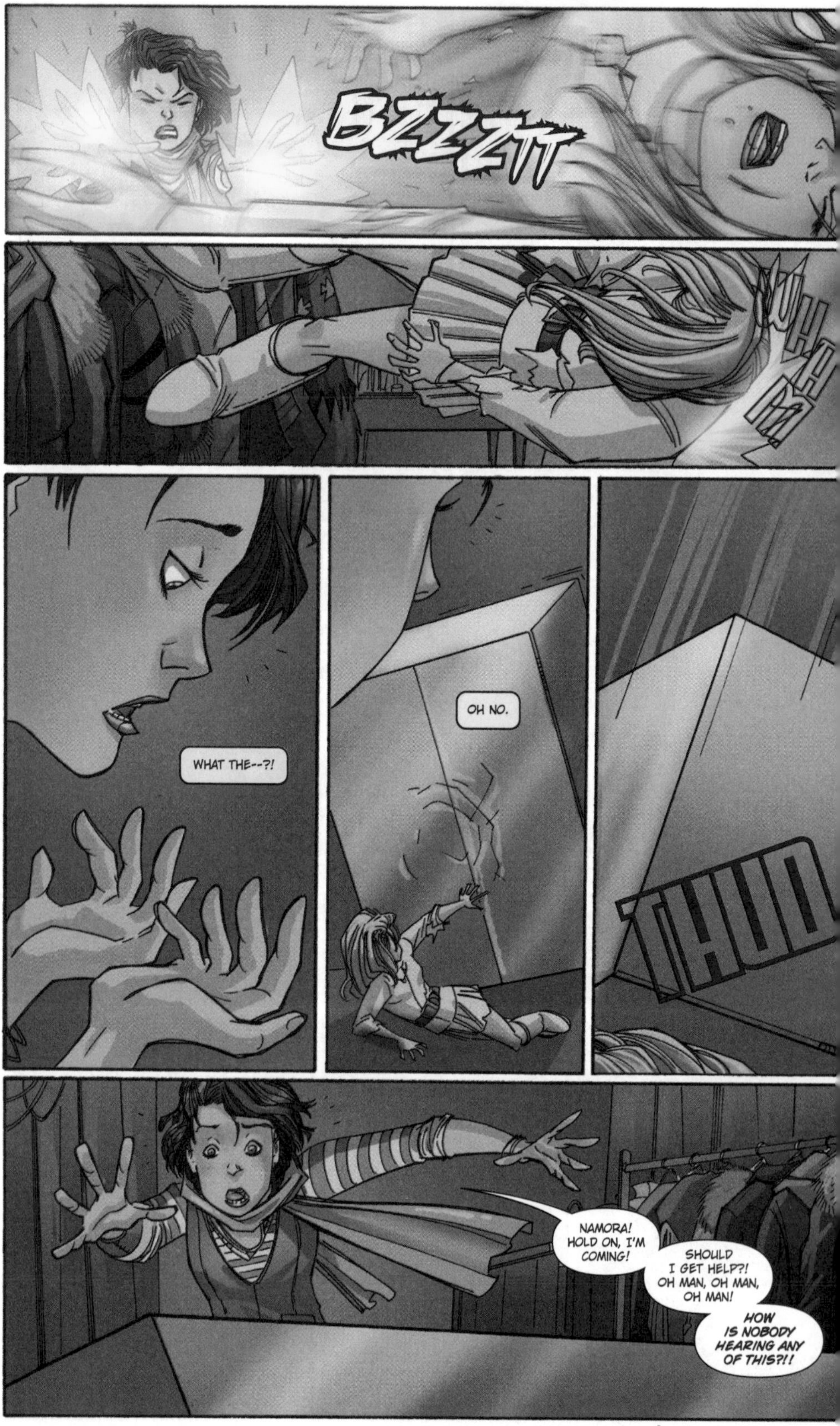
BZZZTT
WHAM
WHAT THE--?!
OH NO.
THUD
NAMORA! HOLD ON, I'M COMING!
SHOULD I GET HELP?! OH MAN, OH MAN, OH MAN!
HOW IS NOBODY HEARING ANY OF THIS?!!

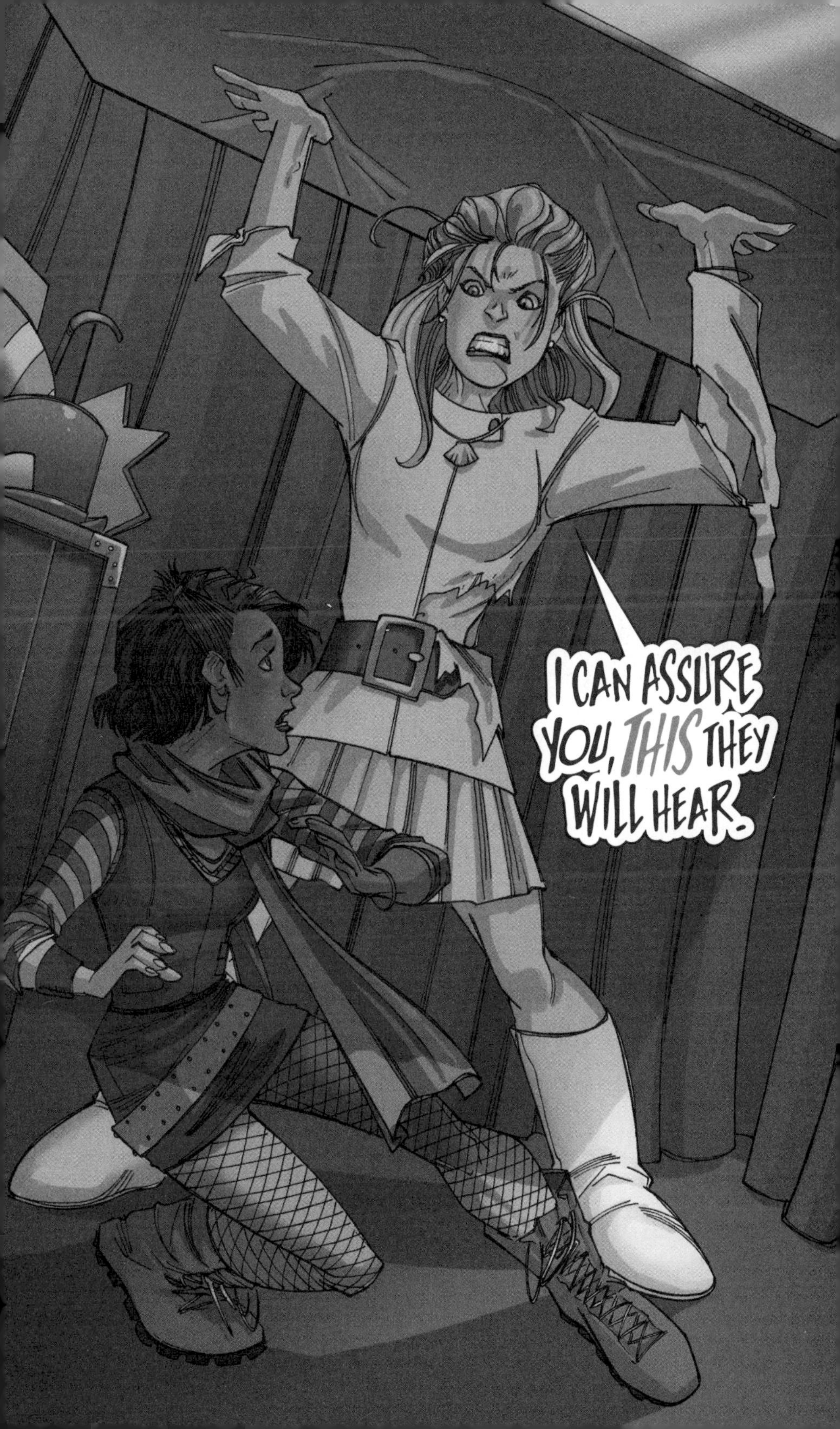
I CAN ASSURE YOU, *THIS* THEY WILL HEAR.

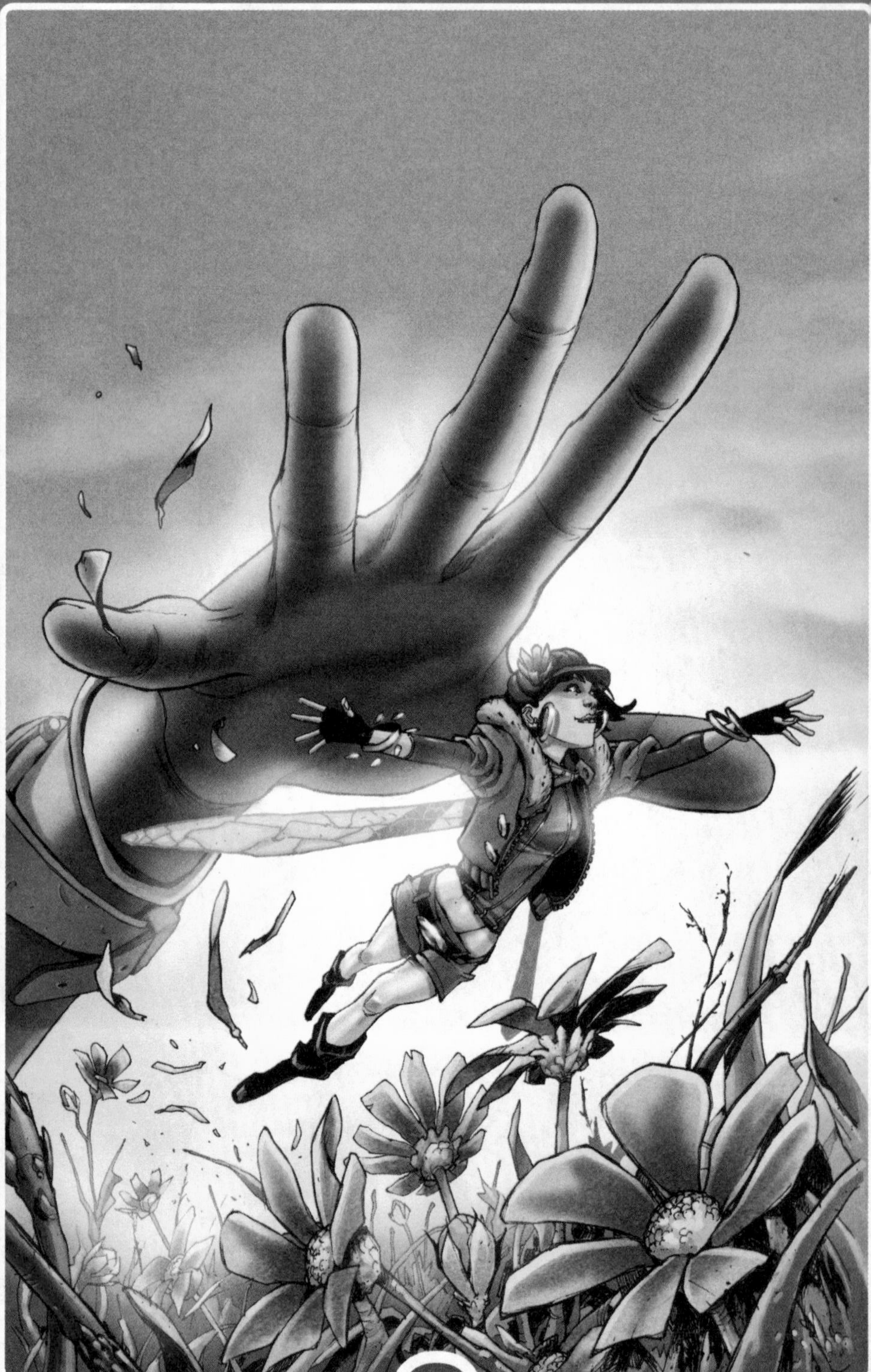

2

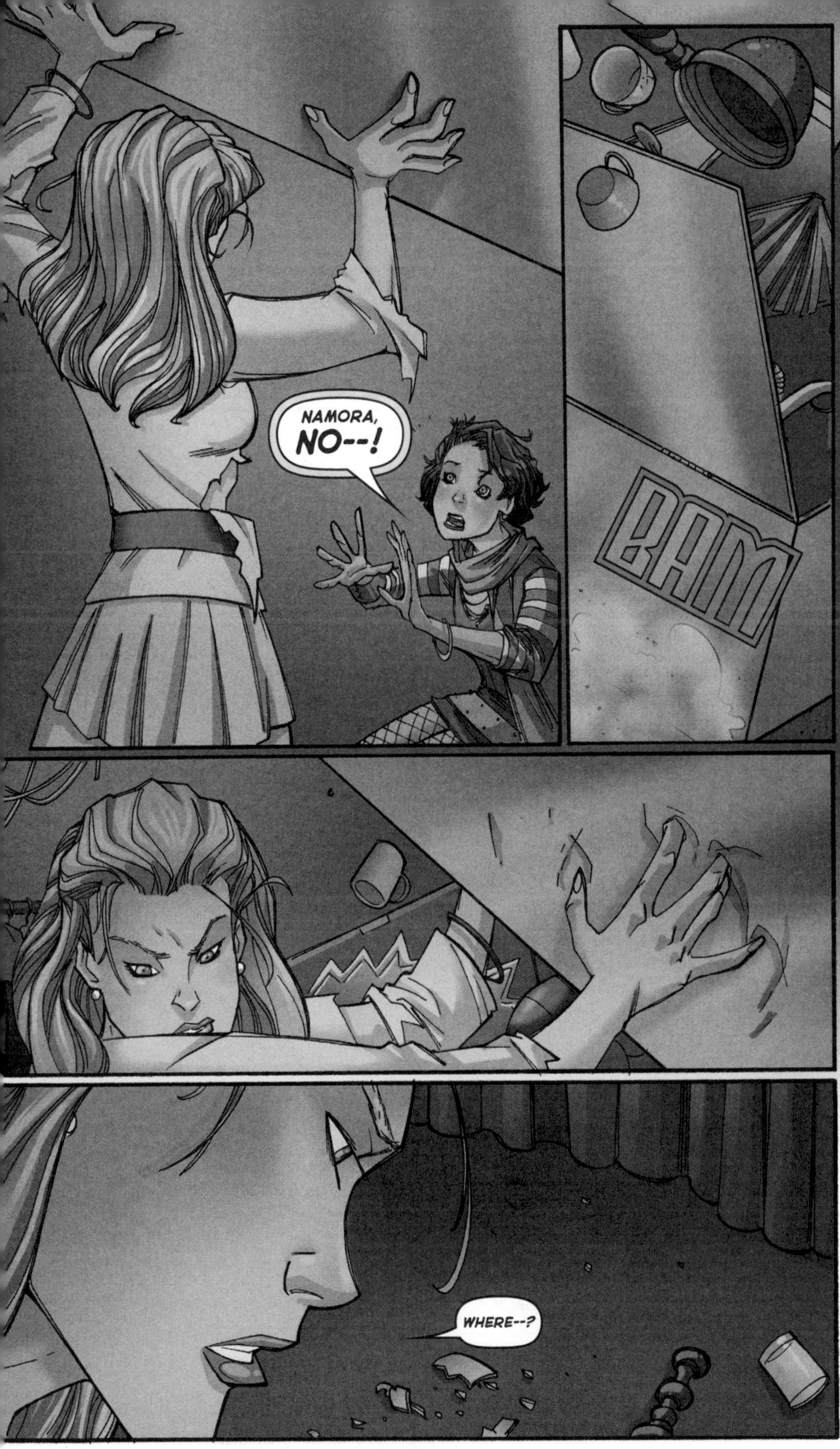
NAMORA, NO--!
BAM
WHERE--?

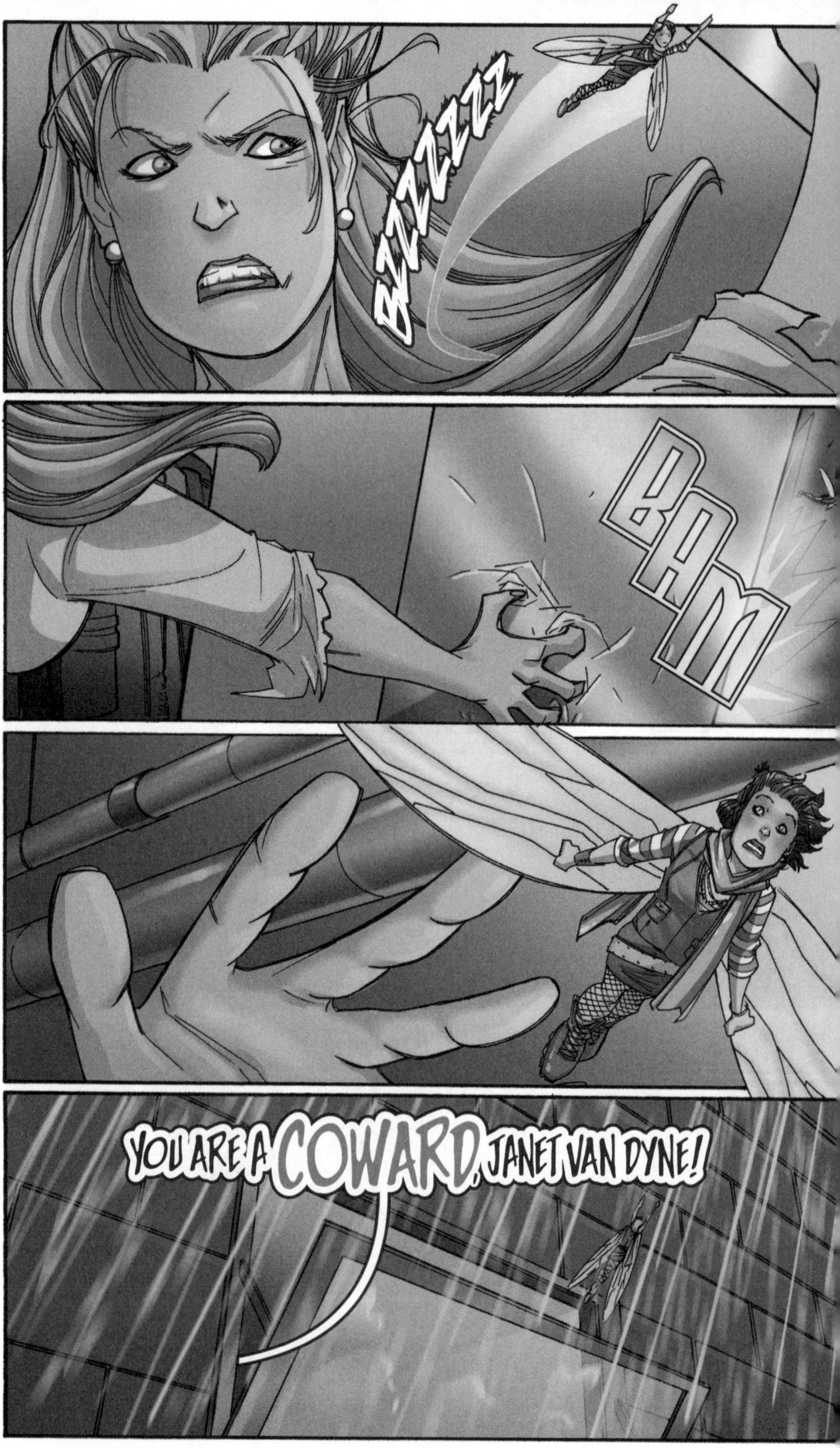
BZZZZZZZZZ
BAM
YOU ARE A COWARD, JANET VAN DYNE!

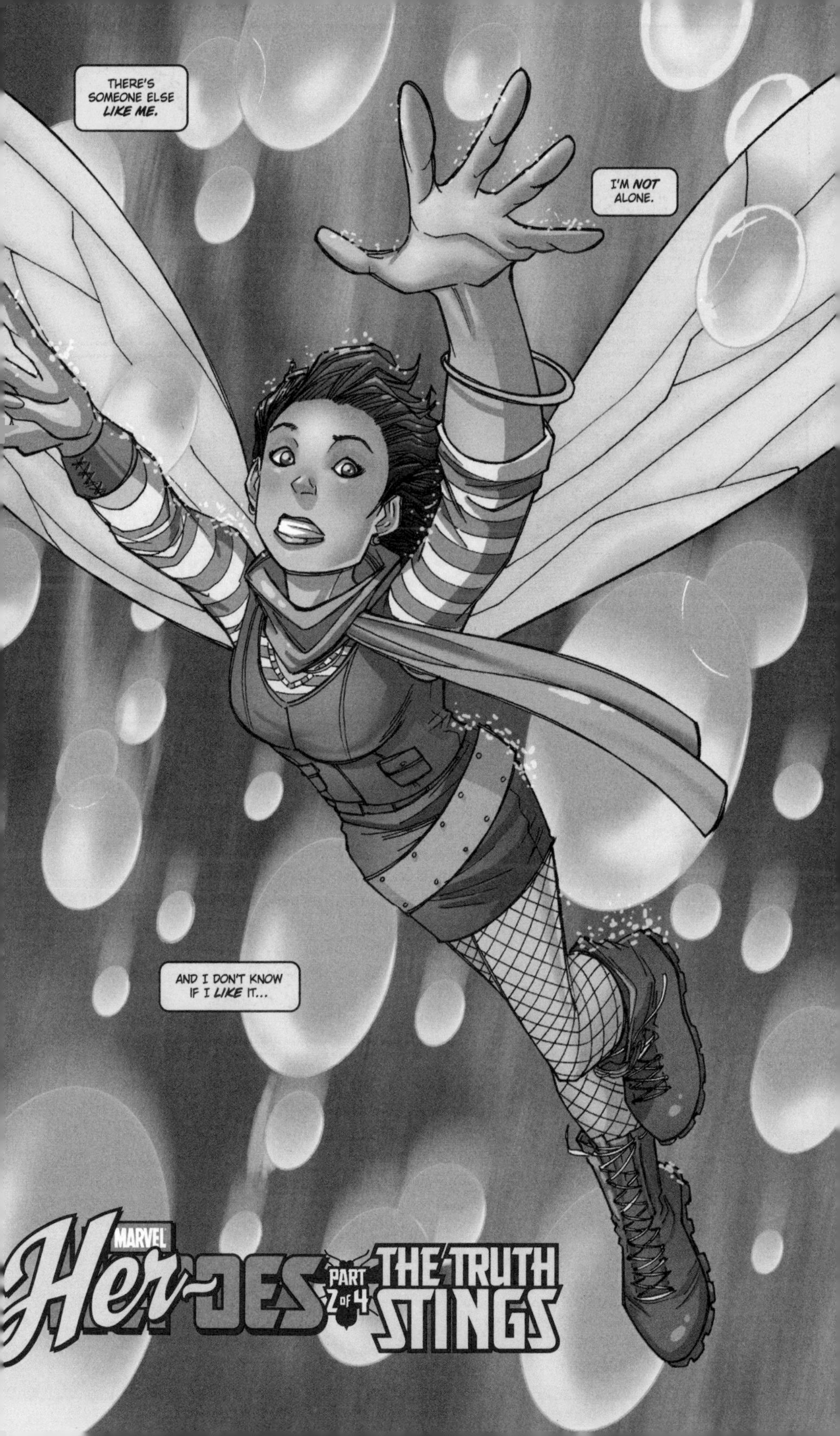
THERE'S SOMEONE ELSE *LIKE ME.*
I'M *NOT* ALONE.
AND I DON'T KNOW IF I *LIKE* IT...
MARVEL
HER-OES
PART 2 OF 4
THE TRUTH STINGS

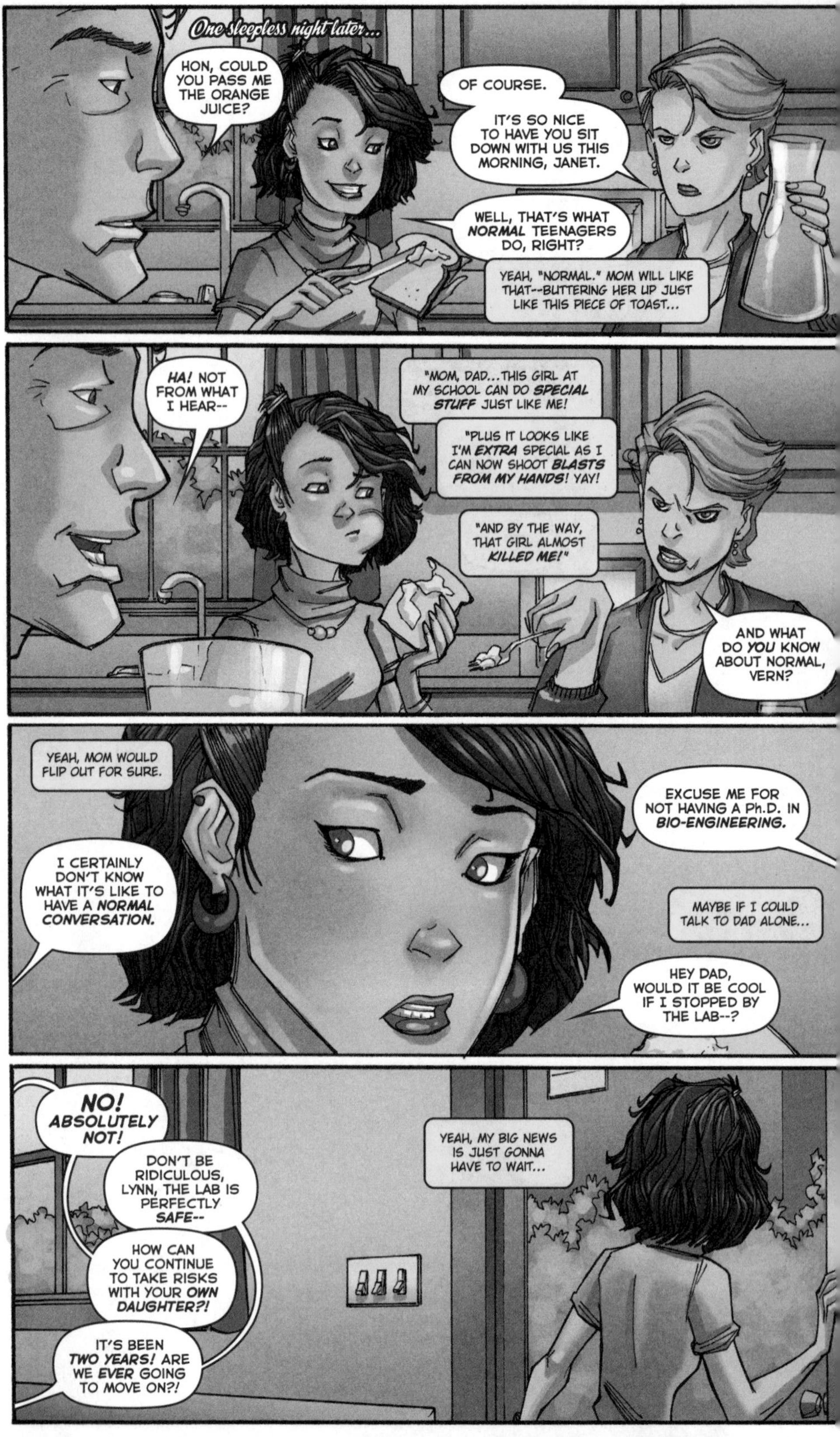
One sleepless night later...
HON, COULD YOU PASS ME THE ORANGE JUICE?
OF COURSE.
IT'S SO NICE TO HAVE YOU SIT DOWN WITH US THIS MORNING, JANET.
WELL, THAT'S WHAT NORMAL TEENAGERS DO, RIGHT?
YEAH, "NORMAL." MOM WILL LIKE THAT--BUTTERING HER UP JUST LIKE THIS PIECE OF TOAST...
HA! NOT FROM WHAT I HEAR--
"MOM, DAD...THIS GIRL AT MY SCHOOL CAN DO SPECIAL STUFF JUST LIKE ME!
"PLUS IT LOOKS LIKE I'M EXTRA SPECIAL AS I CAN NOW SHOOT BLASTS FROM MY HANDS! YAY!
"AND BY THE WAY, THAT GIRL ALMOST KILLED ME!"
AND WHAT DO YOU KNOW ABOUT NORMAL, VERN?
YEAH, MOM WOULD FLIP OUT FOR SURE.
EXCUSE ME FOR NOT HAVING A Ph.D. IN BIO-ENGINEERING.
I CERTAINLY DON'T KNOW WHAT IT'S LIKE TO HAVE A NORMAL CONVERSATION.
MAYBE IF I COULD TALK TO DAD ALONE...
HEY DAD, WOULD IT BE COOL IF I STOPPED BY THE LAB--?
NO! ABSOLUTELY NOT!
DON'T BE RIDICULOUS, LYNN, THE LAB IS PERFECTLY SAFE--
HOW CAN YOU CONTINUE TO TAKE RISKS WITH YOUR OWN DAUGHTER?!
IT'S BEEN TWO YEARS! ARE WE EVER GOING TO MOVE ON?!
YEAH, MY BIG NEWS IS JUST GONNA HAVE TO WAIT...

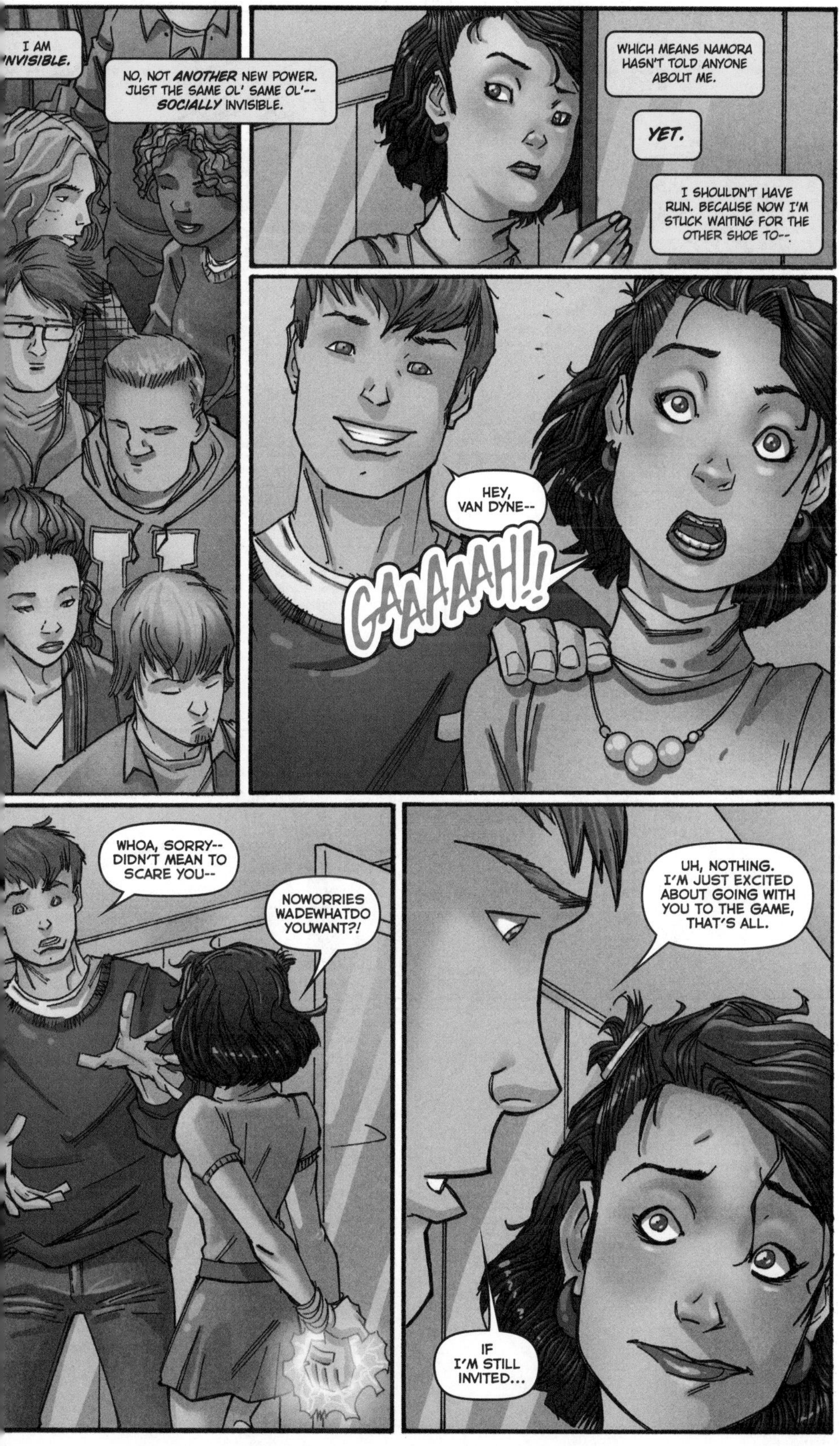
I AM INVISIBLE.
NO, NOT ANOTHER NEW POWER. JUST THE SAME OL' SAME OL'-- SOCIALLY INVISIBLE.
WHICH MEANS NAMORA HASN'T TOLD ANYONE ABOUT ME.
YET.
I SHOULDN'T HAVE RUN. BECAUSE NOW I'M STUCK WAITING FOR THE OTHER SHOE TO--.
HEY, VAN DYNE--
GAAAAAH!!
WHOA, SORRY-- DIDN'T MEAN TO SCARE YOU--
NOWORRIES WADEWHATDO YOUWANT?!
UH, NOTHING. I'M JUST EXCITED ABOUT GOING WITH YOU TO THE GAME, THAT'S ALL.
IF I'M STILL INVITED...

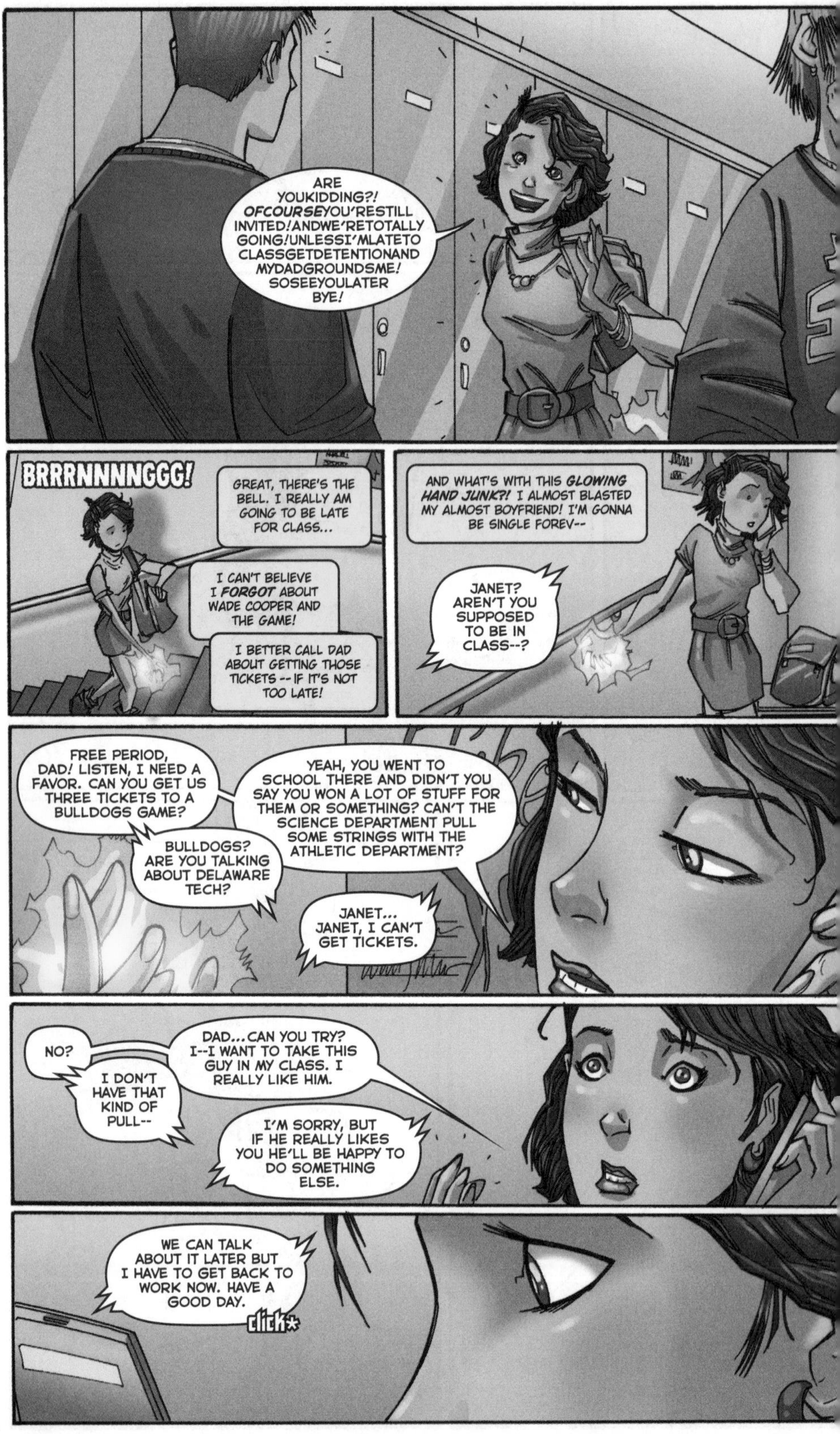
ARE YOUKIDDING?! OFCOURSEYOU'RESTILL INVITED!ANDWE'RETOTALLY GOING!UNLESSI'MLATETO CLASSGETDETENTIONAND MYDADGROUNDSME! SOSEEYOULATER BYE!
BRRRNNNNGGG!
GREAT, THERE'S THE BELL. I REALLY AM GOING TO BE LATE FOR CLASS...
I CAN'T BELIEVE I FORGOT ABOUT WADE COOPER AND THE GAME!
I BETTER CALL DAD ABOUT GETTING THOSE TICKETS -- IF IT'S NOT TOO LATE!
AND WHAT'S WITH THIS GLOWING HAND JUNK?! I ALMOST BLASTED MY ALMOST BOYFRIEND! I'M GONNA BE SINGLE FOREV--
JANET? AREN'T YOU SUPPOSED TO BE IN CLASS--?
FREE PERIOD, DAD! LISTEN, I NEED A FAVOR. CAN YOU GET US THREE TICKETS TO A BULLDOGS GAME?
BULLDOGS? ARE YOU TALKING ABOUT DELAWARE TECH?
YEAH, YOU WENT TO SCHOOL THERE AND DIDN'T YOU SAY YOU WON A LOT OF STUFF FOR THEM OR SOMETHING? CAN'T THE SCIENCE DEPARTMENT PULL SOME STRINGS WITH THE ATHLETIC DEPARTMENT?
JANET... JANET, I CAN'T GET TICKETS.
NO?
I DON'T HAVE THAT KIND OF PULL--
DAD...CAN YOU TRY? I--I WANT TO TAKE THIS GUY IN MY CLASS. I REALLY LIKE HIM.
I'M SORRY, BUT IF HE REALLY LIKES YOU HE'LL BE HAPPY TO DO SOMETHING ELSE.
WE CAN TALK ABOUT IT LATER BUT I HAVE TO GET BACK TO WORK NOW. HAVE A GOOD DAY.
click*

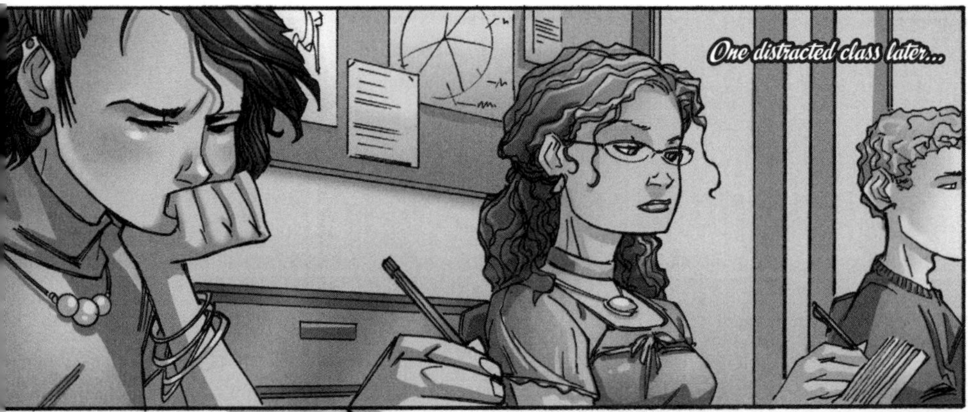
One distracted class later...

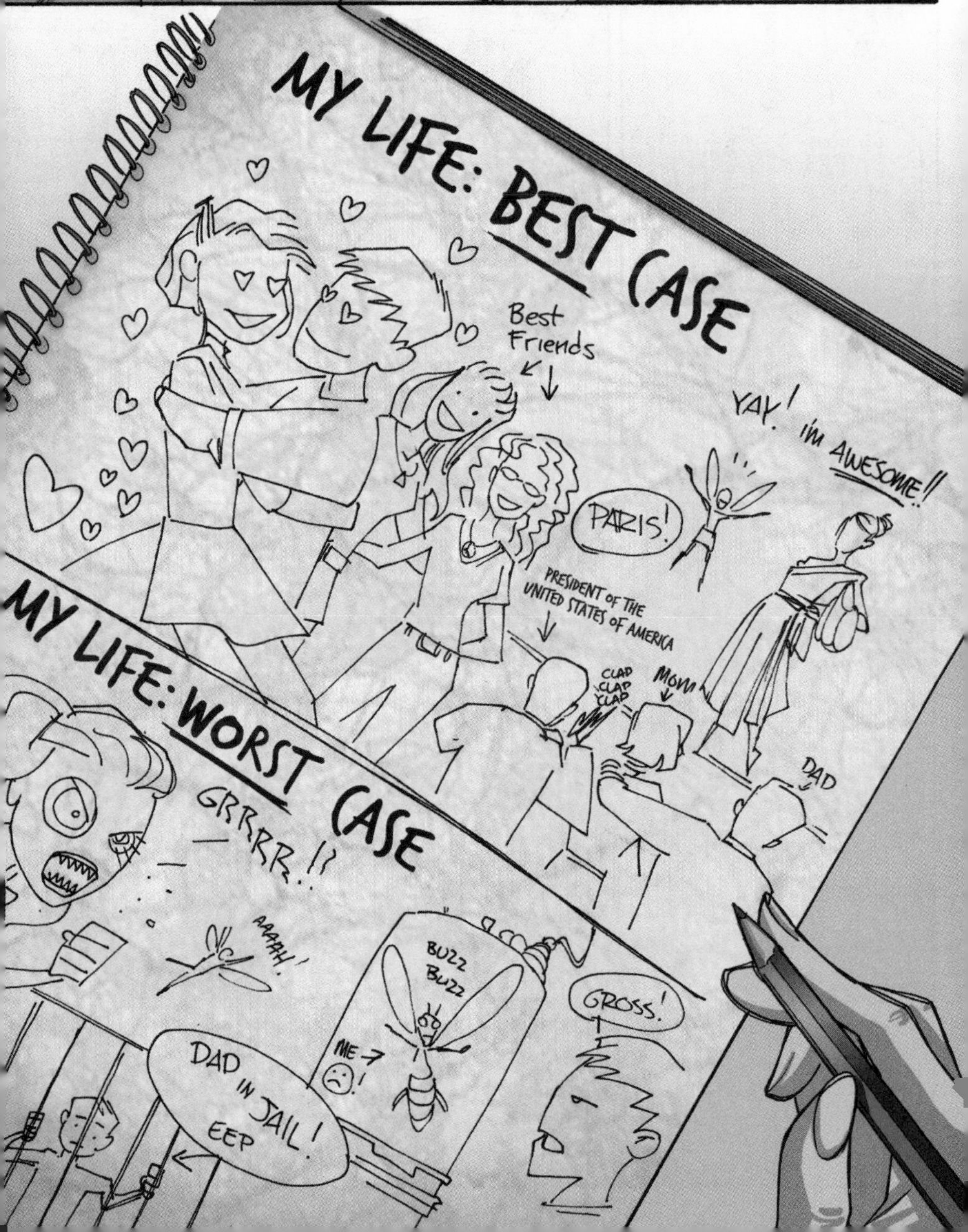
MY LIFE: BEST CASE
Best Friends
YAY! I'M AWESOME!!
PARIS!
PRESIDENT OF THE UNITED STATES OF AMERICA
CLAP CLAP CLAP
MOM
DAD
MY LIFE: WORST CASE
GRRRRR..!!
AAAAH!
BUZZ BUZZ
ME
GROSS!
DAD IN JAIL! EEP

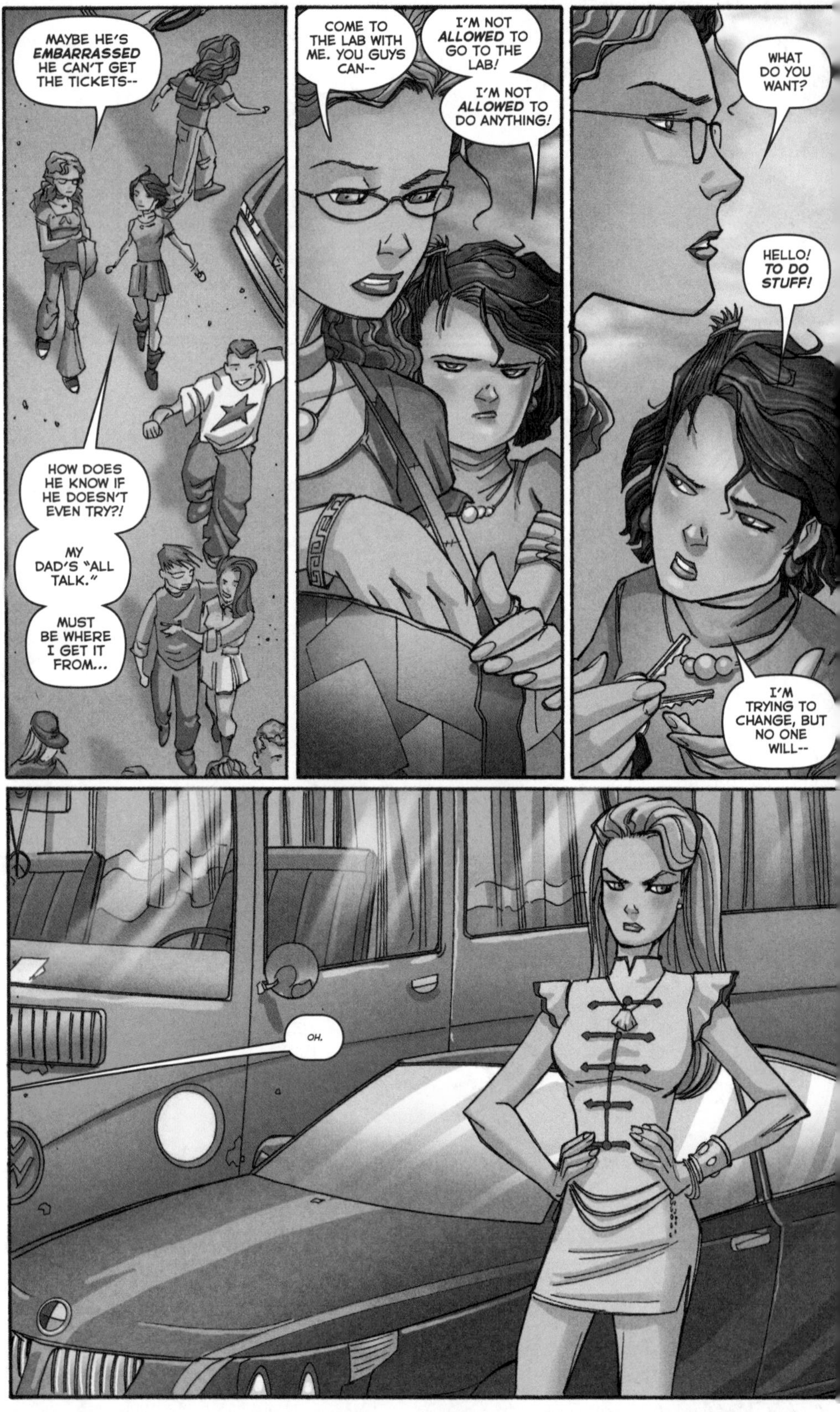
MAYBE HE'S EMBARRASSED HE CAN'T GET THE TICKETS--
HOW DOES HE KNOW IF HE DOESN'T EVEN TRY?!
MY DAD'S "ALL TALK."
MUST BE WHERE I GET IT FROM...
COME TO THE LAB WITH ME. YOU GUYS CAN--
I'M NOT ALLOWED TO GO TO THE LAB!
I'M NOT ALLOWED TO DO ANYTHING!
WHAT DO YOU WANT?
HELLO! TO DO STUFF!
I'M TRYING TO CHANGE, BUT NO ONE WILL--
OH.

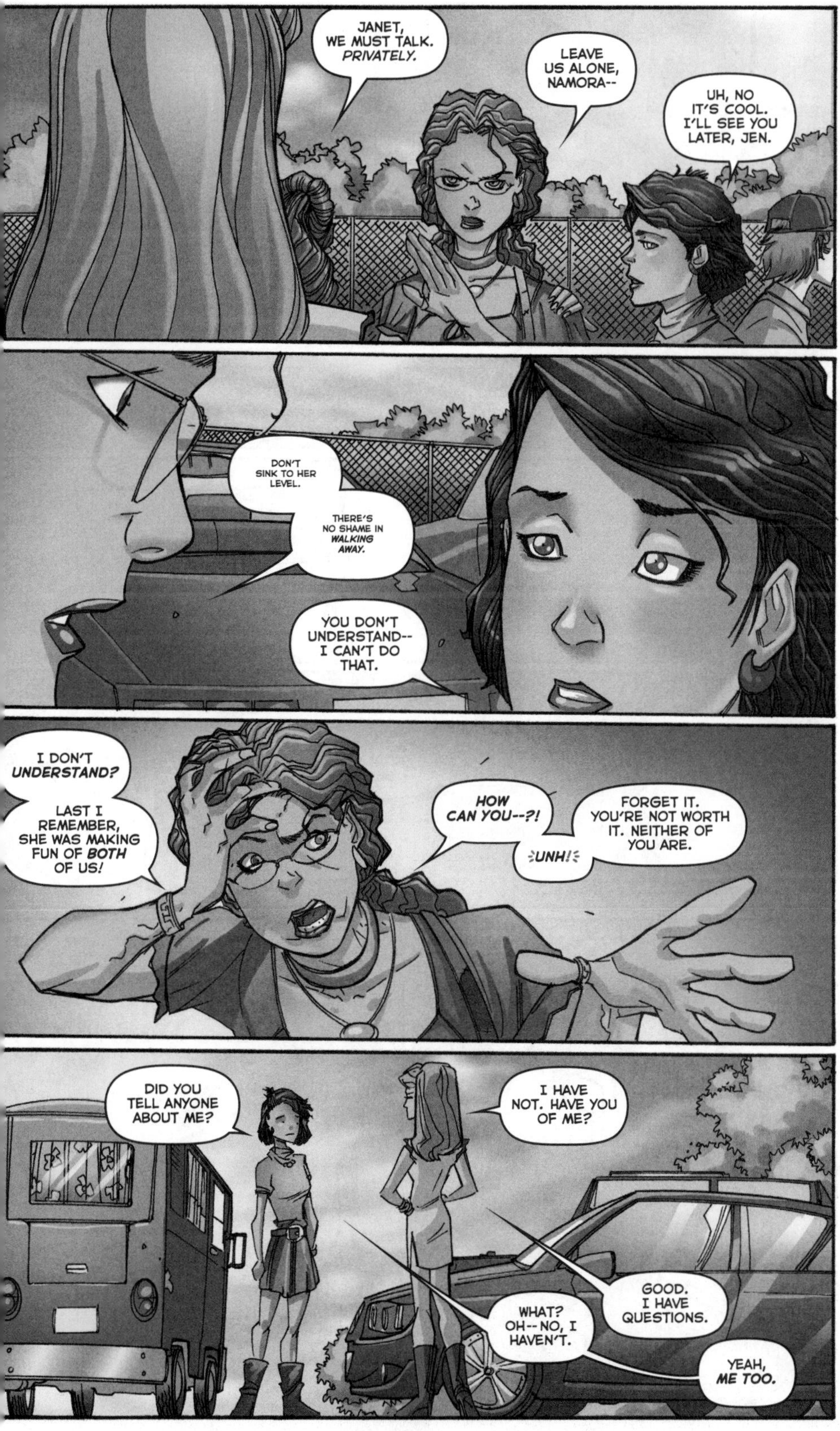
JANET, WE MUST TALK. *PRIVATELY.*
LEAVE US ALONE, NAMORA--
UH, NO IT'S COOL. I'LL SEE YOU LATER, JEN.
DON'T SINK TO HER LEVEL.
THERE'S NO SHAME IN *WALKING AWAY.*
YOU DON'T UNDERSTAND-- I CAN'T DO THAT.
I DON'T *UNDERSTAND?*
LAST I REMEMBER, SHE WAS MAKING FUN OF *BOTH* OF US!
HOW CAN YOU--?!
UNH!
FORGET IT. YOU'RE NOT WORTH IT. NEITHER OF YOU ARE.
DID YOU TELL ANYONE ABOUT ME?
I HAVE NOT. HAVE YOU OF ME?
WHAT? OH-- NO, I HAVEN'T.
GOOD. I HAVE QUESTIONS.
YEAH, *ME TOO.*

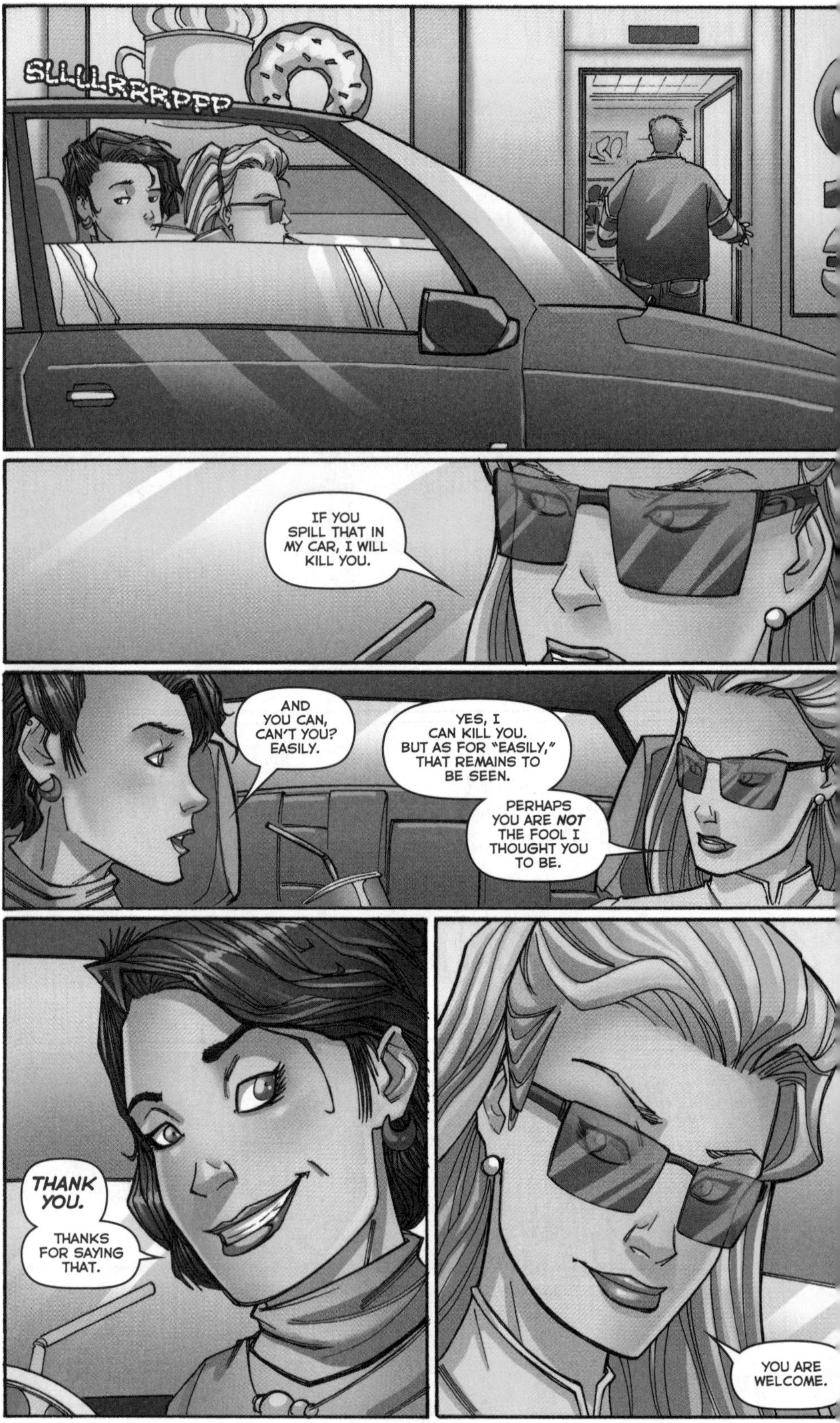
SLLLLRRRPPP
IF YOU SPILL THAT IN MY CAR, I WILL KILL YOU.
AND YOU CAN, CAN'T YOU? EASILY.
YES, I CAN KILL YOU. BUT AS FOR "EASILY," THAT REMAINS TO BE SEEN.
PERHAPS YOU ARE NOT THE FOOL I THOUGHT YOU TO BE.
THANK YOU.
THANKS FOR SAYING THAT.
YOU ARE WELCOME.

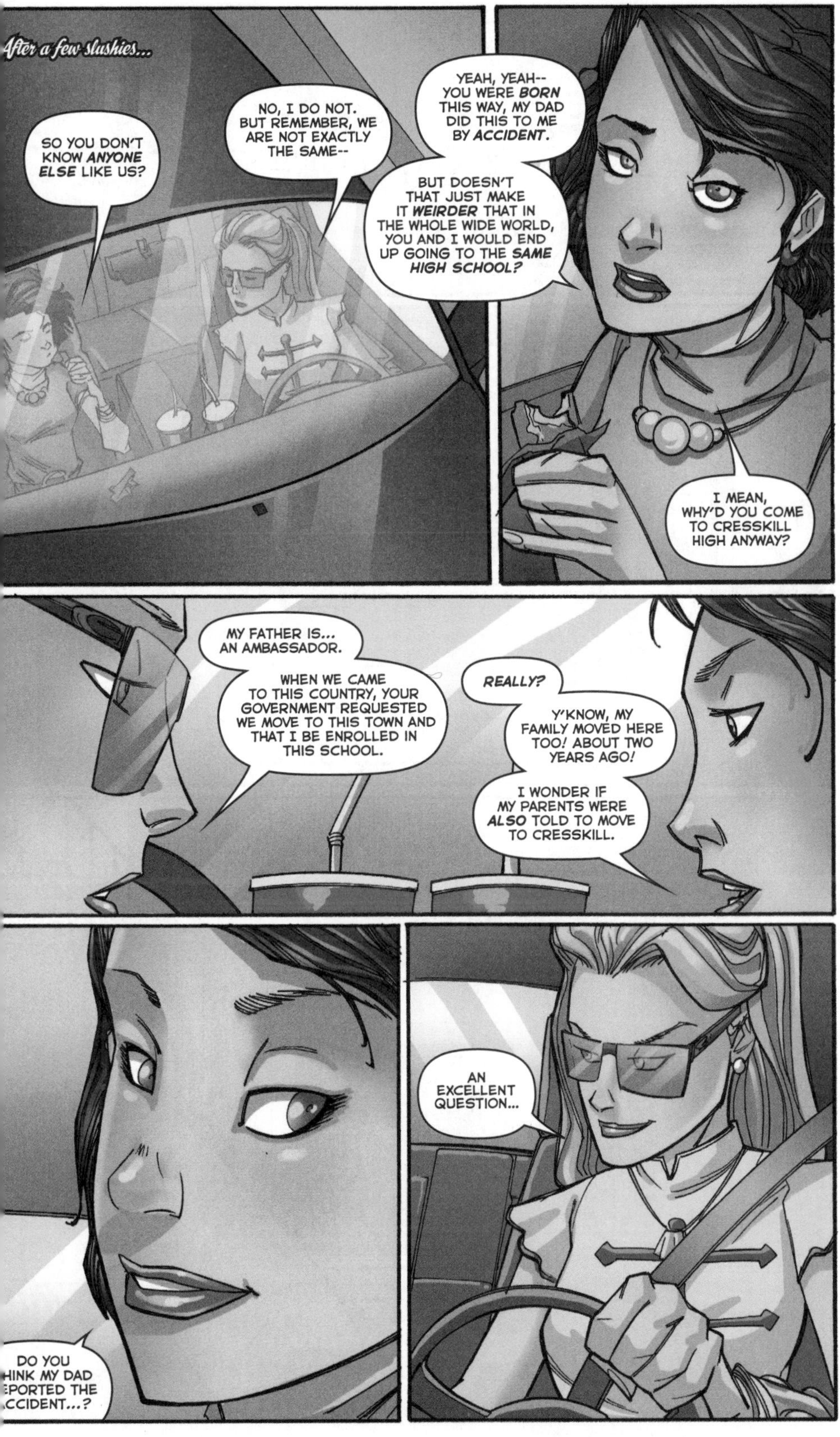
After a few slushies...
SO YOU DON'T KNOW ANYONE ELSE LIKE US?
NO, I DO NOT. BUT REMEMBER, WE ARE NOT EXACTLY THE SAME--
YEAH, YEAH-- YOU WERE BORN THIS WAY, MY DAD DID THIS TO ME BY ACCIDENT.
BUT DOESN'T THAT JUST MAKE IT WEIRDER THAT IN THE WHOLE WIDE WORLD, YOU AND I WOULD END UP GOING TO THE SAME HIGH SCHOOL?
I MEAN, WHY'D YOU COME TO CRESSKILL HIGH ANYWAY?
MY FATHER IS... AN AMBASSADOR.
WHEN WE CAME TO THIS COUNTRY, YOUR GOVERNMENT REQUESTED WE MOVE TO THIS TOWN AND THAT I BE ENROLLED IN THIS SCHOOL.
REALLY?
Y'KNOW, MY FAMILY MOVED HERE TOO! ABOUT TWO YEARS AGO!
I WONDER IF MY PARENTS WERE ALSO TOLD TO MOVE TO CRESSKILL.
DO YOU HINK MY DAD EPORTED THE CCIDENT...?
AN EXCELLENT QUESTION...

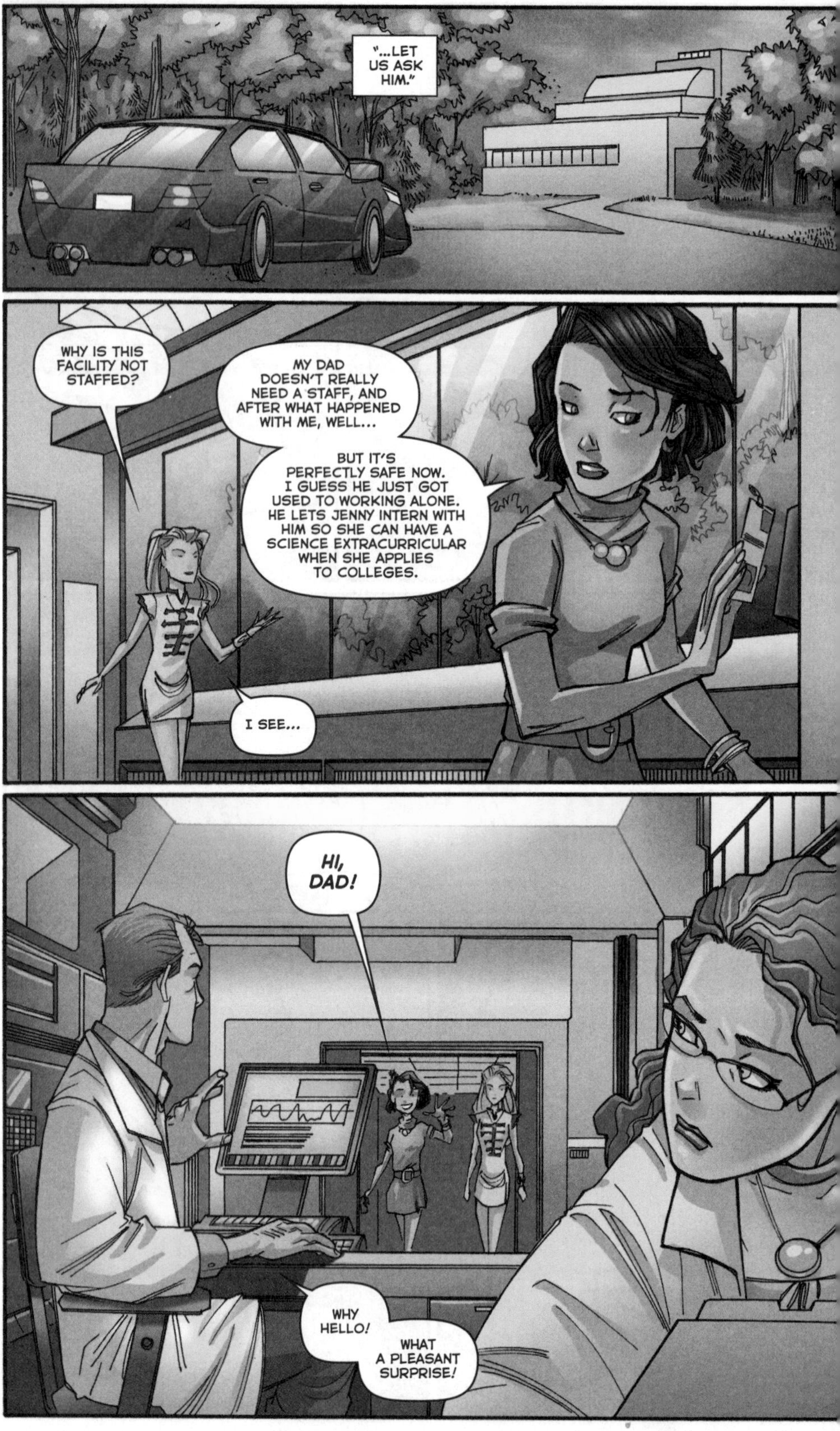
"...LET US ASK HIM."
WHY IS THIS FACILITY NOT STAFFED?
MY DAD DOESN'T REALLY NEED A STAFF, AND AFTER WHAT HAPPENED WITH ME, WELL...
BUT IT'S PERFECTLY SAFE NOW. I GUESS HE JUST GOT USED TO WORKING ALONE. HE LETS JENNY INTERN WITH HIM SO SHE CAN HAVE A SCIENCE EXTRACURRICULAR WHEN SHE APPLIES TO COLLEGES.
I SEE...
HI, DAD!
WHY HELLO!
WHAT A PLEASANT SURPRISE!

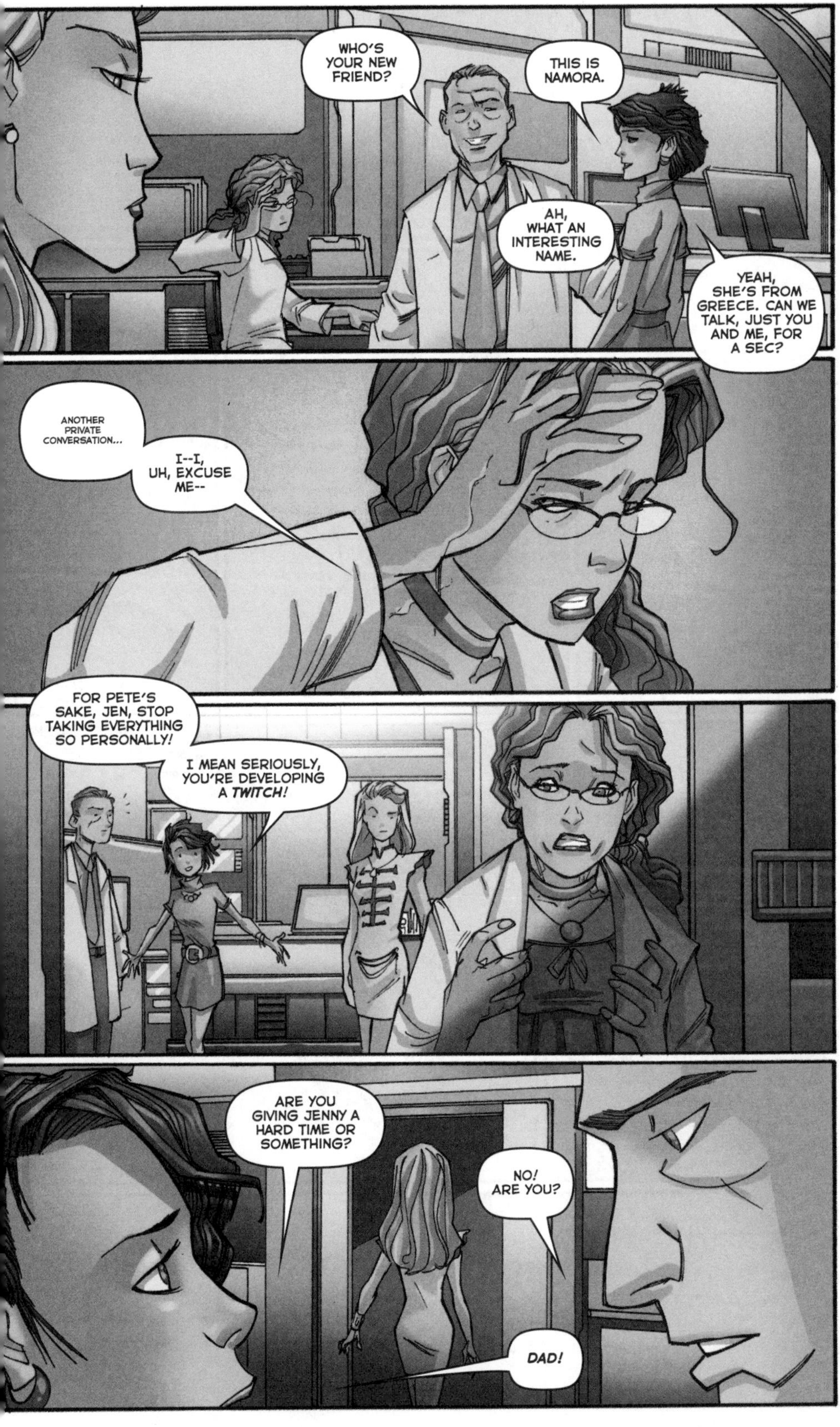
WHO'S YOUR NEW FRIEND?
THIS IS NAMORA.
AH, WHAT AN INTERESTING NAME.
YEAH, SHE'S FROM GREECE. CAN WE TALK, JUST YOU AND ME, FOR A SEC?
ANOTHER PRIVATE CONVERSATION...
I--I, UH, EXCUSE ME--
FOR PETE'S SAKE, JEN, STOP TAKING EVERYTHING SO PERSONALLY!
I MEAN SERIOUSLY, YOU'RE DEVELOPING A *TWITCH*!
ARE YOU GIVING JENNY A HARD TIME OR SOMETHING?
NO! ARE YOU?
DAD!

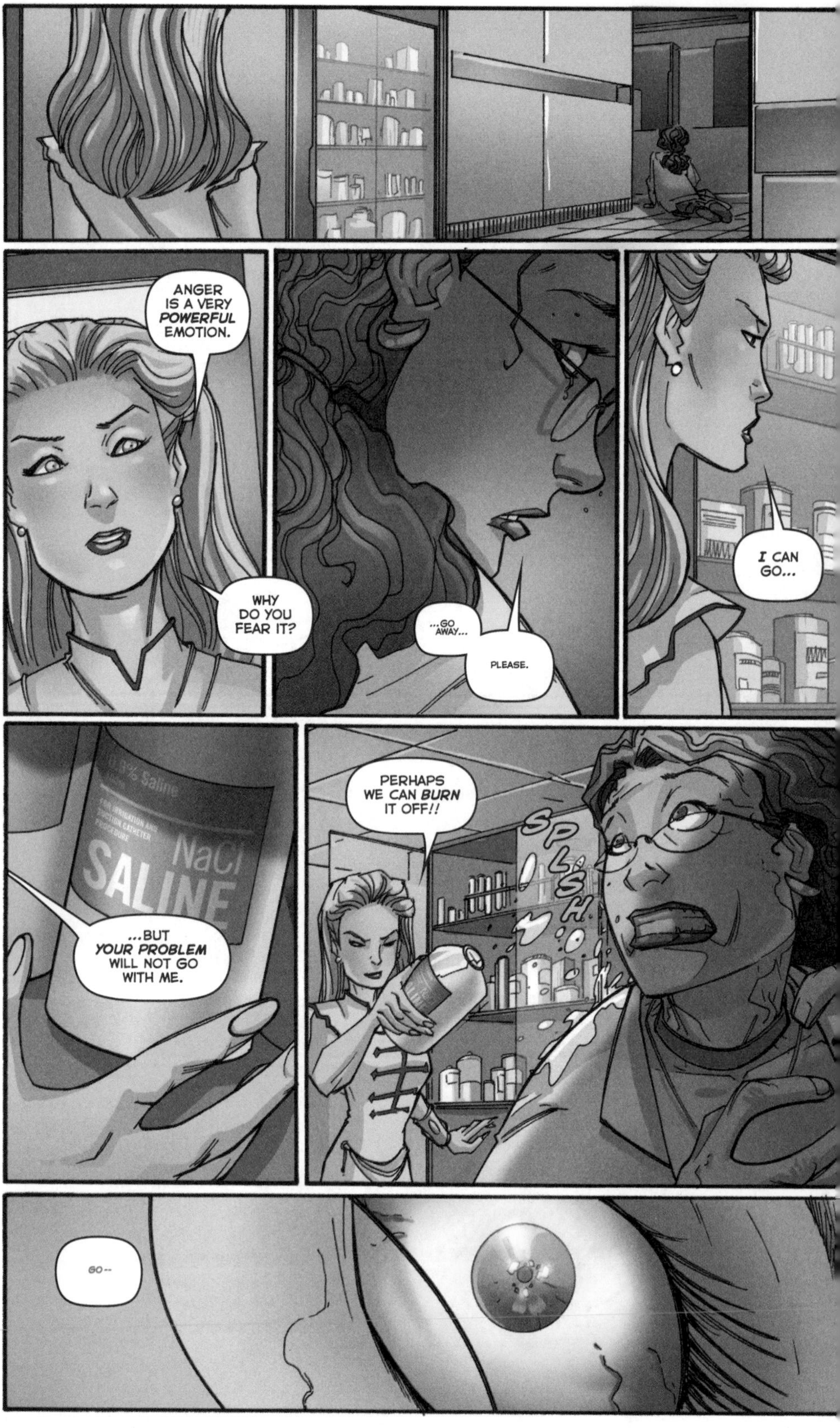
ANGER IS A VERY *POWERFUL* EMOTION.
WHY DO YOU FEAR IT?
...GO AWAY...
PLEASE.
I CAN GO...
NaCl
SALINE
...BUT *YOUR PROBLEM* WILL NOT GO WITH ME.
PERHAPS WE CAN *BURN* IT OFF!!
SPLSH
GO--

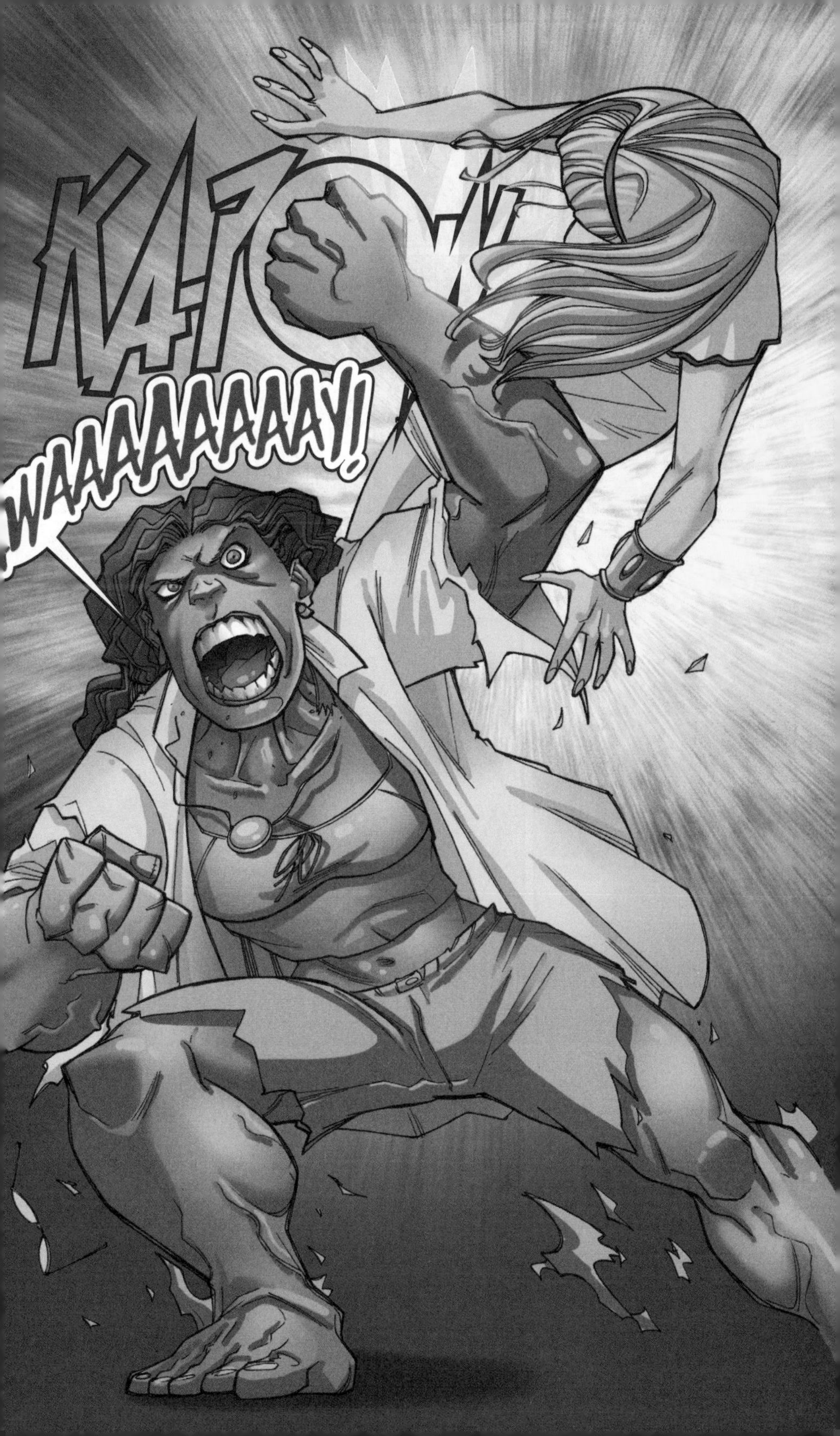
KA-TOW
WAAAAAAAAY!

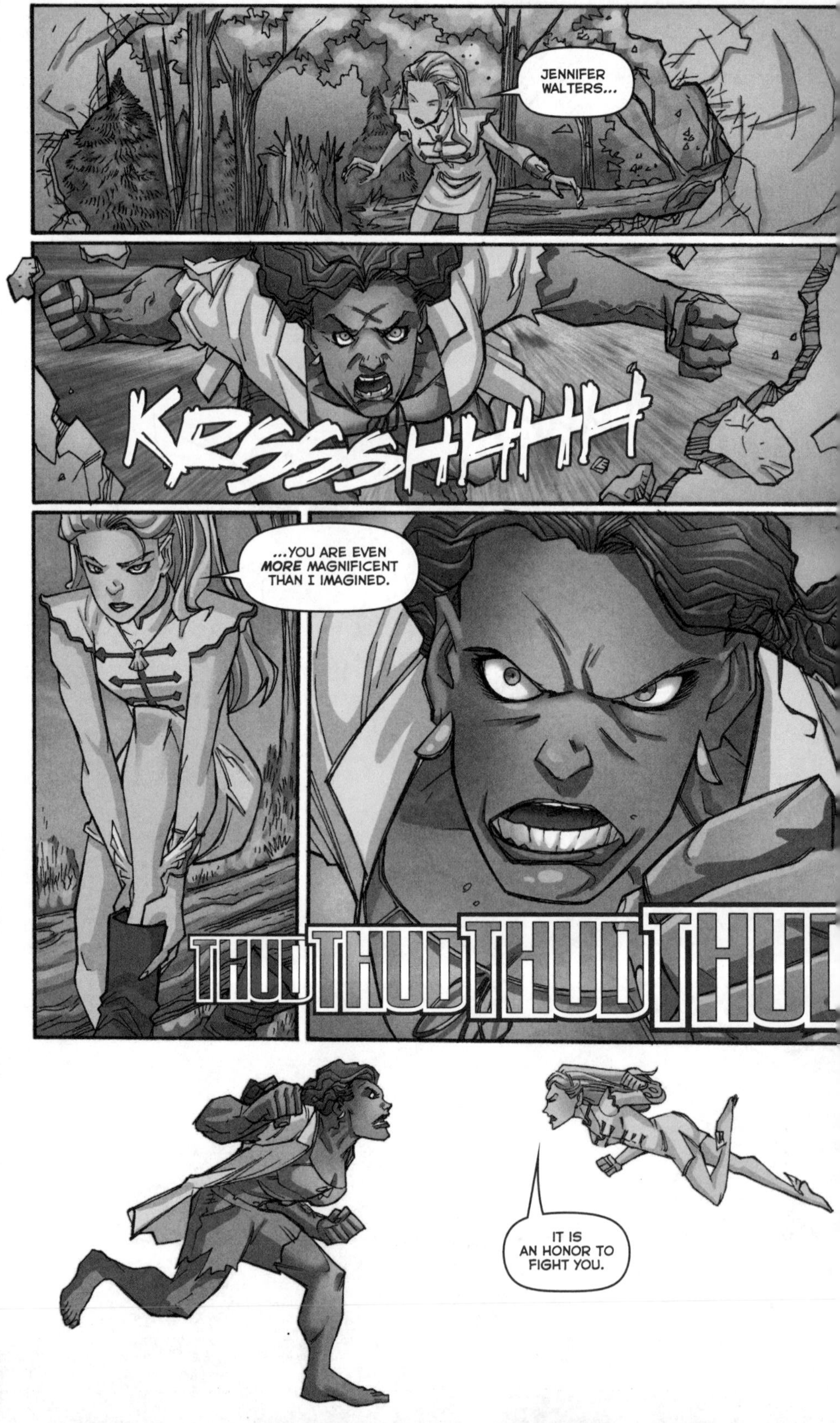
JENNIFER WALTERS...
KRSSSHHHH
...YOU ARE EVEN *MORE* MAGNIFICENT THAN I IMAGINED.
THUD THUD THUD THUD
IT IS AN HONOR TO FIGHT YOU.

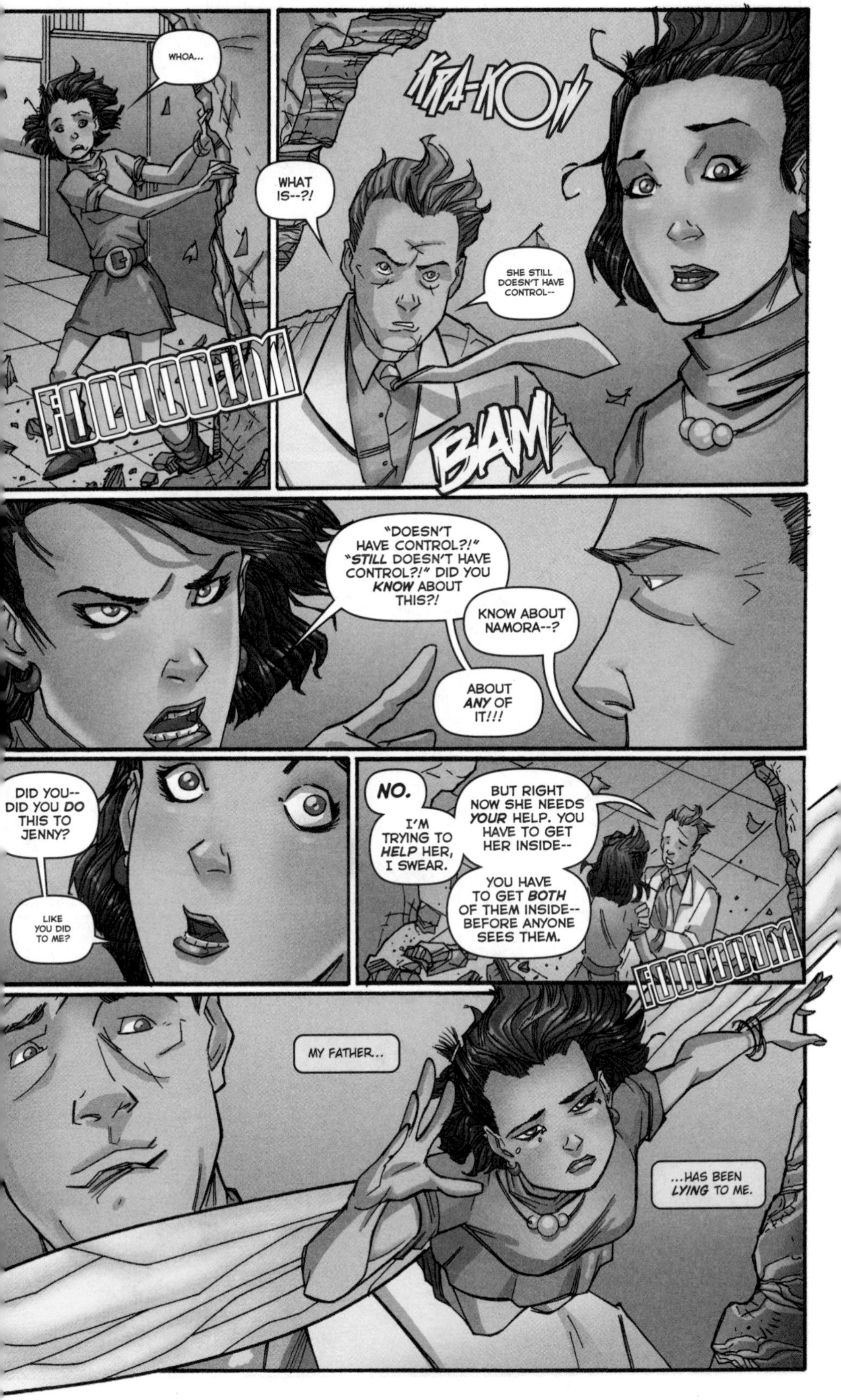
WHOA...
FOOOOOOM
WHAT IS--?!
KRA-KOW
SHE STILL DOESN'T HAVE CONTROL--
BAM
"DOESN'T HAVE CONTROL?!" "STILL DOESN'T HAVE CONTROL?!" DID YOU KNOW ABOUT THIS?!
KNOW ABOUT NAMORA--?
ABOUT ANY OF IT!!!
DID YOU-- DID YOU DO THIS TO JENNY?
LIKE YOU DID TO ME?
NO.
I'M TRYING TO HELP HER, I SWEAR.
BUT RIGHT NOW SHE NEEDS YOUR HELP. YOU HAVE TO GET HER INSIDE--
YOU HAVE TO GET BOTH OF THEM INSIDE-- BEFORE ANYONE SEES THEM.
FOOOOOOM
MY FATHER..
...HAS BEEN LYING TO ME.

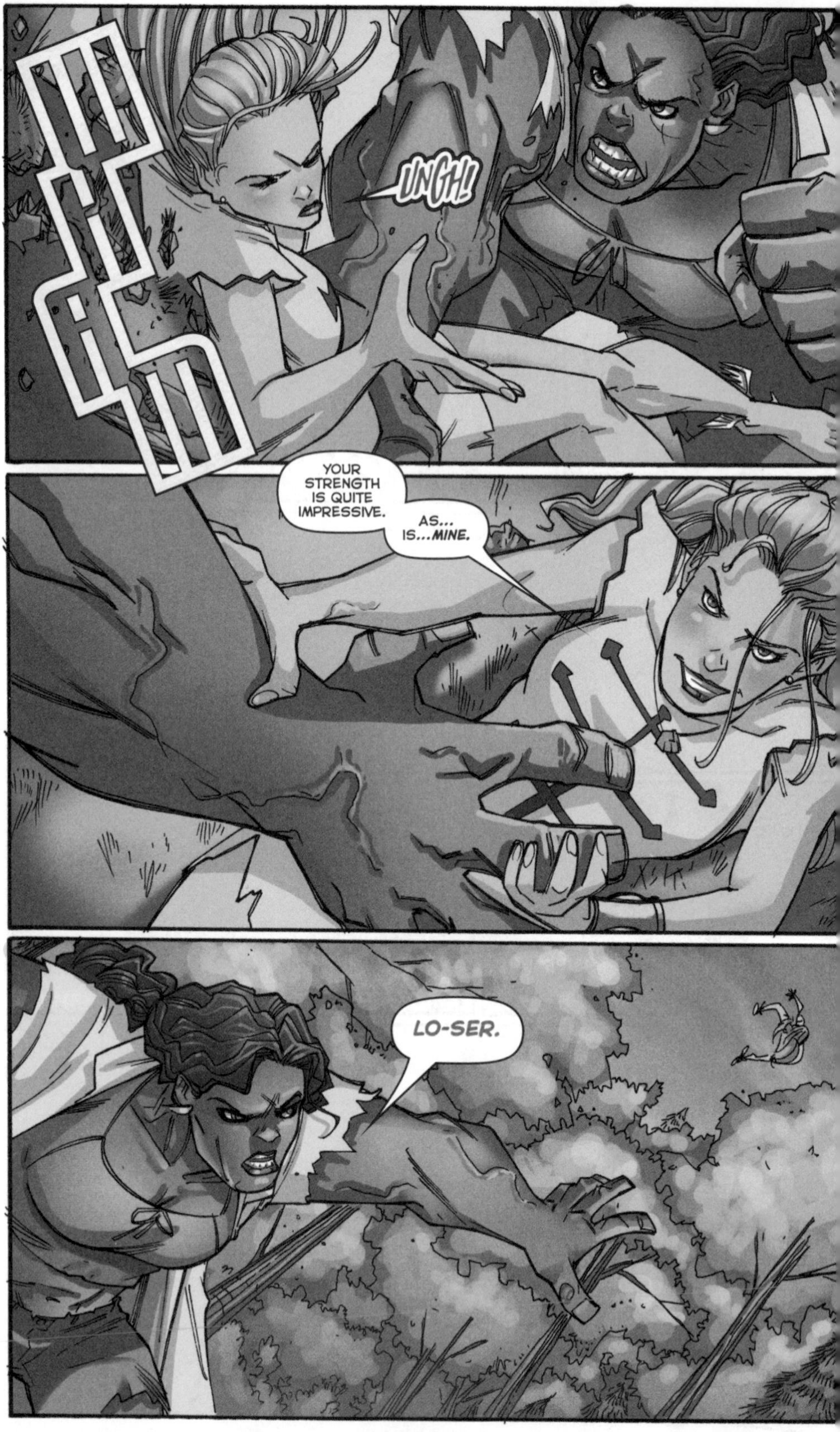
UNGH!
YOUR STRENGTH IS QUITE IMPRESSIVE.
AS... IS...MINE.
LO-SER.

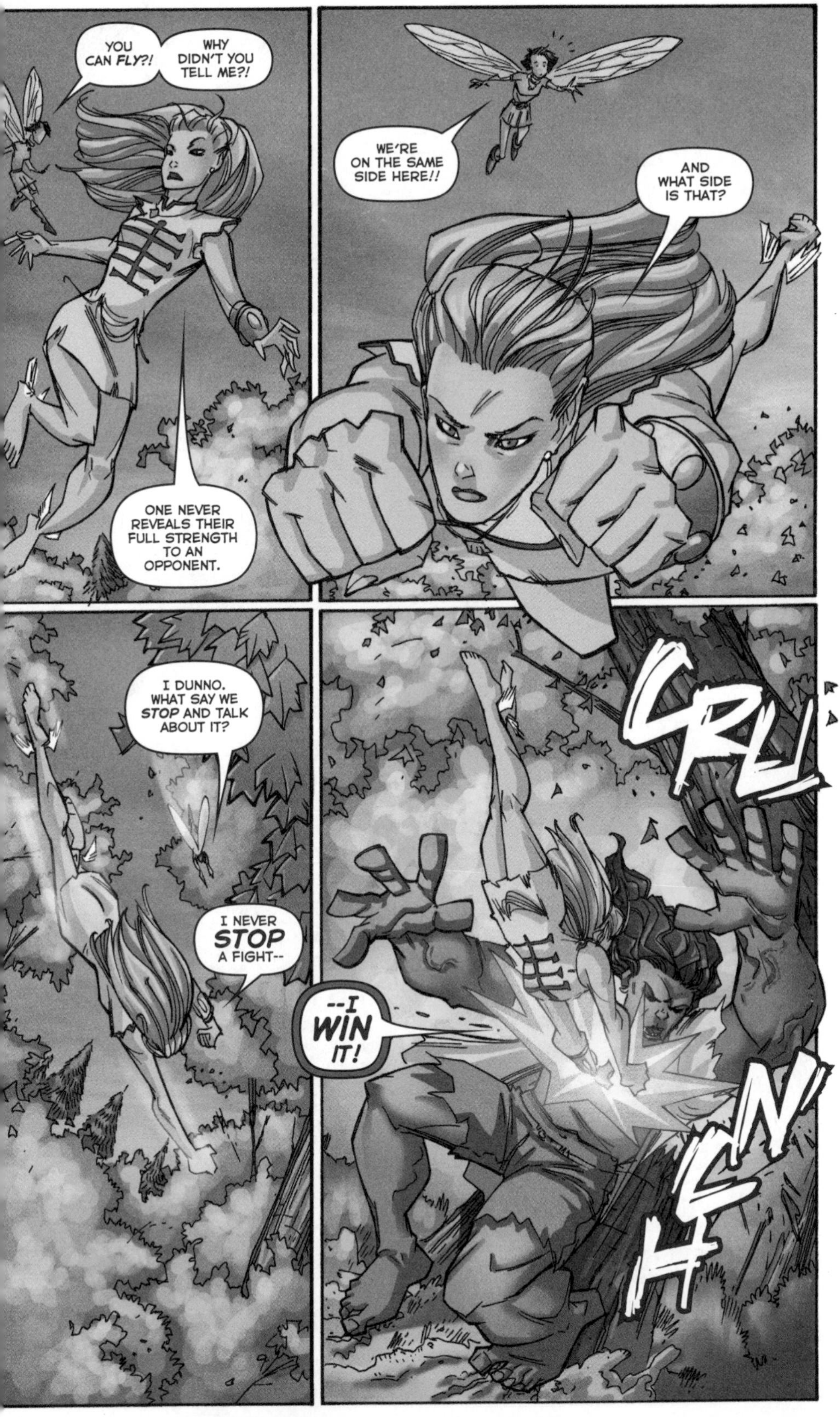
YOU CAN *FLY*?!
WHY DIDN'T YOU TELL ME?!
ONE NEVER REVEALS THEIR FULL STRENGTH TO AN OPPONENT.
WE'RE ON THE SAME SIDE HERE!!
AND WHAT SIDE IS THAT?
I DUNNO. WHAT SAY WE *STOP* AND TALK ABOUT IT?
I NEVER **STOP** A FIGHT--
--I **WIN** IT!
CRUNCH

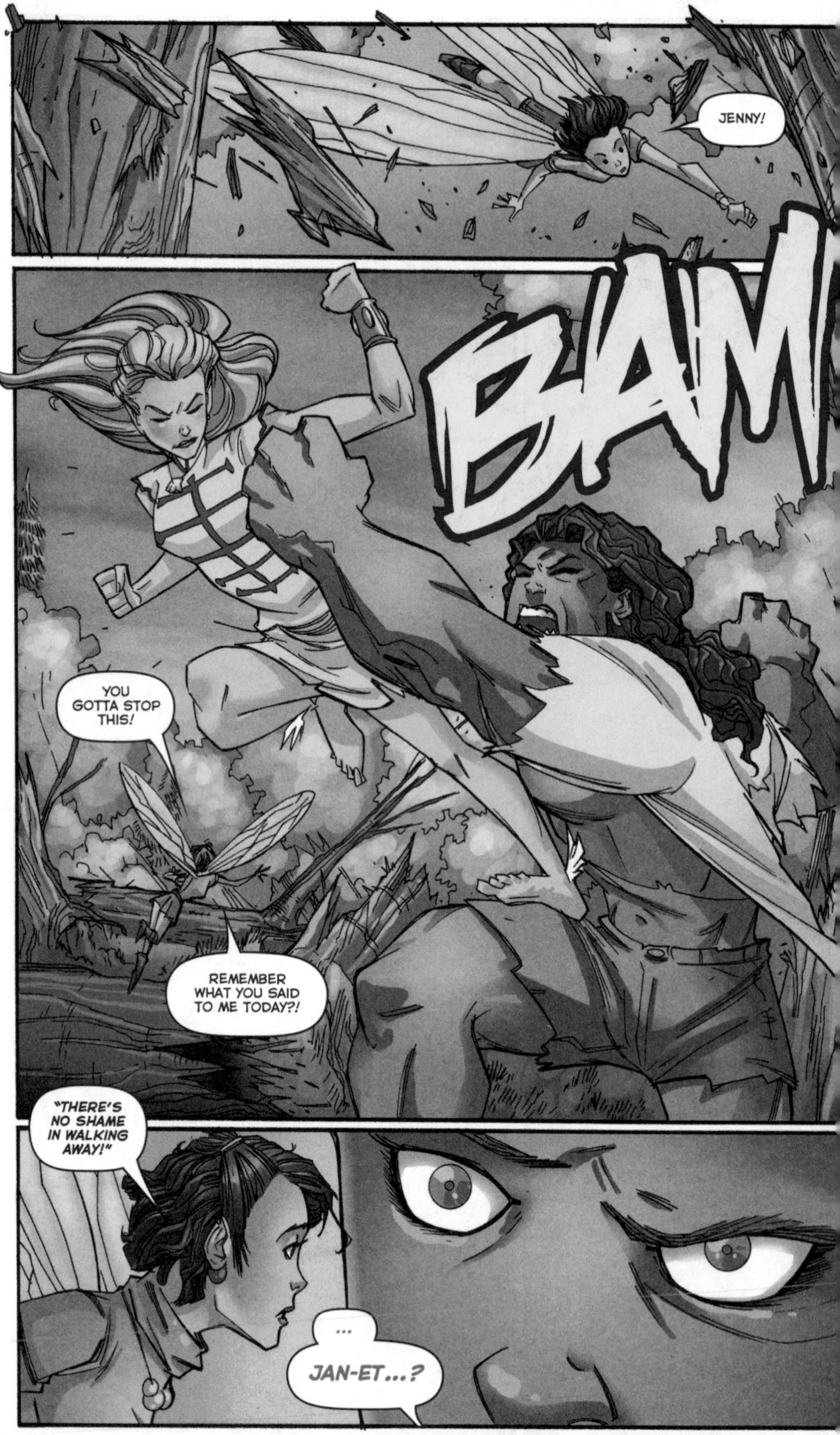
JENNY!
BAM
YOU GOTTA STOP THIS!
REMEMBER WHAT YOU SAID TO ME TODAY?!
"THERE'S NO SHAME IN WALKING AWAY!"
...
JAN-ET...?

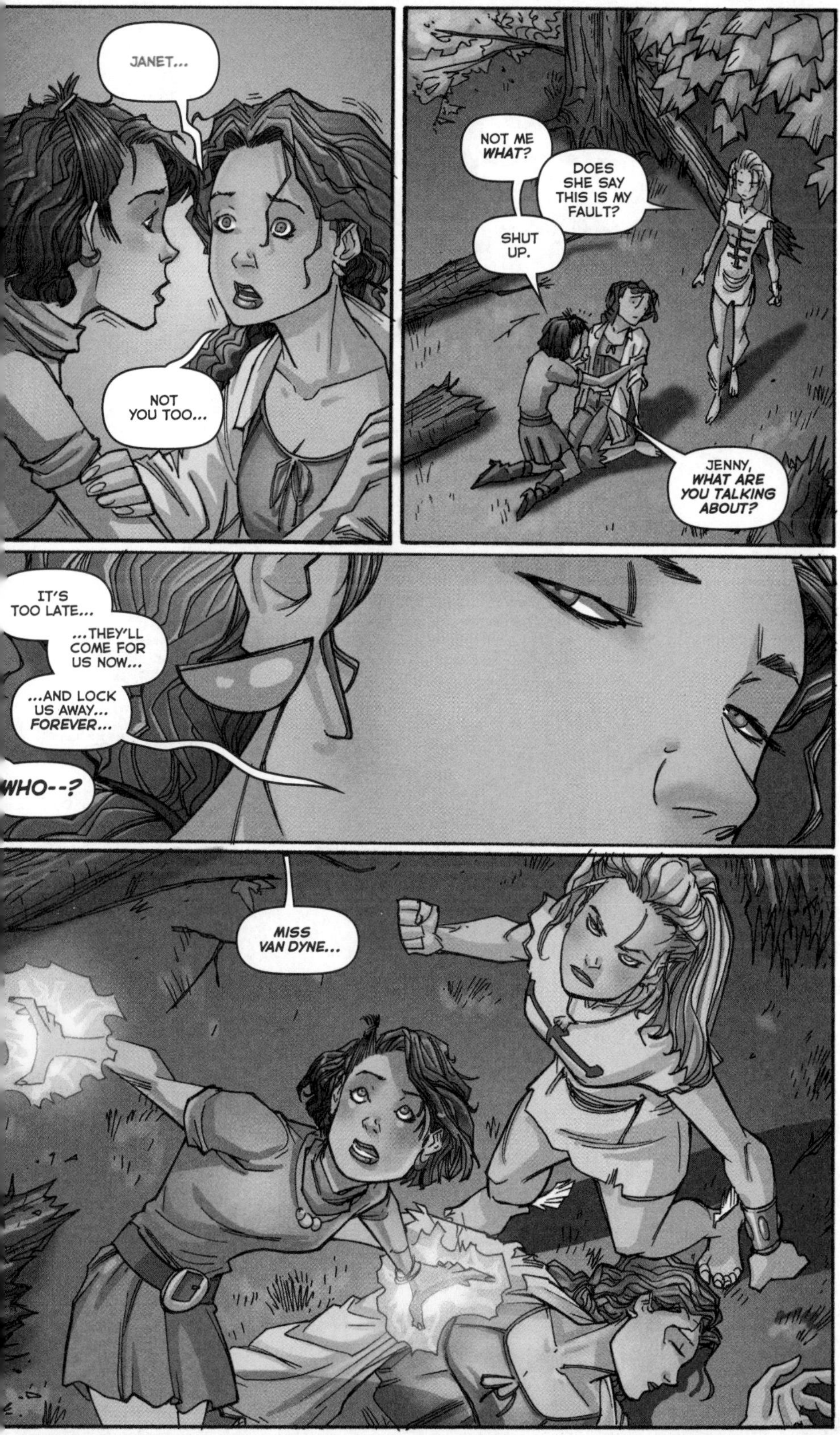
JANET...
NOT YOU TOO...
NOT ME *WHAT?*
DOES SHE SAY THIS IS MY FAULT?
SHUT UP.
JENNY, *WHAT ARE YOU TALKING ABOUT?*
IT'S TOO LATE...
...THEY'LL COME FOR US NOW...
...AND LOCK US AWAY... *FOREVER...*
WHO--?
MISS VAN DYNE...

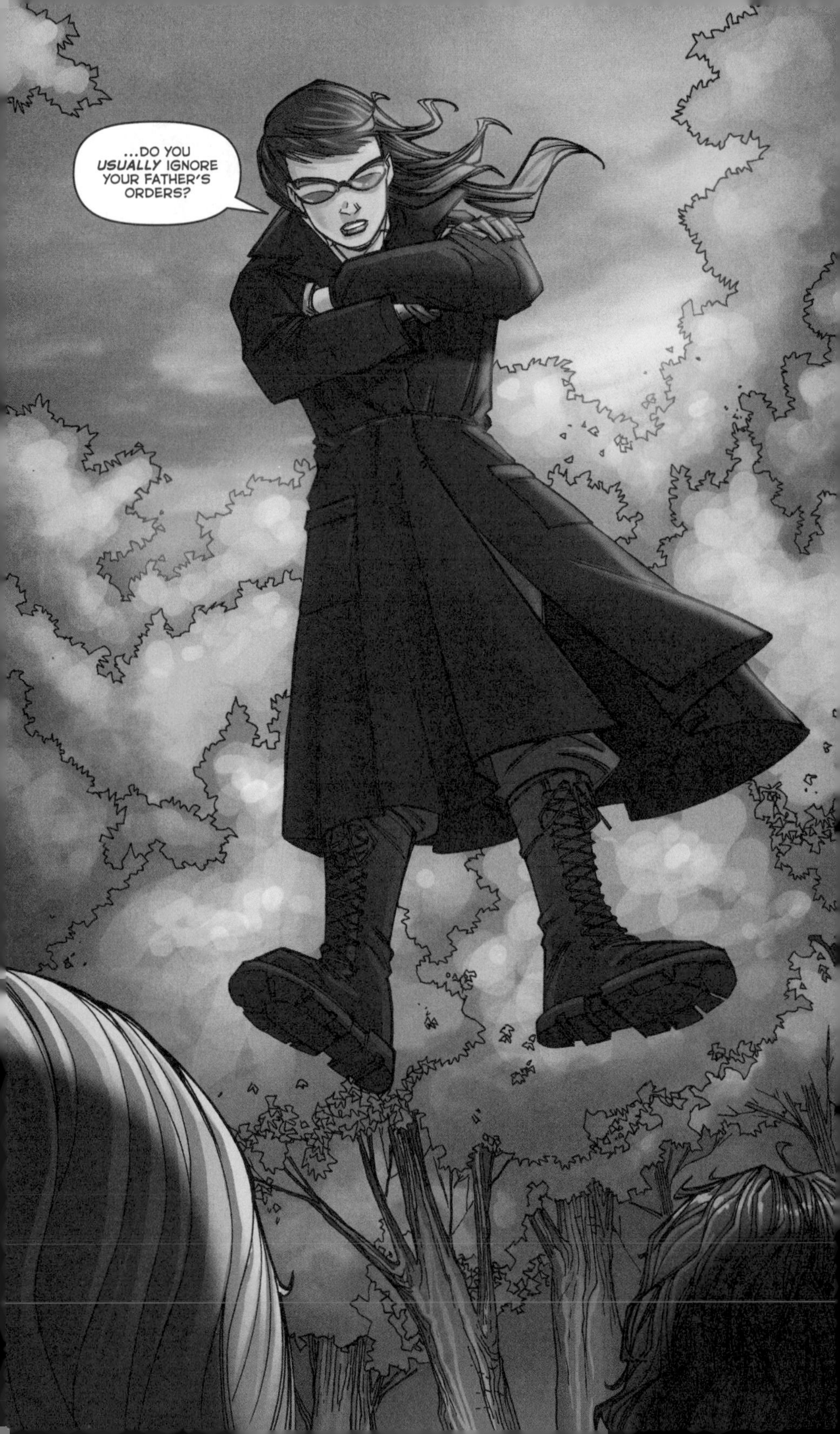
...DO YOU USUALLY IGNORE YOUR FATHER'S ORDERS?

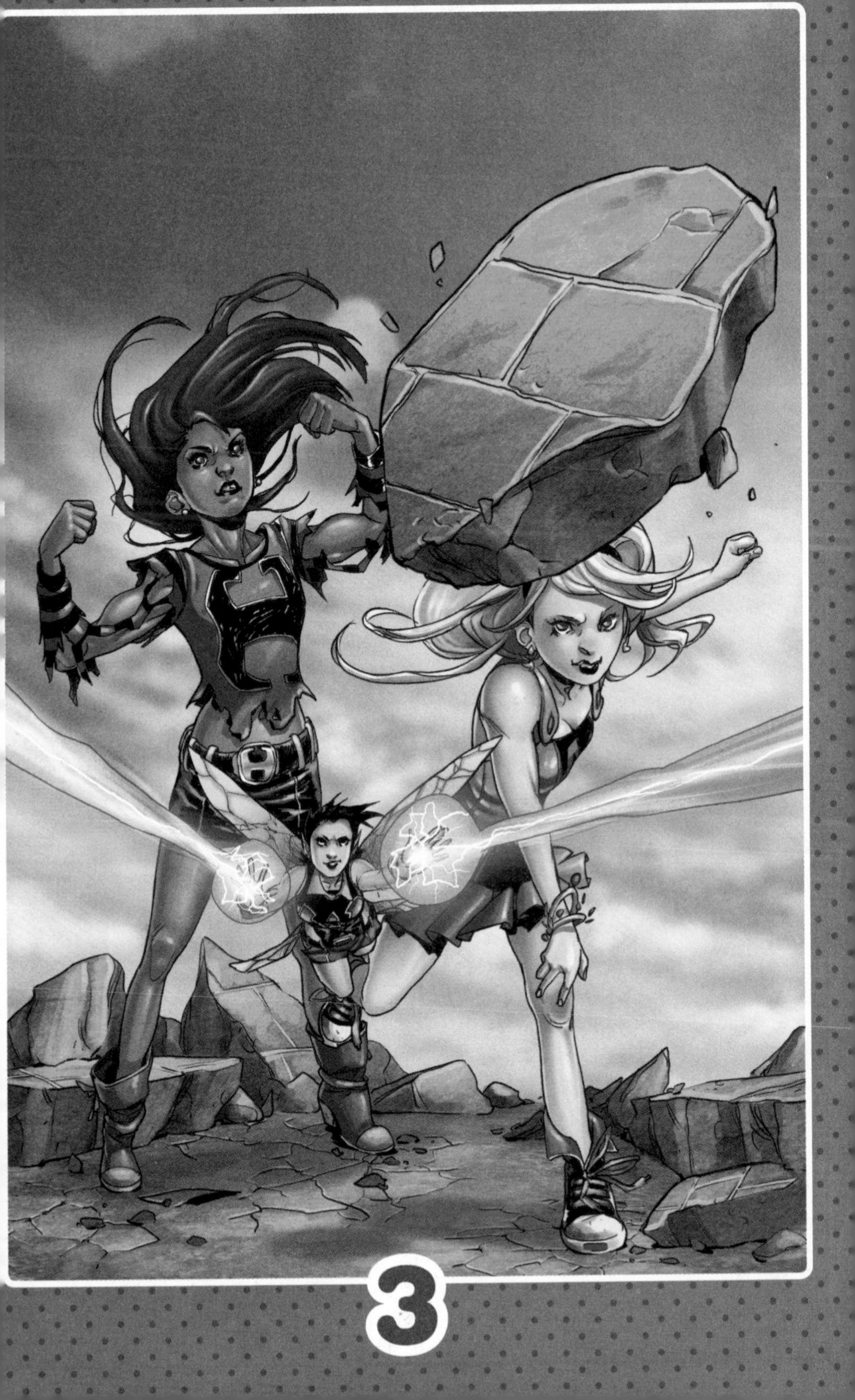

3

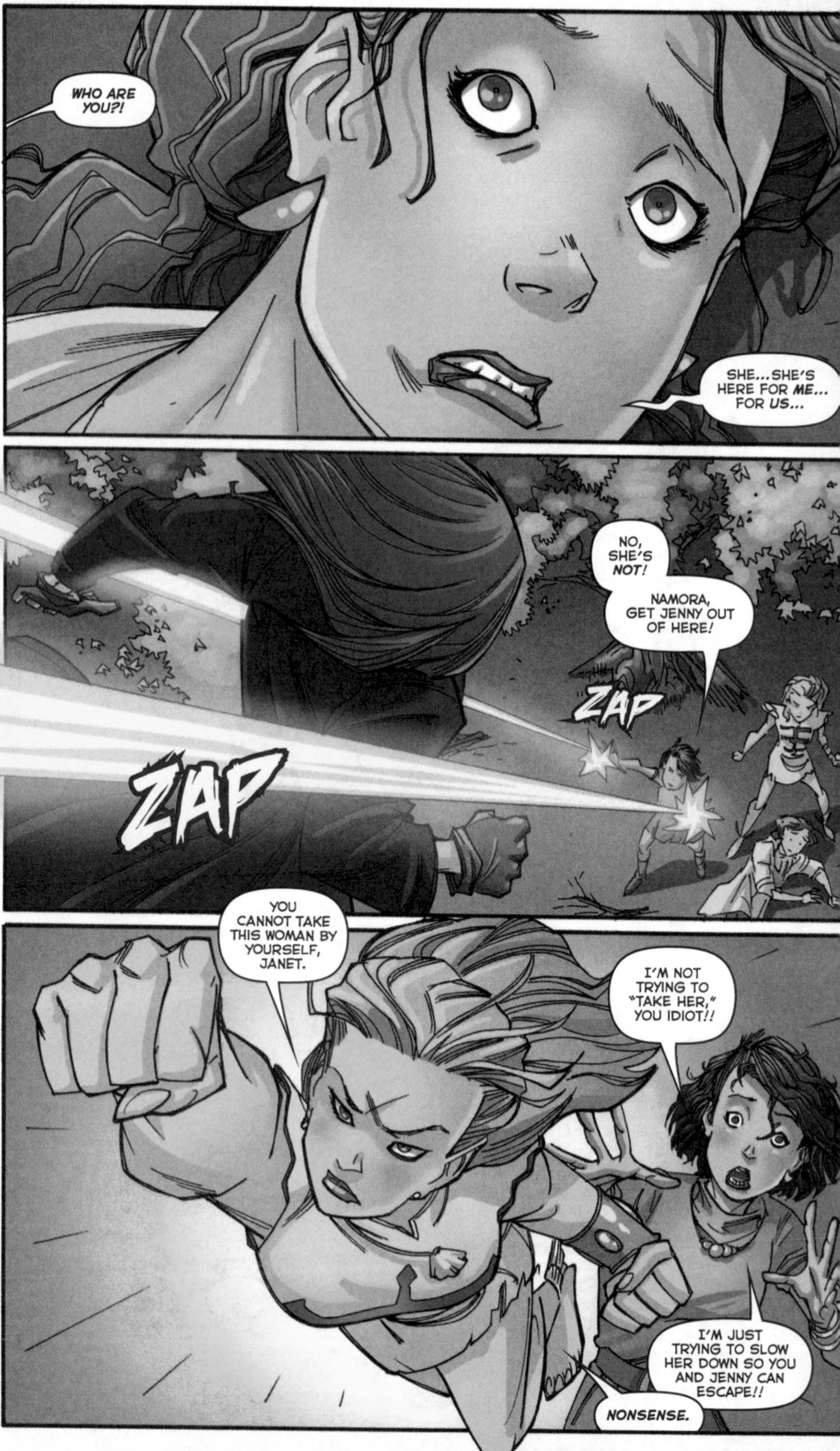
WHO ARE YOU?!
SHE...SHE'S HERE FOR ME... FOR US...
NO, SHE'S NOT!
NAMORA, GET JENNY OUT OF HERE!
ZAP
ZAP
YOU CANNOT TAKE THIS WOMAN BY YOURSELF, JANET.
I'M NOT TRYING TO "TAKE HER," YOU IDIOT!!
I'M JUST TRYING TO SLOW HER DOWN SO YOU AND JENNY CAN ESCAPE!!
NONSENSE.

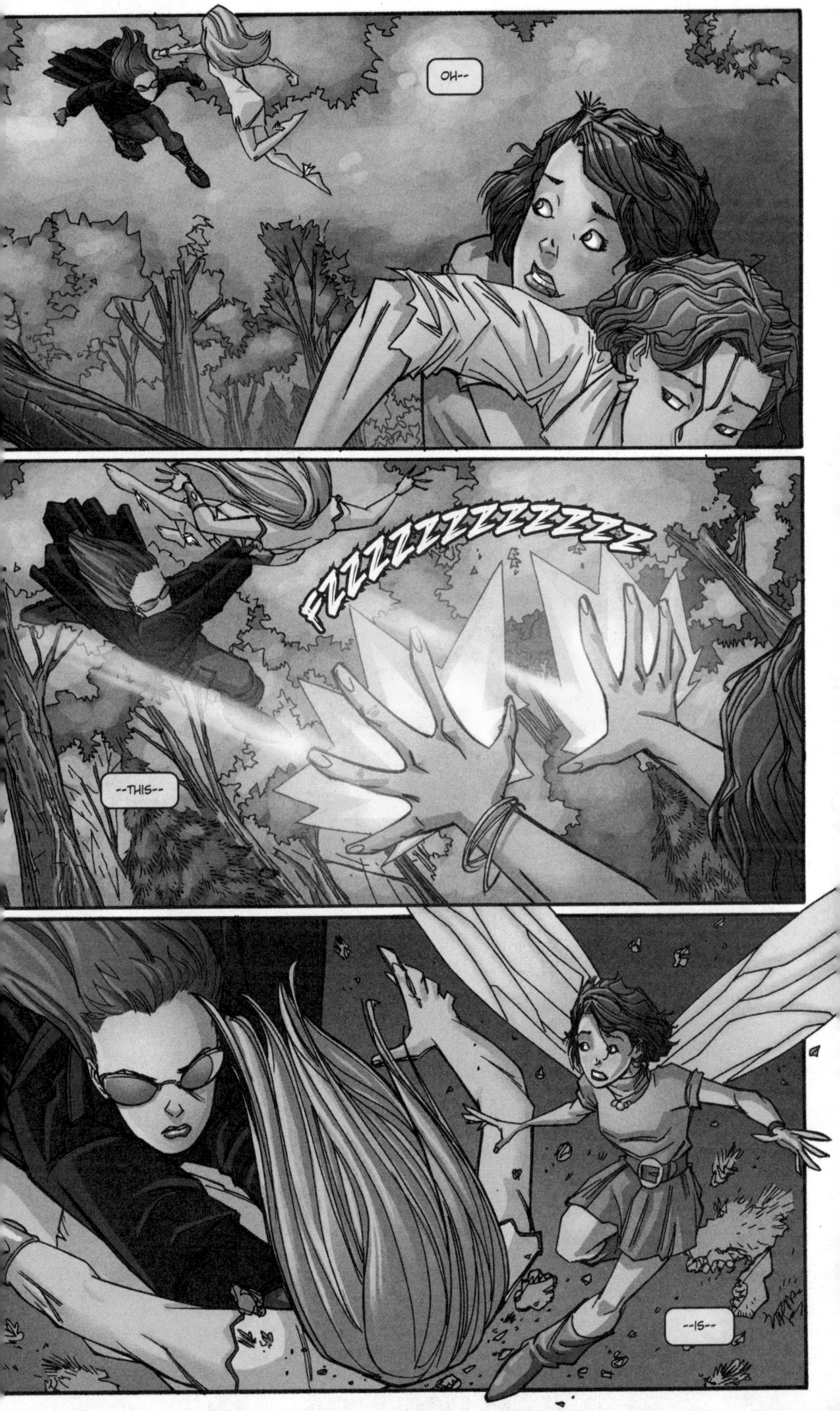
OH--
FZZZZZZZZZZZZZZZZ
--THIS--
--IS--

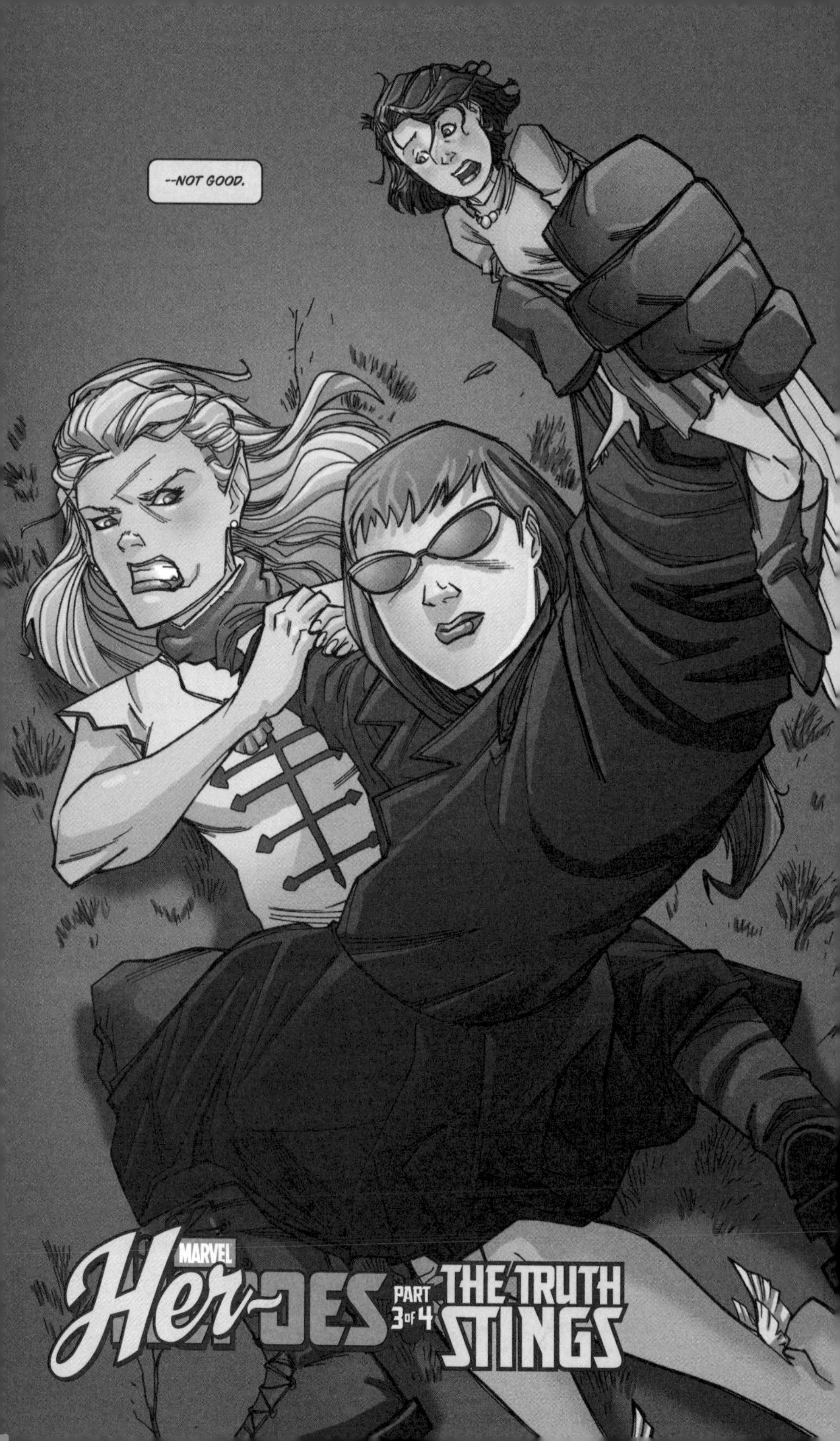
--NOT GOOD.
MARVEL Her-oes PART 3 of 4 THE TRUTH STINGS

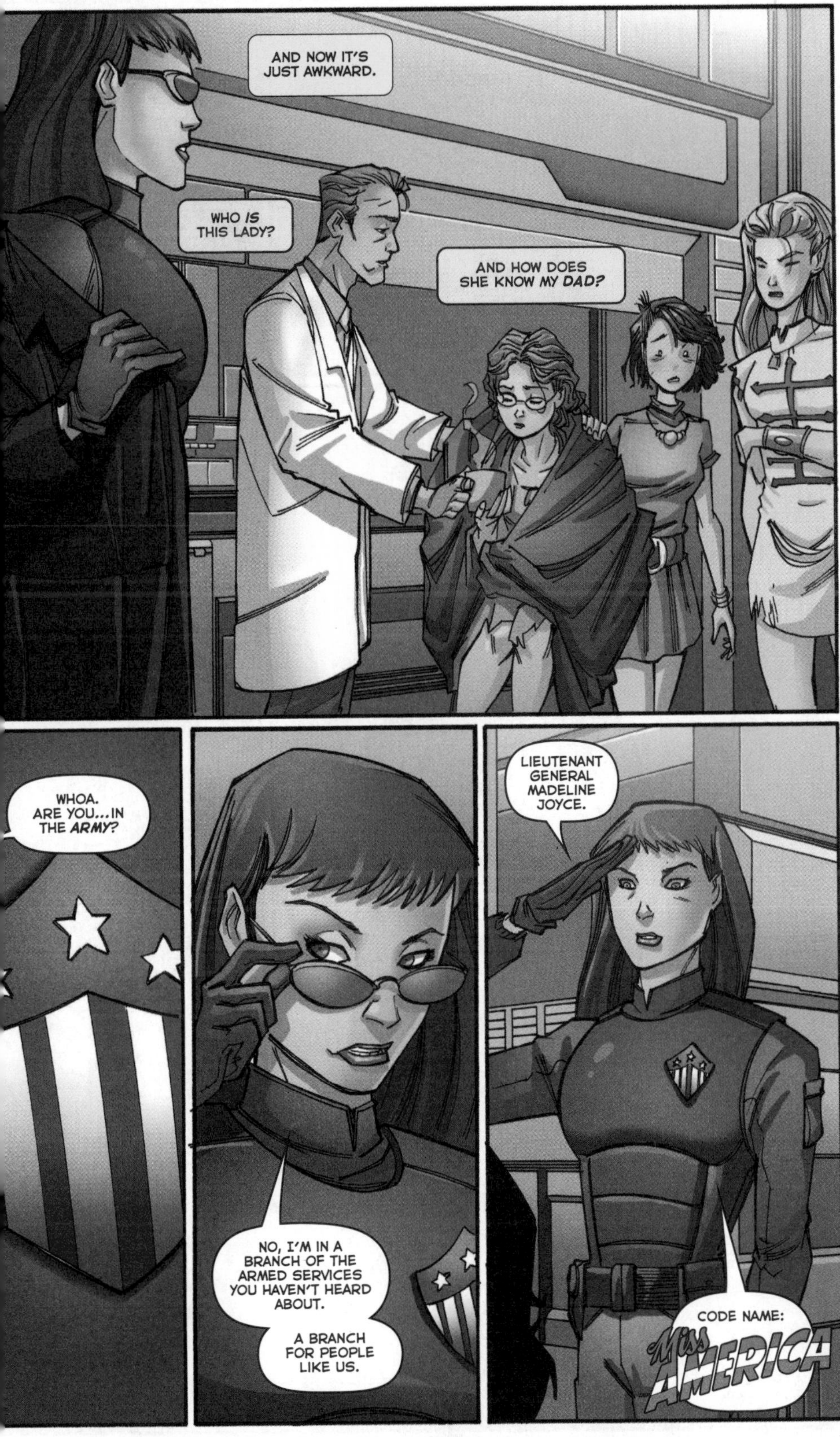
AND NOW IT'S JUST AWKWARD.
WHO *IS* THIS LADY?
AND HOW DOES SHE KNOW MY *DAD?*
WHOA. ARE YOU...IN THE *ARMY?*
NO, I'M IN A BRANCH OF THE ARMED SERVICES YOU HAVEN'T HEARD ABOUT.
A BRANCH FOR PEOPLE LIKE US.
LIEUTENANT GENERAL MADELINE JOYCE.
CODE NAME:
Miss AMERICA

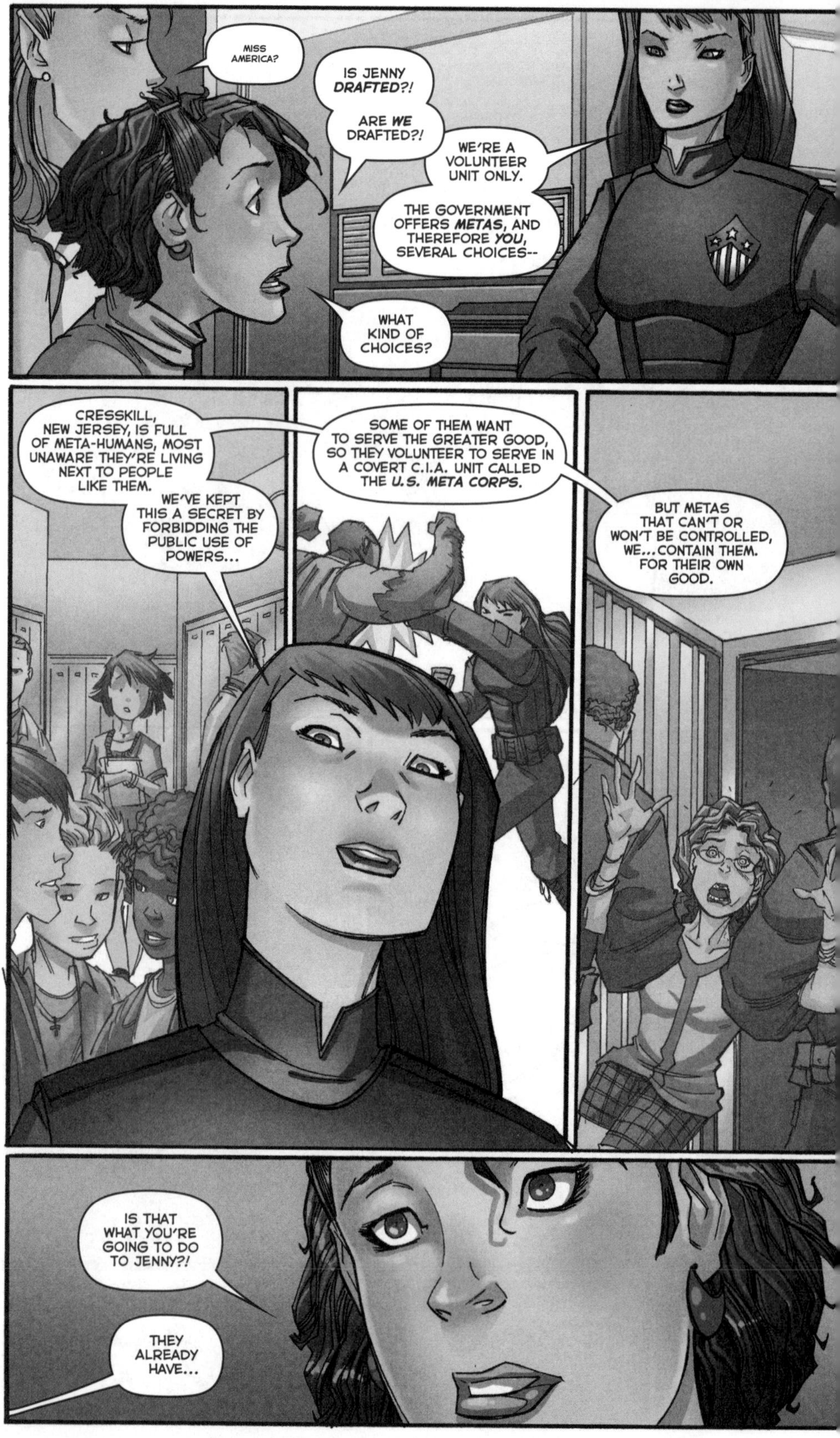
MISS AMERICA?
IS JENNY DRAFTED?!
ARE WE DRAFTED?!
WE'RE A VOLUNTEER UNIT ONLY.
THE GOVERNMENT OFFERS METAS, AND THEREFORE YOU, SEVERAL CHOICES--
WHAT KIND OF CHOICES?
CRESSKILL, NEW JERSEY, IS FULL OF META-HUMANS, MOST UNAWARE THEY'RE LIVING NEXT TO PEOPLE LIKE THEM.
WE'VE KEPT THIS A SECRET BY FORBIDDING THE PUBLIC USE OF POWERS...
SOME OF THEM WANT TO SERVE THE GREATER GOOD, SO THEY VOLUNTEER TO SERVE IN A COVERT C.I.A. UNIT CALLED THE U.S. META CORPS.
BUT METAS THAT CAN'T OR WON'T BE CONTROLLED, WE...CONTAIN THEM. FOR THEIR OWN GOOD.
IS THAT WHAT YOU'RE GOING TO DO TO JENNY?!
THEY ALREADY HAVE...

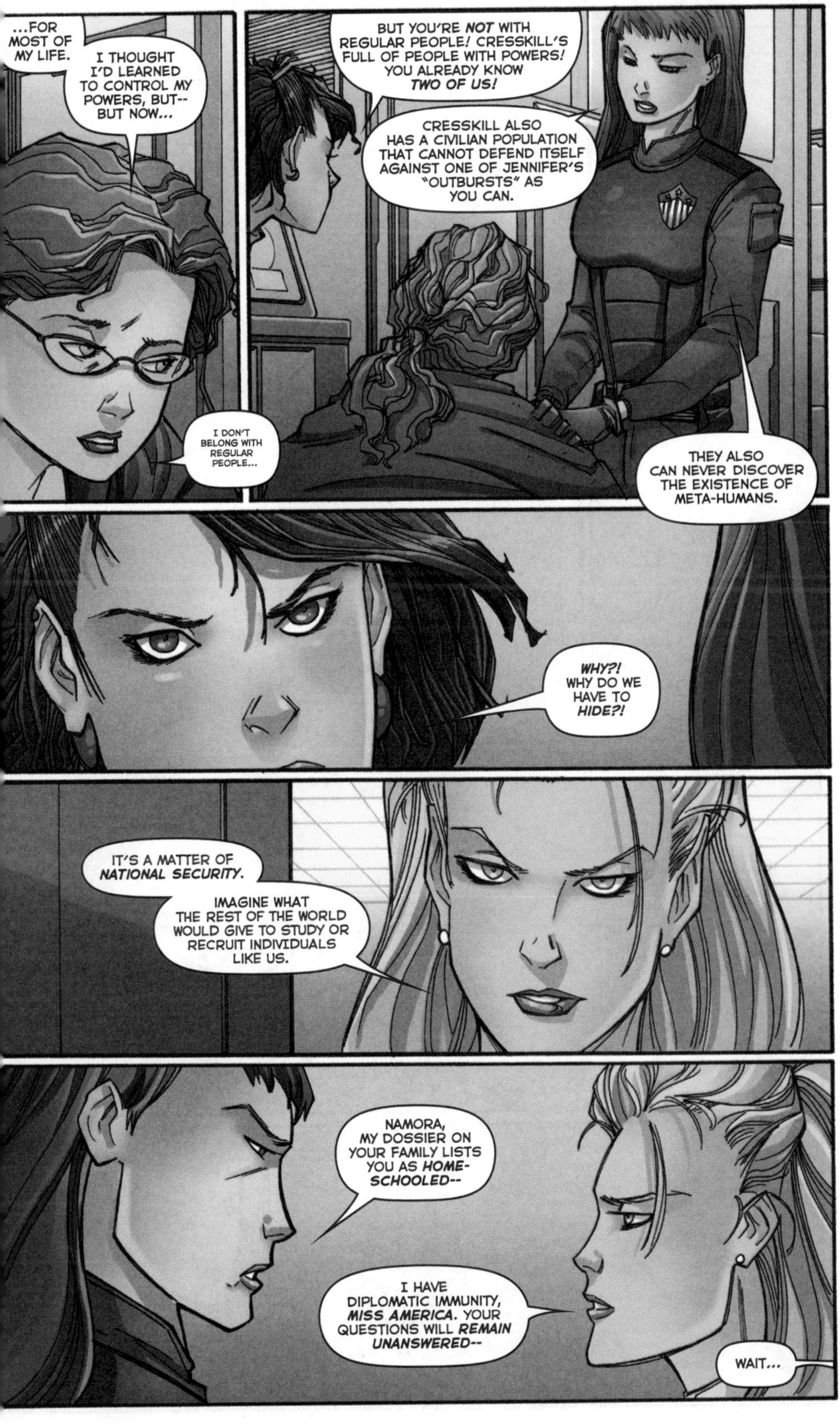
...FOR MOST OF MY LIFE.
I THOUGHT I'D LEARNED TO CONTROL MY POWERS, BUT-- BUT NOW...
I DON'T BELONG WITH REGULAR PEOPLE...
BUT YOU'RE NOT WITH REGULAR PEOPLE! CRESSKILL'S FULL OF PEOPLE WITH POWERS! YOU ALREADY KNOW TWO OF US!
CRESSKILL ALSO HAS A CIVILIAN POPULATION THAT CANNOT DEFEND ITSELF AGAINST ONE OF JENNIFER'S "OUTBURSTS" AS YOU CAN.
THEY ALSO CAN NEVER DISCOVER THE EXISTENCE OF META-HUMANS.
WHY?! WHY DO WE HAVE TO HIDE?!
IT'S A MATTER OF NATIONAL SECURITY.
IMAGINE WHAT THE REST OF THE WORLD WOULD GIVE TO STUDY OR RECRUIT INDIVIDUALS LIKE US.
NAMORA, MY DOSSIER ON YOUR FAMILY LISTS YOU AS HOME-SCHOOLED--
I HAVE DIPLOMATIC IMMUNITY, MISS AMERICA. YOUR QUESTIONS WILL REMAIN UNANSWERED--
WAIT...

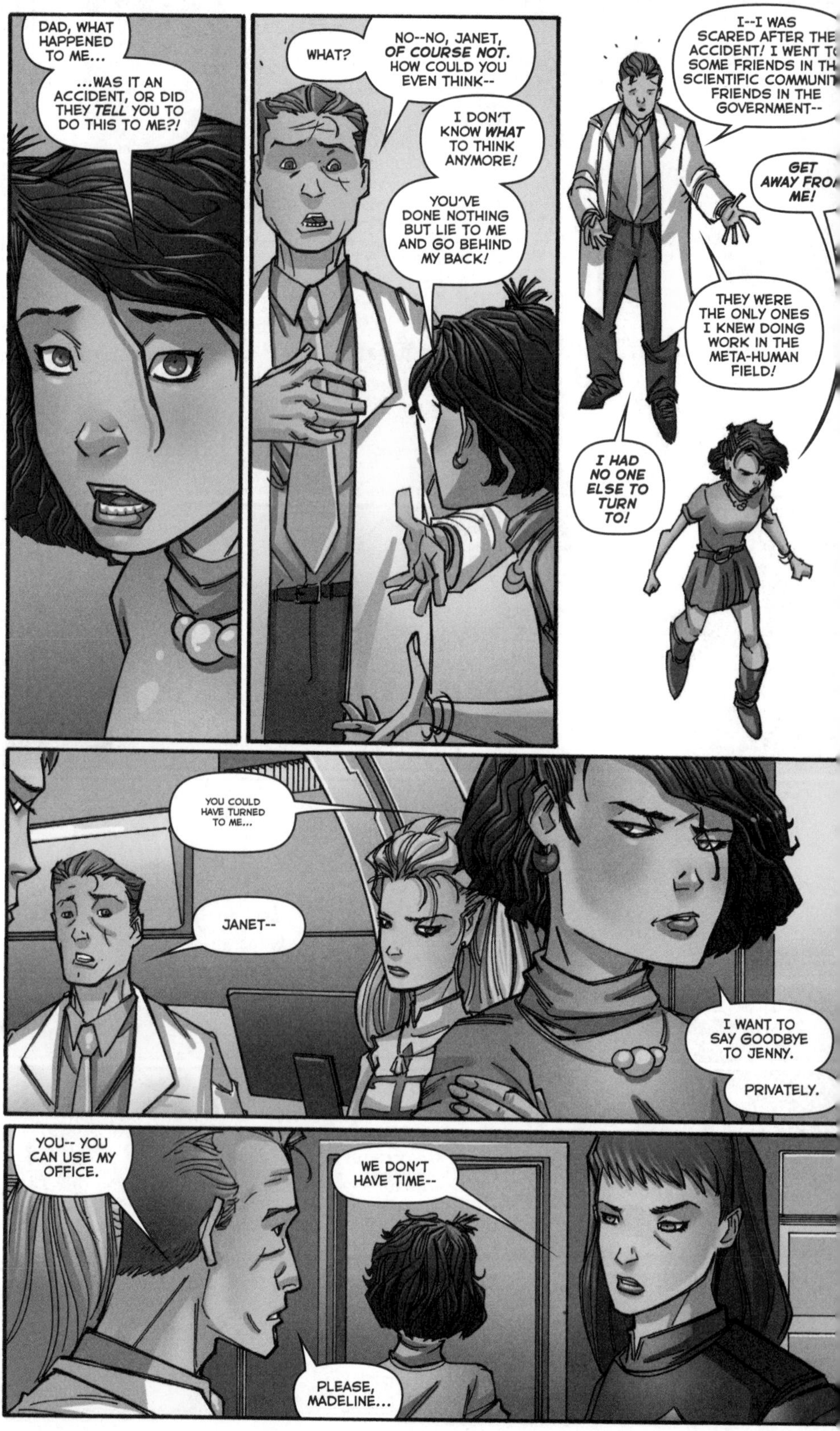
DAD, WHAT HAPPENED TO ME...
...WAS IT AN ACCIDENT, OR DID THEY *TELL* YOU TO DO THIS TO ME?!
WHAT?
NO--NO, JANET, *OF COURSE NOT*. HOW COULD YOU EVEN THINK--
I DON'T KNOW *WHAT* TO THINK ANYMORE!
YOU'VE DONE NOTHING BUT LIE TO ME AND GO BEHIND MY BACK!
I--I WAS SCARED AFTER THE ACCIDENT! I WENT TO SOME FRIENDS IN THE SCIENTIFIC COMMUNITY, FRIENDS IN THE GOVERNMENT--
GET AWAY FROM ME!
THEY WERE THE ONLY ONES I KNEW DOING WORK IN THE META-HUMAN FIELD!
I HAD NO ONE ELSE TO TURN TO!
YOU COULD HAVE TURNED TO ME...
JANET--
I WANT TO SAY GOODBYE TO JENNY.
PRIVATELY.
YOU-- YOU CAN USE MY OFFICE.
WE DON'T HAVE TIME--
PLEASE, MADELINE...

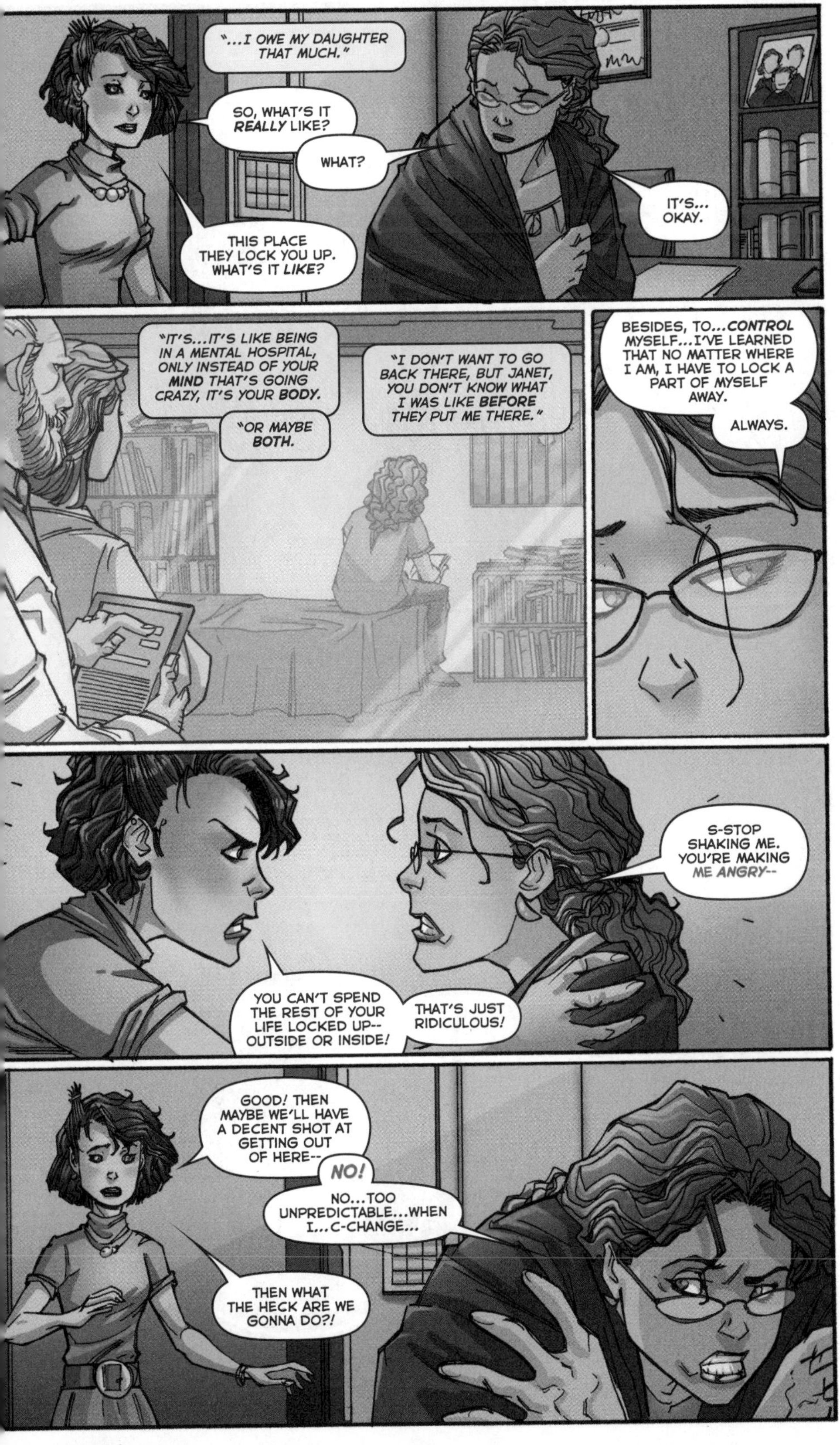
"...I OWE MY DAUGHTER THAT MUCH."
SO, WHAT'S IT *REALLY* LIKE?
WHAT?
THIS PLACE THEY LOCK YOU UP. WHAT'S IT *LIKE*?
IT'S... OKAY.
"IT'S...IT'S LIKE BEING IN A MENTAL HOSPITAL, ONLY INSTEAD OF YOUR *MIND* THAT'S GOING CRAZY, IT'S YOUR *BODY*.
"OR MAYBE *BOTH*.
"I DON'T WANT TO GO BACK THERE, BUT JANET, YOU DON'T KNOW WHAT I WAS LIKE *BEFORE* THEY PUT ME THERE."
BESIDES, TO...*CONTROL* MYSELF...I'VE LEARNED THAT NO MATTER WHERE I AM, I HAVE TO LOCK A PART OF MYSELF AWAY.
ALWAYS.
S-STOP SHAKING ME. YOU'RE MAKING *ME ANGRY*--
YOU CAN'T SPEND THE REST OF YOUR LIFE LOCKED UP-- OUTSIDE OR INSIDE!
THAT'S JUST RIDICULOUS!
GOOD! THEN MAYBE WE'LL HAVE A DECENT SHOT AT GETTING OUT OF HERE--
NO!
NO...TOO UNPREDICTABLE...WHEN I...C-CHANGE...
THEN WHAT THE HECK ARE WE GONNA DO?!

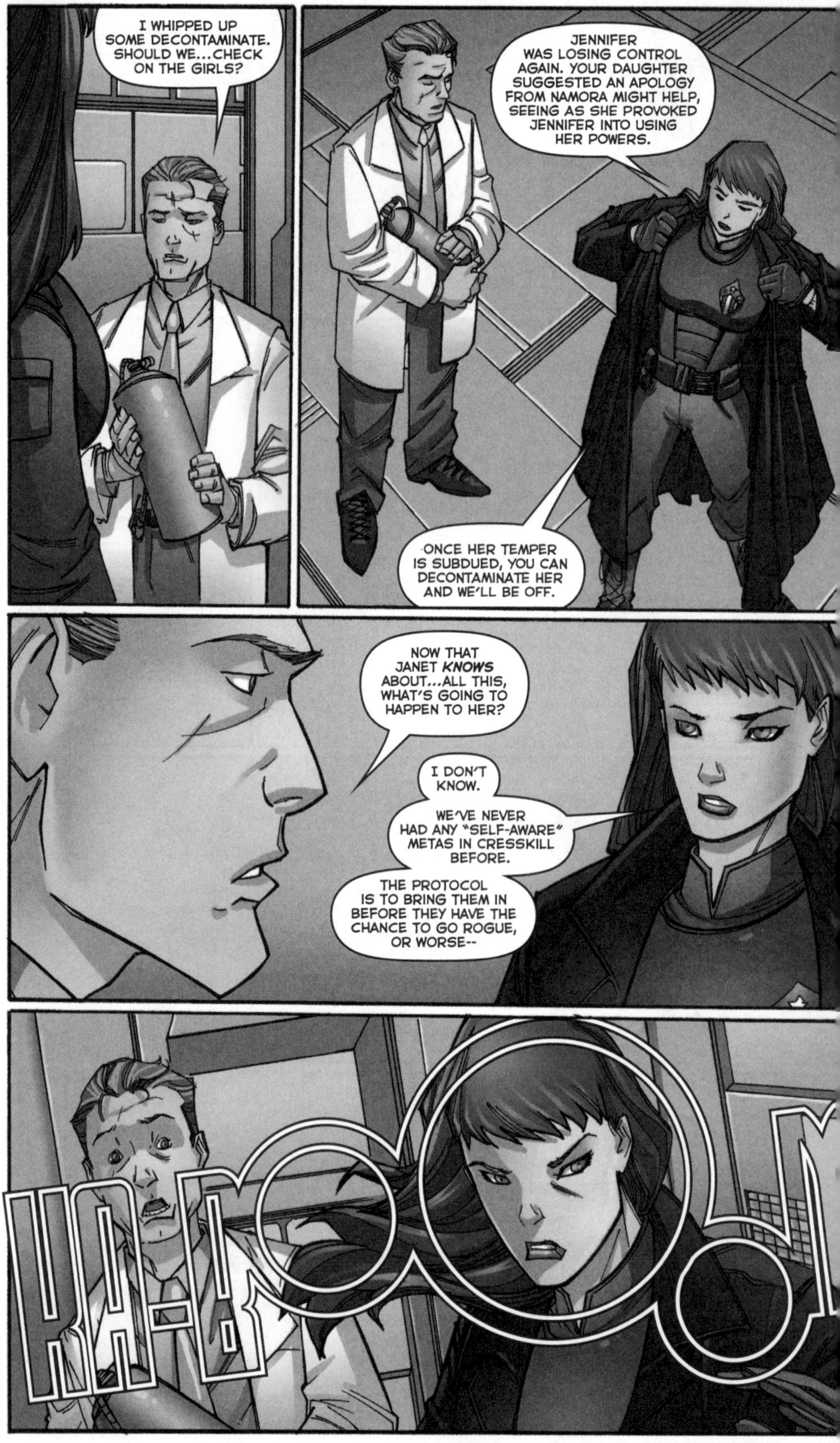
I WHIPPED UP SOME DECONTAMINATE. SHOULD WE...CHECK ON THE GIRLS?
JENNIFER WAS LOSING CONTROL AGAIN. YOUR DAUGHTER SUGGESTED AN APOLOGY FROM NAMORA MIGHT HELP, SEEING AS SHE PROVOKED JENNIFER INTO USING HER POWERS.
ONCE HER TEMPER IS SUBDUED, YOU CAN DECONTAMINATE HER AND WE'LL BE OFF.
NOW THAT JANET *KNOWS* ABOUT...ALL THIS, WHAT'S GOING TO HAPPEN TO HER?
I DON'T KNOW.
WE'VE NEVER HAD ANY "SELF-AWARE" METAS IN CRESSKILL BEFORE.
THE PROTOCOL IS TO BRING THEM IN BEFORE THEY HAVE THE CHANCE TO GO ROGUE, OR WORSE--
KA-BOOOM

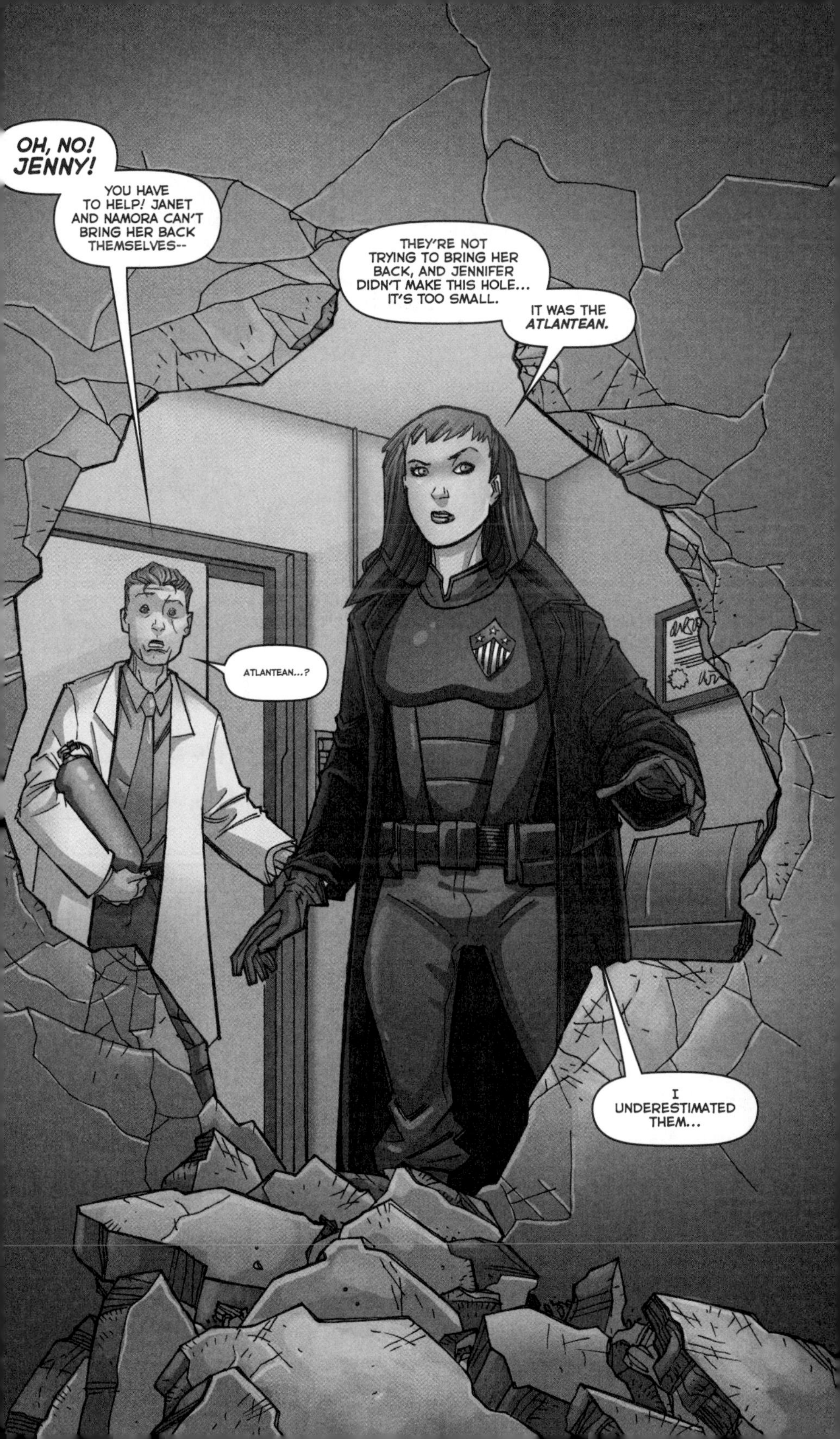
OH, NO! JENNY!
YOU HAVE TO HELP! JANET AND NAMORA CAN'T BRING HER BACK THEMSELVES--
THEY'RE NOT TRYING TO BRING HER BACK, AND JENNIFER DIDN'T MAKE THIS HOLE... IT'S TOO SMALL.
IT WAS THE *ATLANTEAN.*
ATLANTEAN...?
I UNDERESTIMATED THEM...

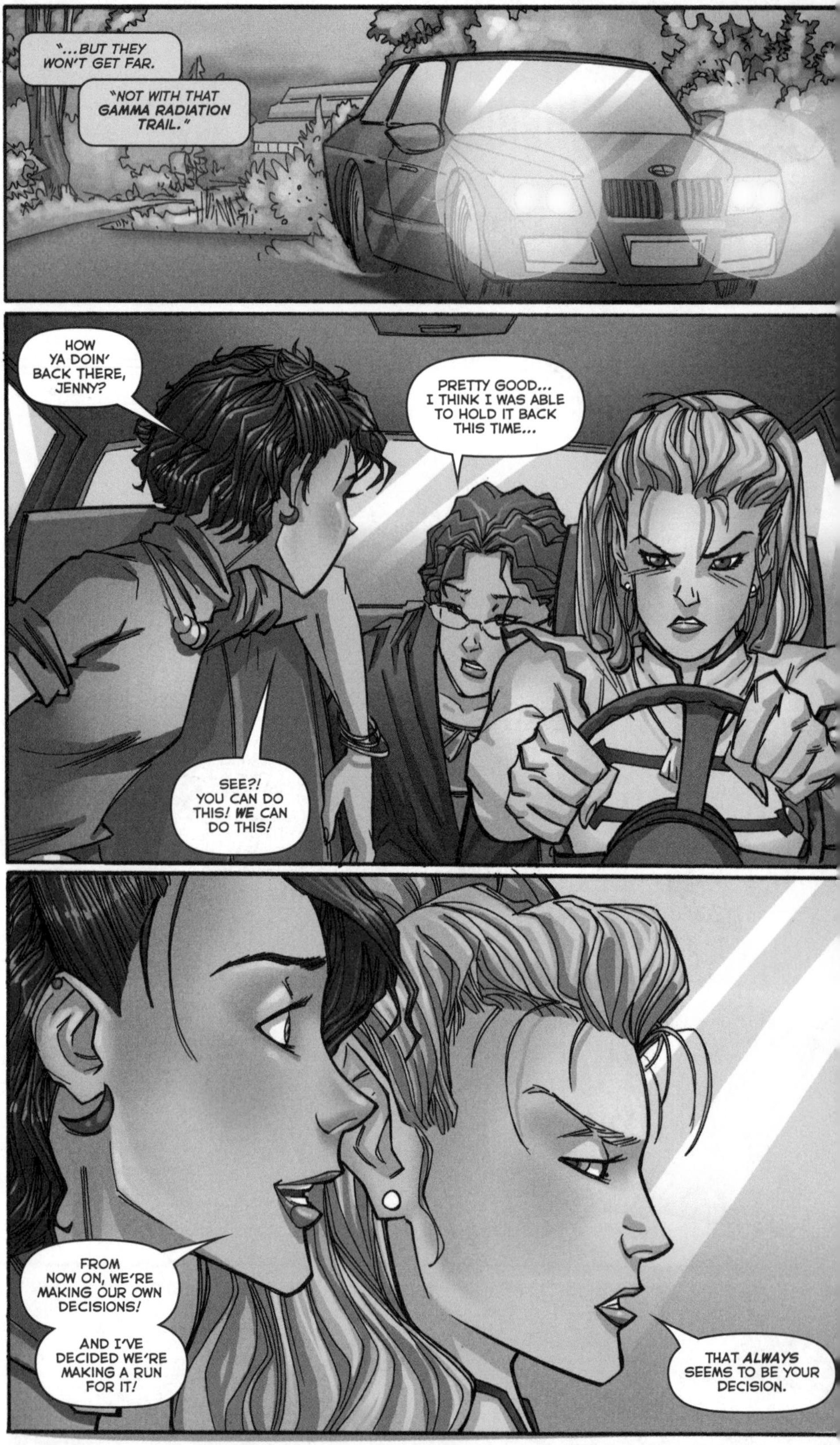
"...BUT THEY WON'T GET FAR.
"NOT WITH THAT GAMMA RADIATION TRAIL."
HOW YA DOIN' BACK THERE, JENNY?
PRETTY GOOD... I THINK I WAS ABLE TO HOLD IT BACK THIS TIME...
SEE?! YOU CAN DO THIS! WE CAN DO THIS!
FROM NOW ON, WE'RE MAKING OUR OWN DECISIONS!
AND I'VE DECIDED WE'RE MAKING A RUN FOR IT!
THAT ALWAYS SEEMS TO BE YOUR DECISION.

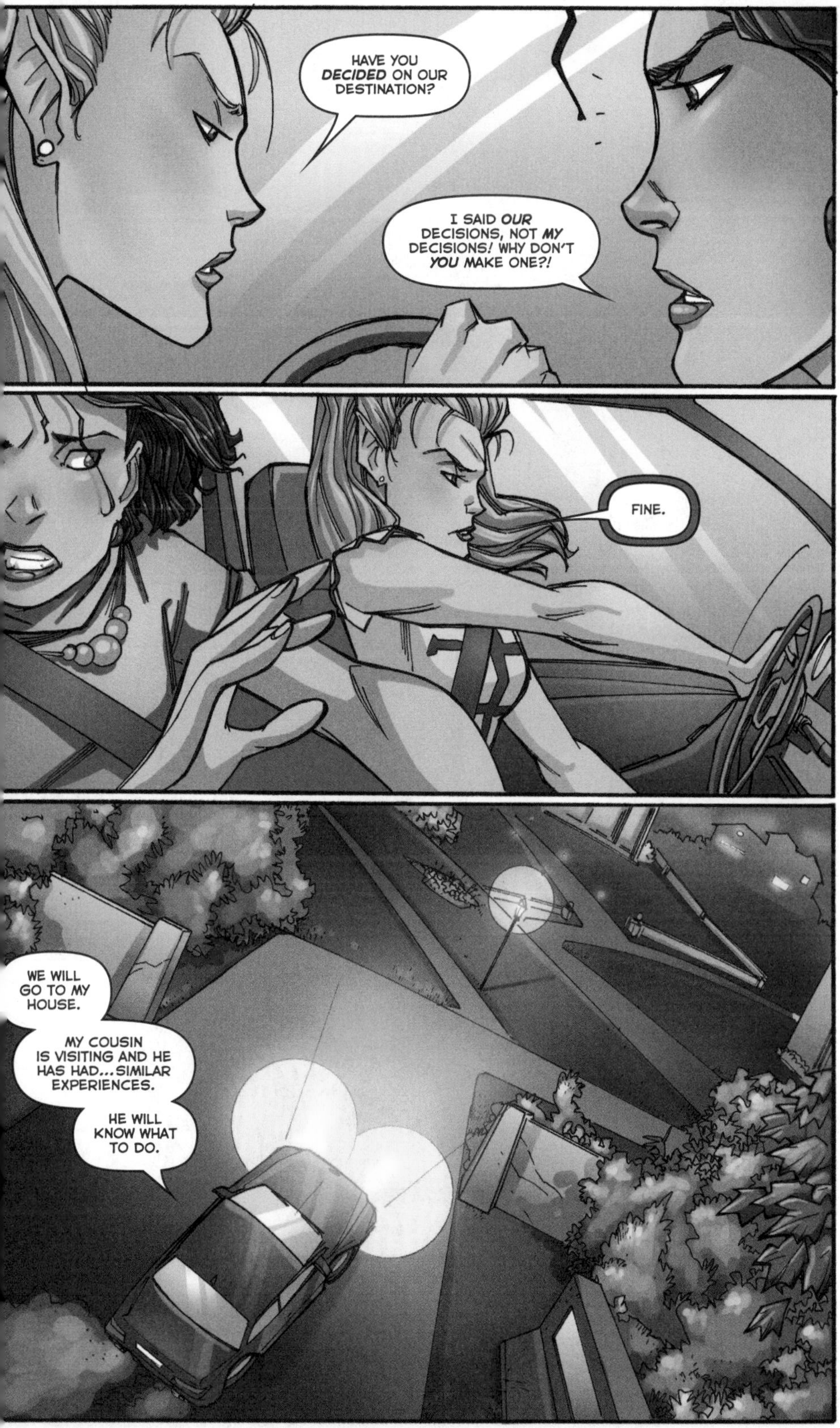
HAVE YOU DECIDED ON OUR DESTINATION?
I SAID OUR DECISIONS, NOT MY DECISIONS! WHY DON'T YOU MAKE ONE?!
FINE.
WE WILL GO TO MY HOUSE.
MY COUSIN IS VISITING AND HE HAS HAD... SIMILAR EXPERIENCES.
HE WILL KNOW WHAT TO DO.

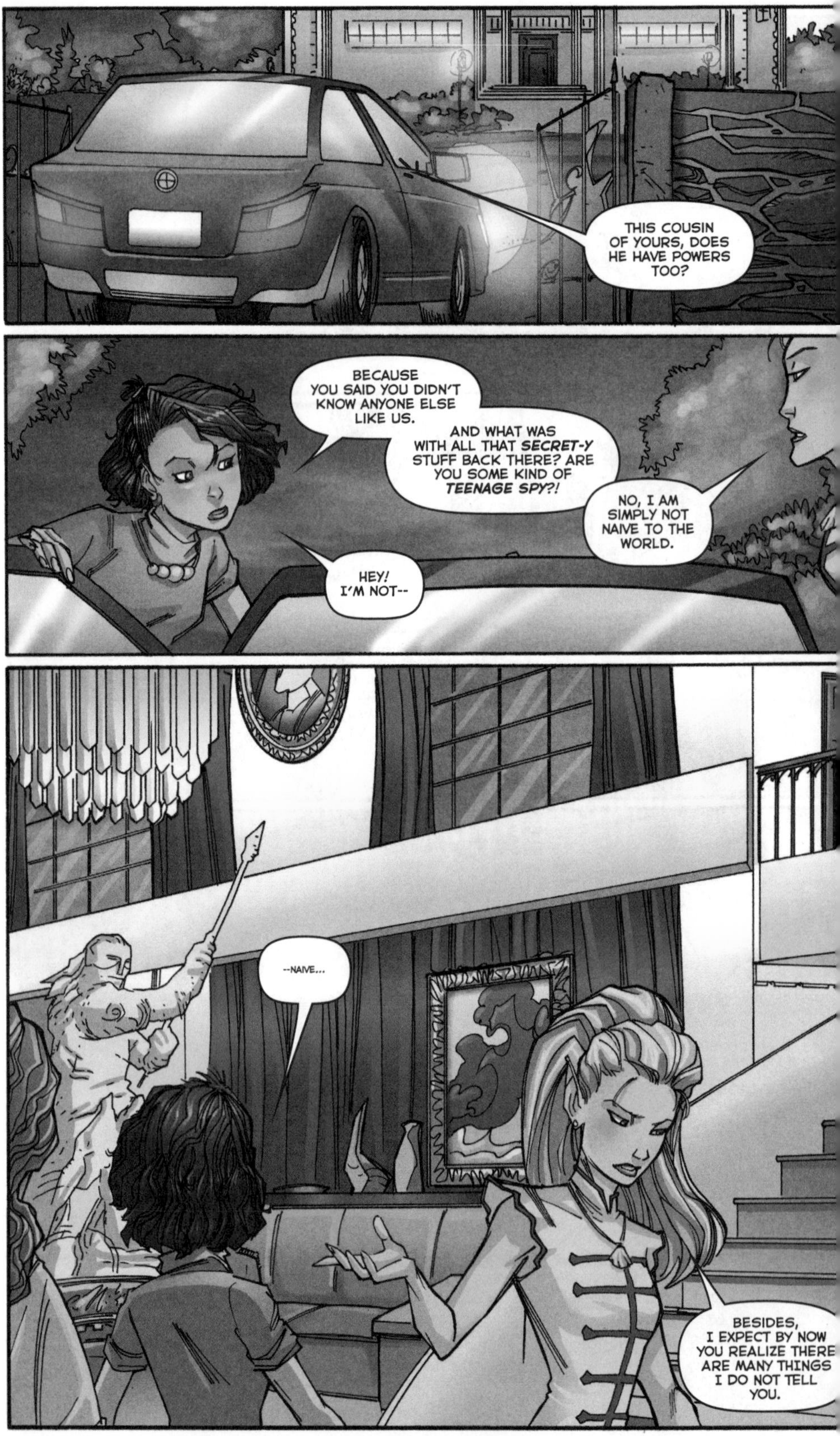
THIS COUSIN OF YOURS, DOES HE HAVE POWERS TOO?
BECAUSE YOU SAID YOU DIDN'T KNOW ANYONE ELSE LIKE US.
AND WHAT WAS WITH ALL THAT *SECRET-Y* STUFF BACK THERE? ARE YOU SOME KIND OF *TEENAGE SPY?!*
NO, I AM SIMPLY NOT NAIVE TO THE WORLD.
HEY! I'M NOT--
--NAIVE...
BESIDES, I EXPECT BY NOW YOU REALIZE THERE ARE MANY THINGS I DO NOT TELL YOU.

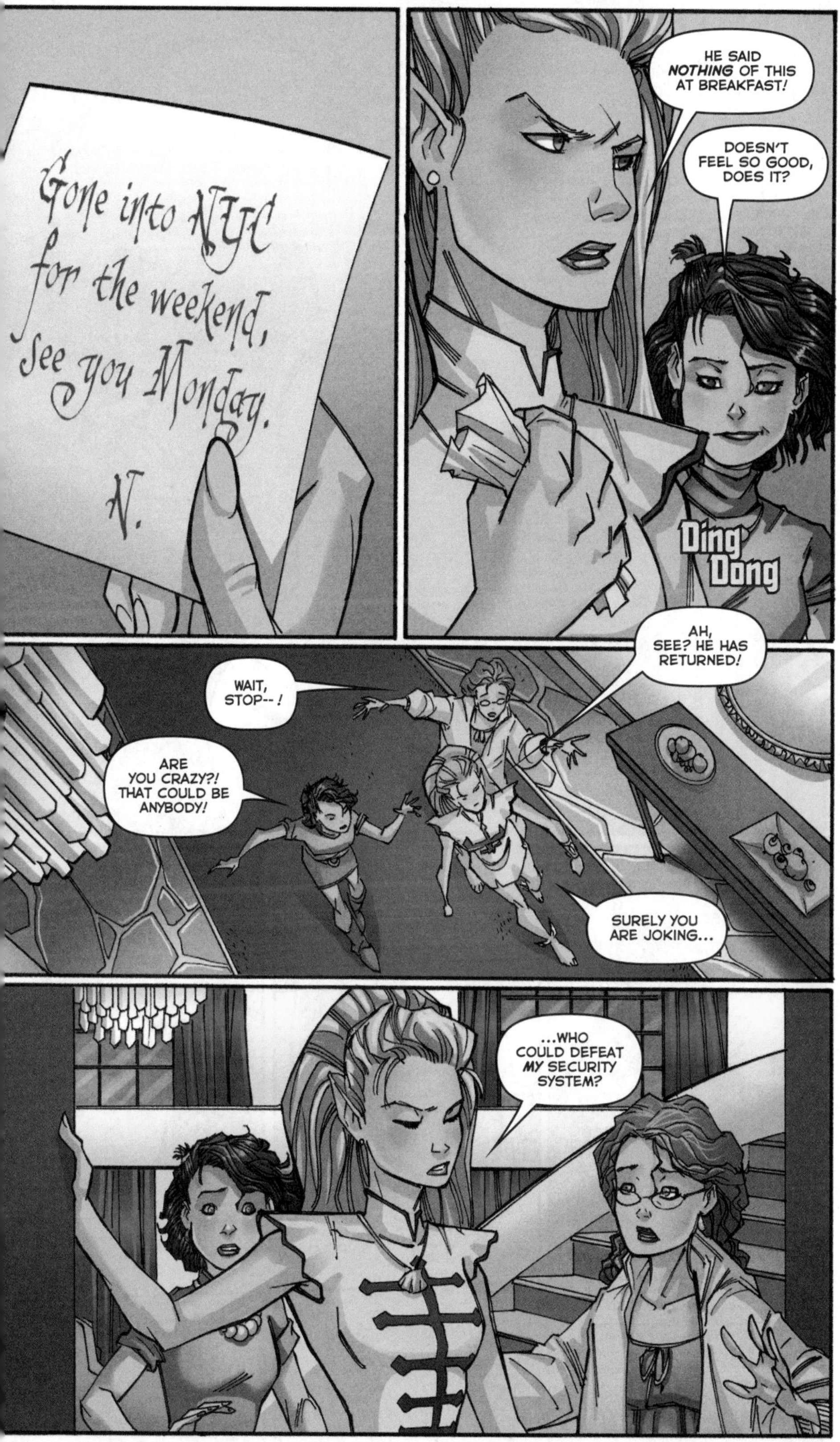
Gone into NYC for the weekend, see you Monday.
N.
HE SAID NOTHING OF THIS AT BREAKFAST!
DOESN'T FEEL SO GOOD, DOES IT?
Ding Dong
AH, SEE? HE HAS RETURNED!
WAIT, STOP-- !
ARE YOU CRAZY?! THAT COULD BE ANYBODY!
SURELY YOU ARE JOKING...
...WHO COULD DEFEAT MY SECURITY SYSTEM?

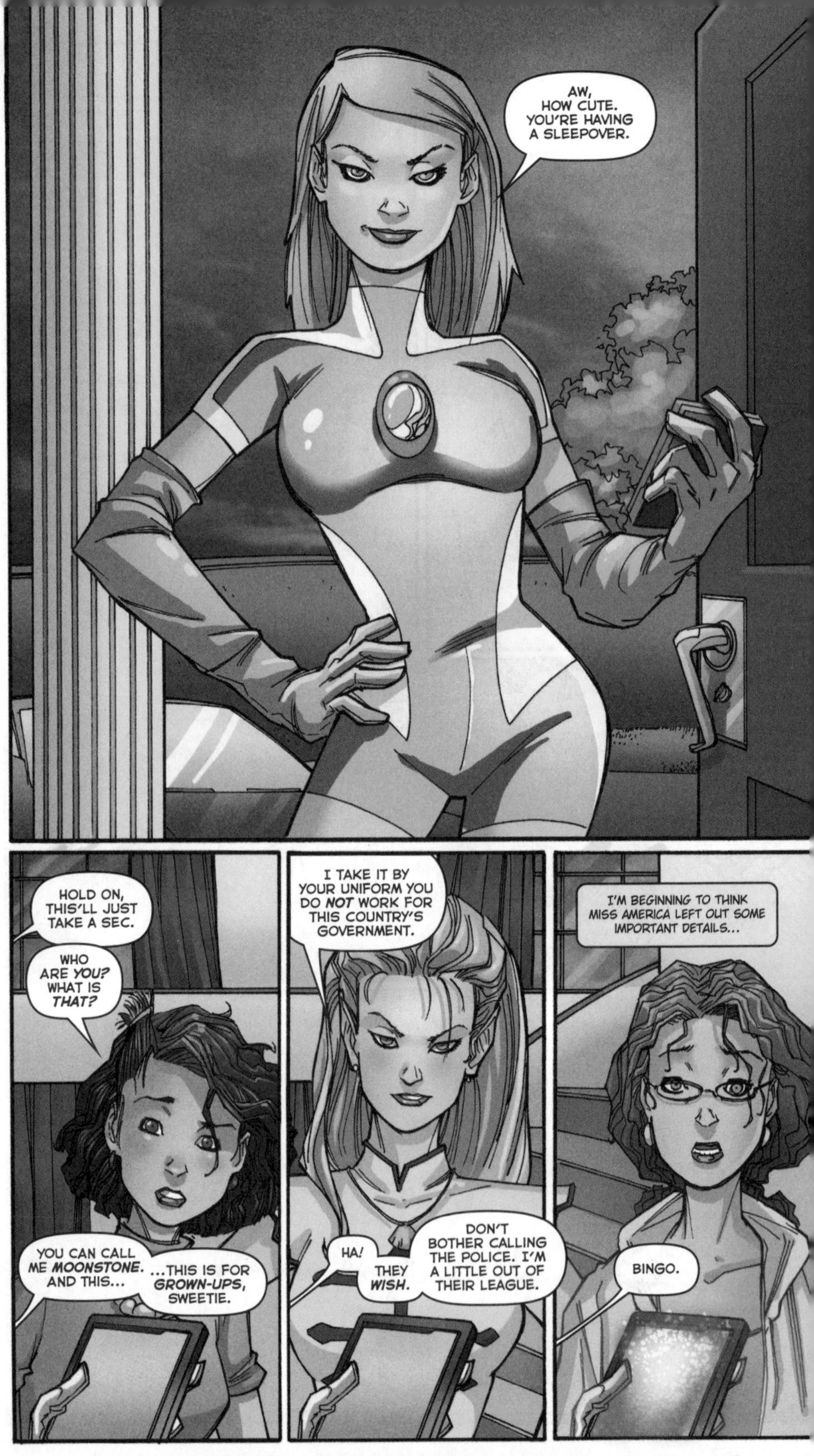
AW, HOW CUTE. YOU'RE HAVING A SLEEPOVER.
HOLD ON, THIS'LL JUST TAKE A SEC.
WHO ARE *YOU?* WHAT IS *THAT?*
YOU CAN CALL ME ***MOONSTONE.*** AND THIS...
...THIS IS FOR ***GROWN-UPS,*** SWEETIE.
I TAKE IT BY YOUR UNIFORM YOU DO ***NOT*** WORK FOR THIS COUNTRY'S GOVERNMENT.
HA!
THEY ***WISH.***
DON'T BOTHER CALLING THE POLICE. I'M A LITTLE OUT OF THEIR LEAGUE.
I'M BEGINNING TO THINK MISS AMERICA LEFT OUT SOME IMPORTANT DETAILS...
BINGO.

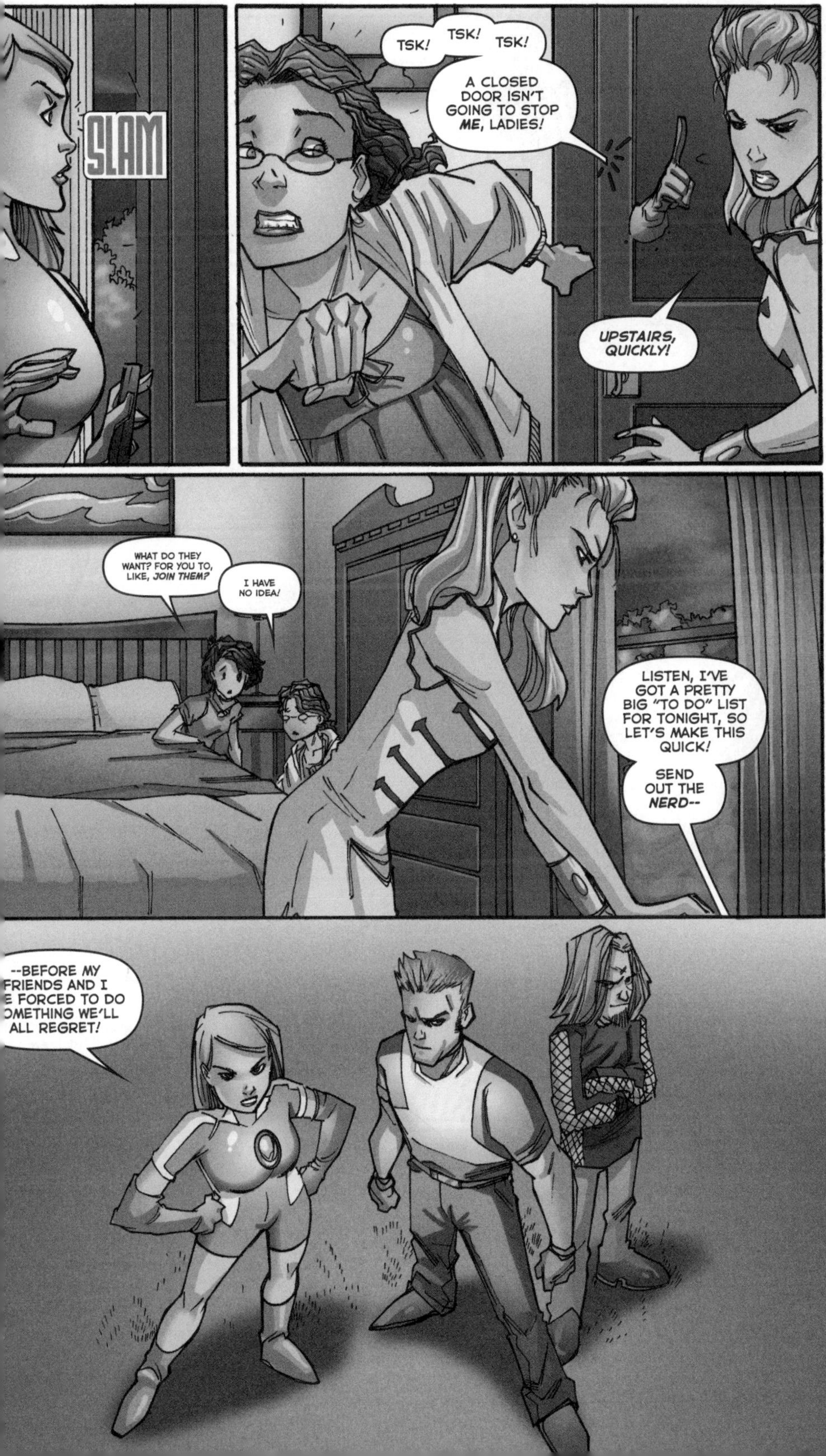
SLAM
TSK! TSK! TSK!
A CLOSED DOOR ISN'T GOING TO STOP ME, LADIES!
UPSTAIRS, QUICKLY!
WHAT DO THEY WANT? FOR YOU TO, LIKE, JOIN THEM?
I HAVE NO IDEA!
LISTEN, I'VE GOT A PRETTY BIG "TO DO" LIST FOR TONIGHT, SO LET'S MAKE THIS QUICK!
SEND OUT THE NERD--
--BEFORE MY FRIENDS AND I E FORCED TO DO OMETHING WE'LL ALL REGRET!

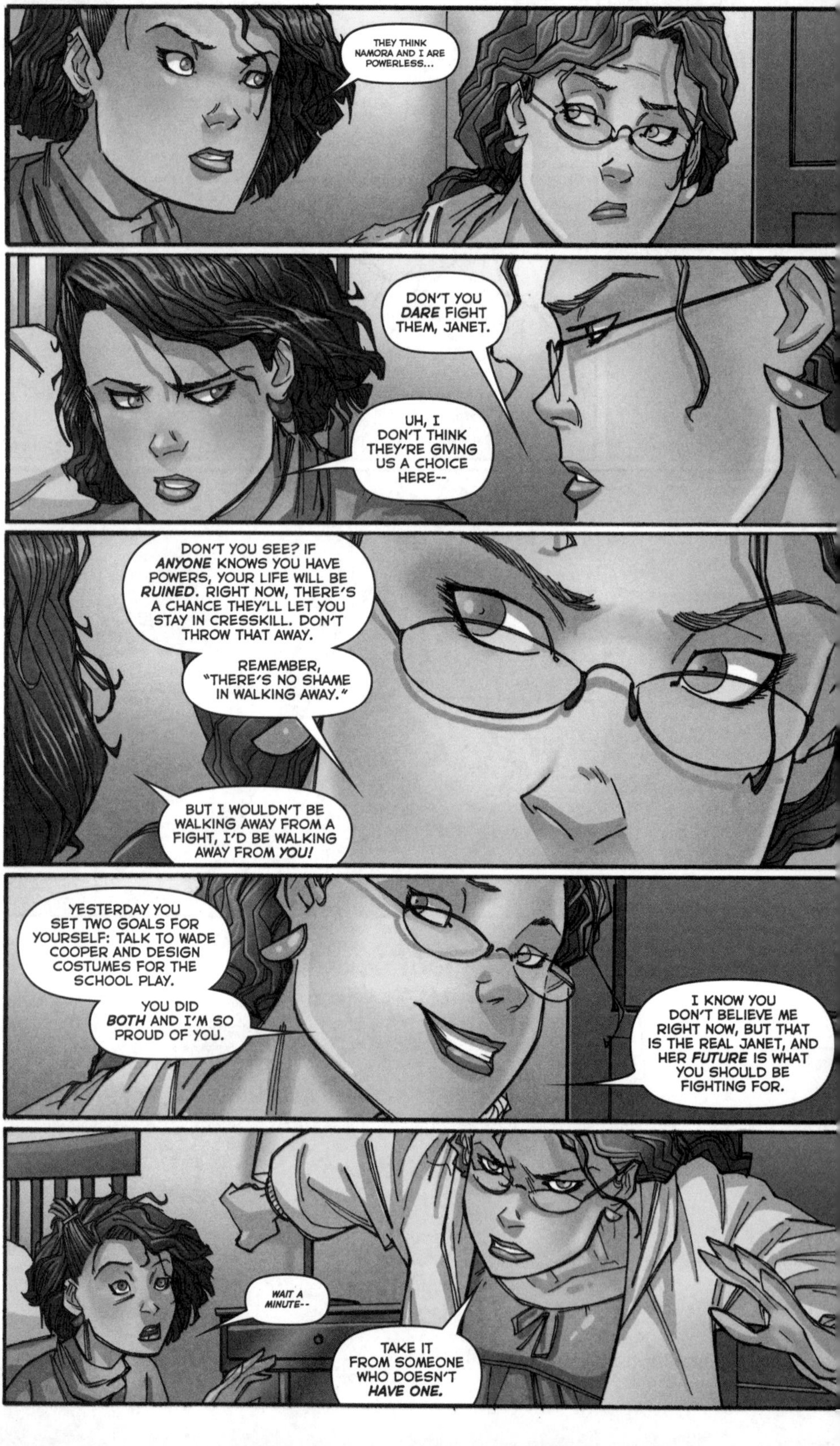

THEY THINK NAMORA AND I ARE POWERLESS...
DON'T YOU *DARE* FIGHT THEM, JANET.
UH, I DON'T THINK THEY'RE GIVING US A CHOICE HERE--
DON'T YOU SEE? IF *ANYONE* KNOWS YOU HAVE POWERS, YOUR LIFE WILL BE *RUINED*. RIGHT NOW, THERE'S A CHANCE THEY'LL LET YOU STAY IN CRESSKILL. DON'T THROW THAT AWAY.
REMEMBER, "THERE'S NO SHAME IN WALKING AWAY."
BUT I WOULDN'T BE WALKING AWAY FROM A FIGHT, I'D BE WALKING AWAY FROM *YOU!*
YESTERDAY YOU SET TWO GOALS FOR YOURSELF: TALK TO WADE COOPER AND DESIGN COSTUMES FOR THE SCHOOL PLAY.
YOU DID *BOTH* AND I'M SO PROUD OF YOU.
I KNOW YOU DON'T BELIEVE ME RIGHT NOW, BUT THAT IS THE REAL JANET, AND HER *FUTURE* IS WHAT YOU SHOULD BE FIGHTING FOR.
WAIT A MINUTE--
TAKE IT FROM SOMEONE WHO DOESN'T *HAVE ONE.*

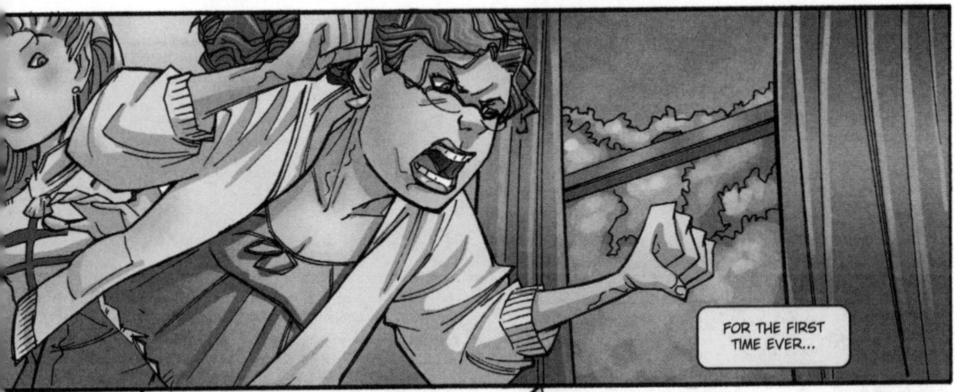
FOR THE FIRST TIME EVER...

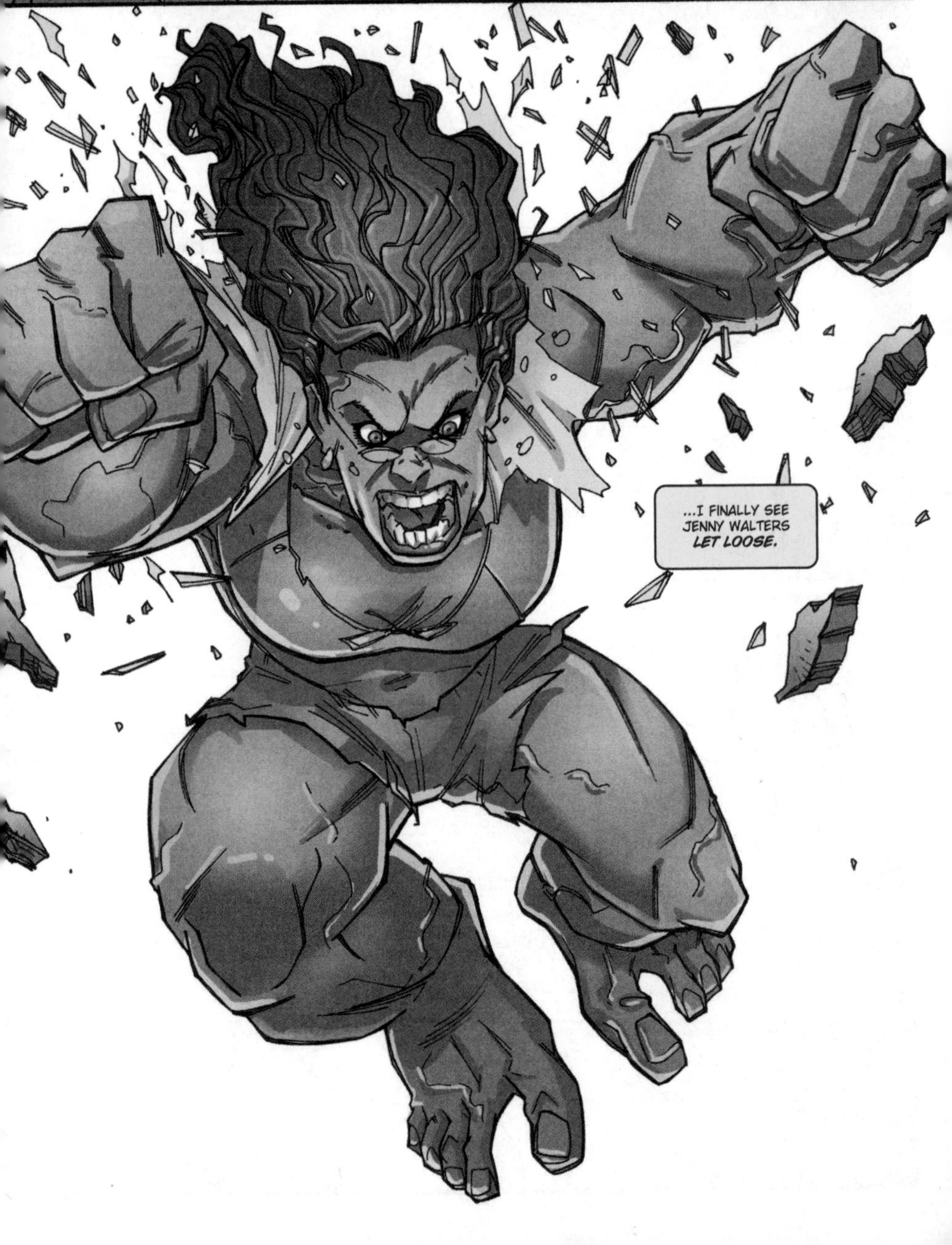
...I FINALLY SEE JENNY WALTERS LET LOOSE.

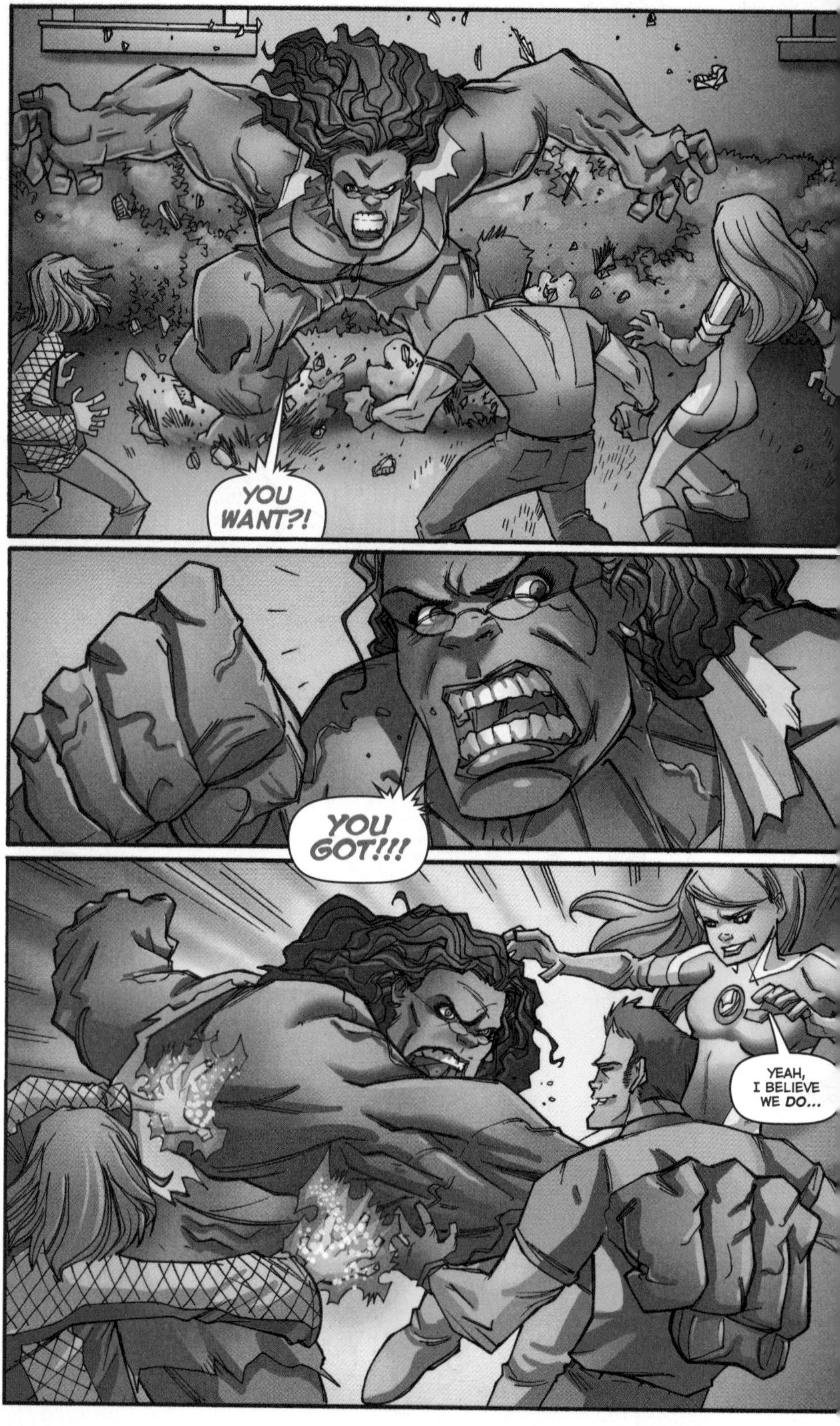
YOU WANT?!
YOU GOT!!!
YEAH, I BELIEVE WE DO...

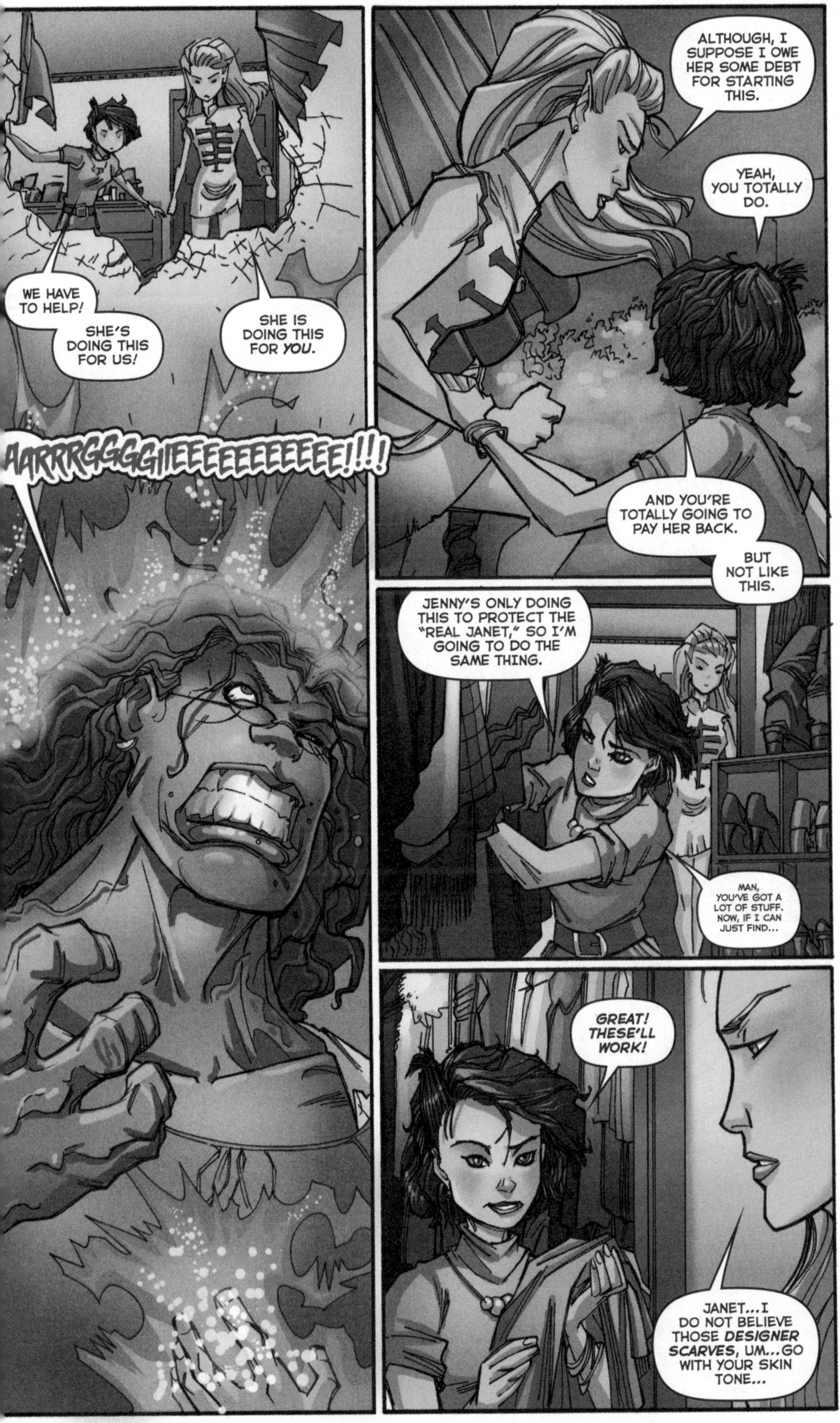
WE HAVE TO HELP!
SHE'S DOING THIS FOR US!
SHE IS DOING THIS FOR *YOU*.
AARRRGGGGIIEEEEEEEEEEEE!!!!
ALTHOUGH, I SUPPOSE I OWE HER SOME DEBT FOR STARTING THIS.
YEAH, YOU TOTALLY DO.
AND YOU'RE TOTALLY GOING TO PAY HER BACK.
BUT NOT LIKE THIS.
JENNY'S ONLY DOING THIS TO PROTECT THE "REAL JANET," SO I'M GOING TO DO THE SAME THING.
MAN, YOU'VE GOT A LOT OF STUFF. NOW, IF I CAN JUST FIND...
GREAT! THESE'LL WORK!
JANET...I DO NOT BELIEVE THOSE *DESIGNER SCARVES*, UM...GO WITH YOUR SKIN TONE...

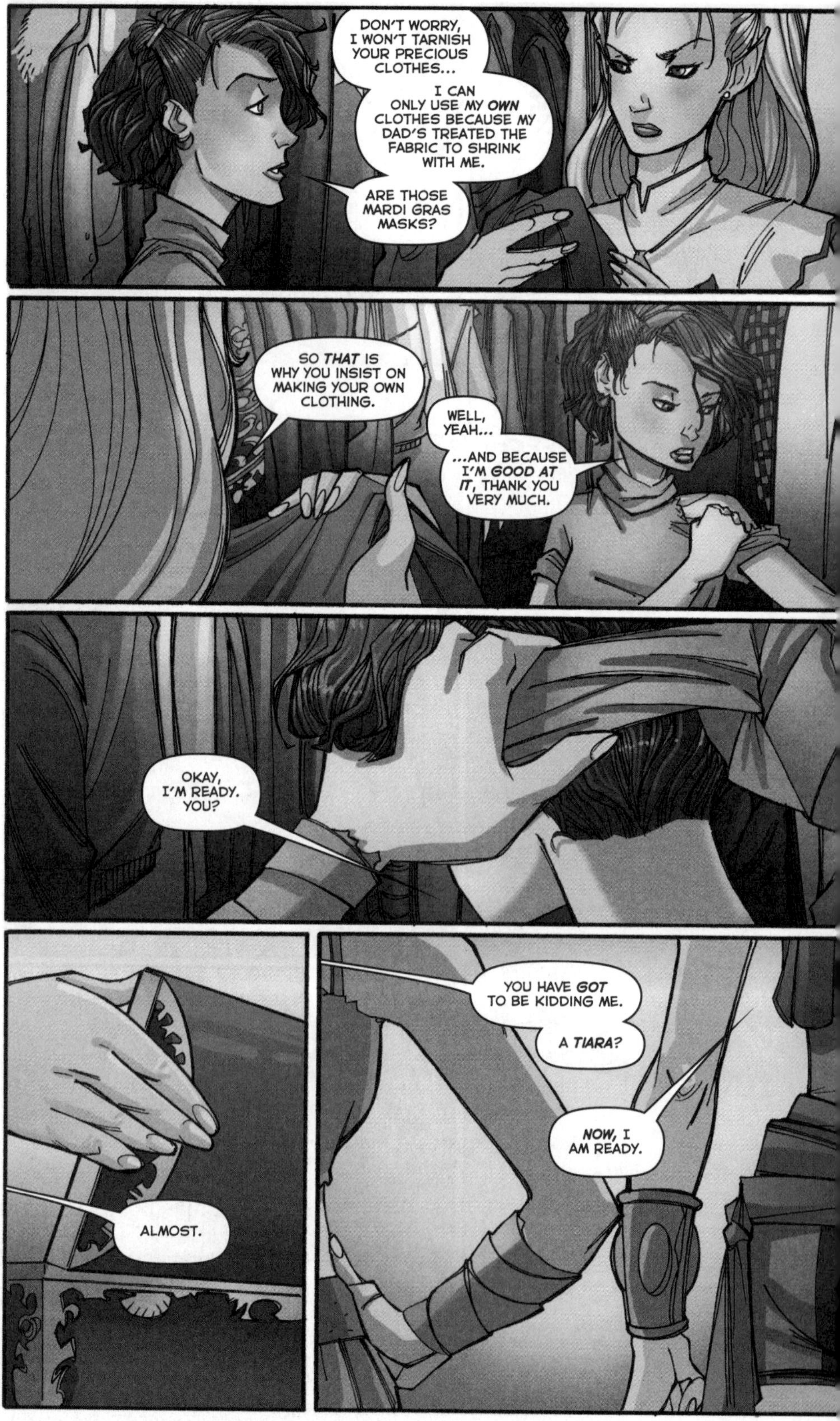
DON'T WORRY, I WON'T TARNISH YOUR PRECIOUS CLOTHES...
I CAN ONLY USE MY OWN CLOTHES BECAUSE MY DAD'S TREATED THE FABRIC TO SHRINK WITH ME.
ARE THOSE MARDI GRAS MASKS?
SO THAT IS WHY YOU INSIST ON MAKING YOUR OWN CLOTHING.
WELL, YEAH...
...AND BECAUSE I'M GOOD AT IT, THANK YOU VERY MUCH.
OKAY, I'M READY. YOU?
ALMOST.
YOU HAVE GOT TO BE KIDDING ME.
A TIARA?
NOW, I AM READY.

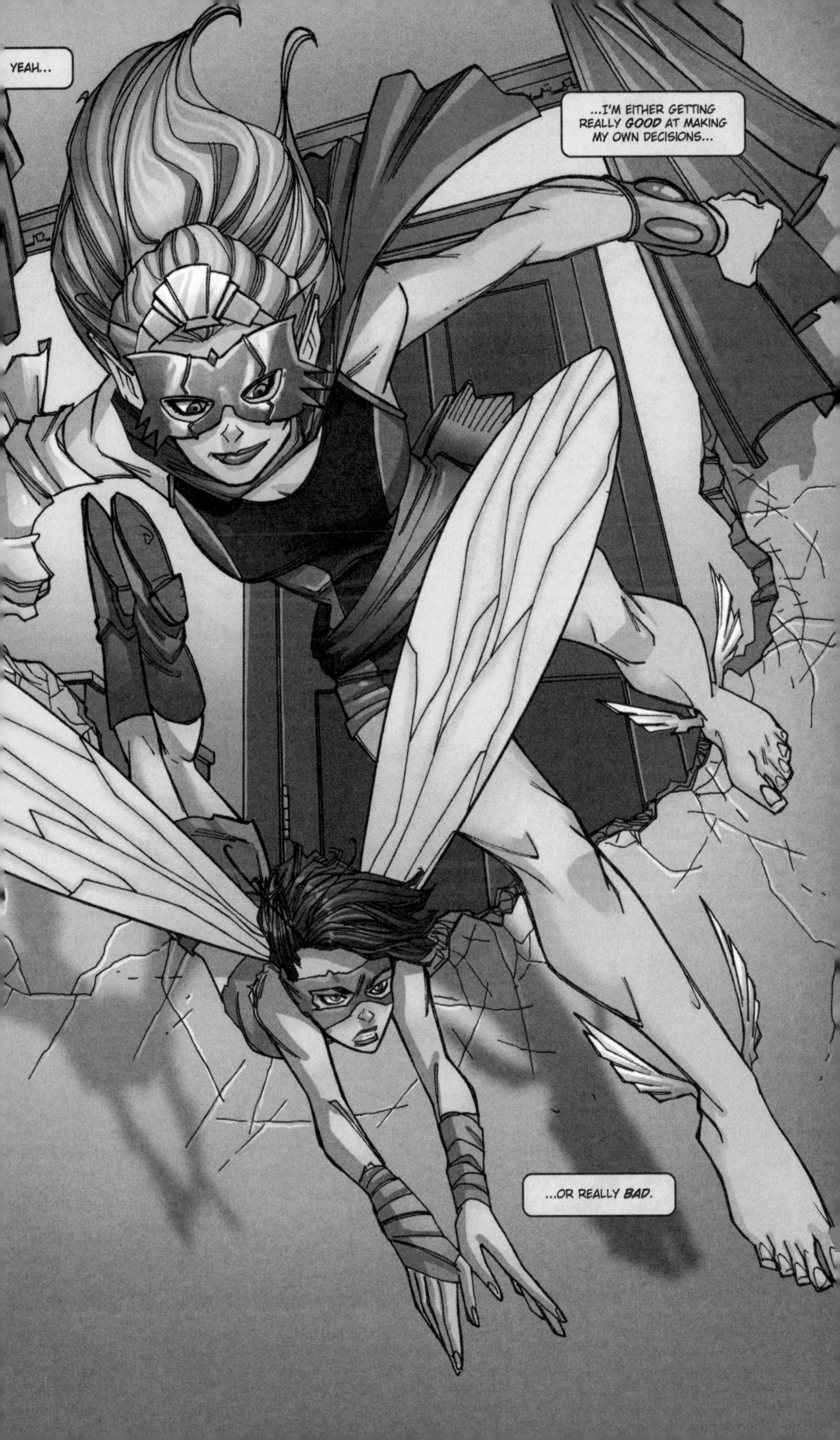
YEAH...
...I'M EITHER GETTING REALLY GOOD AT MAKING MY OWN DECISIONS...
...OR REALLY BAD.

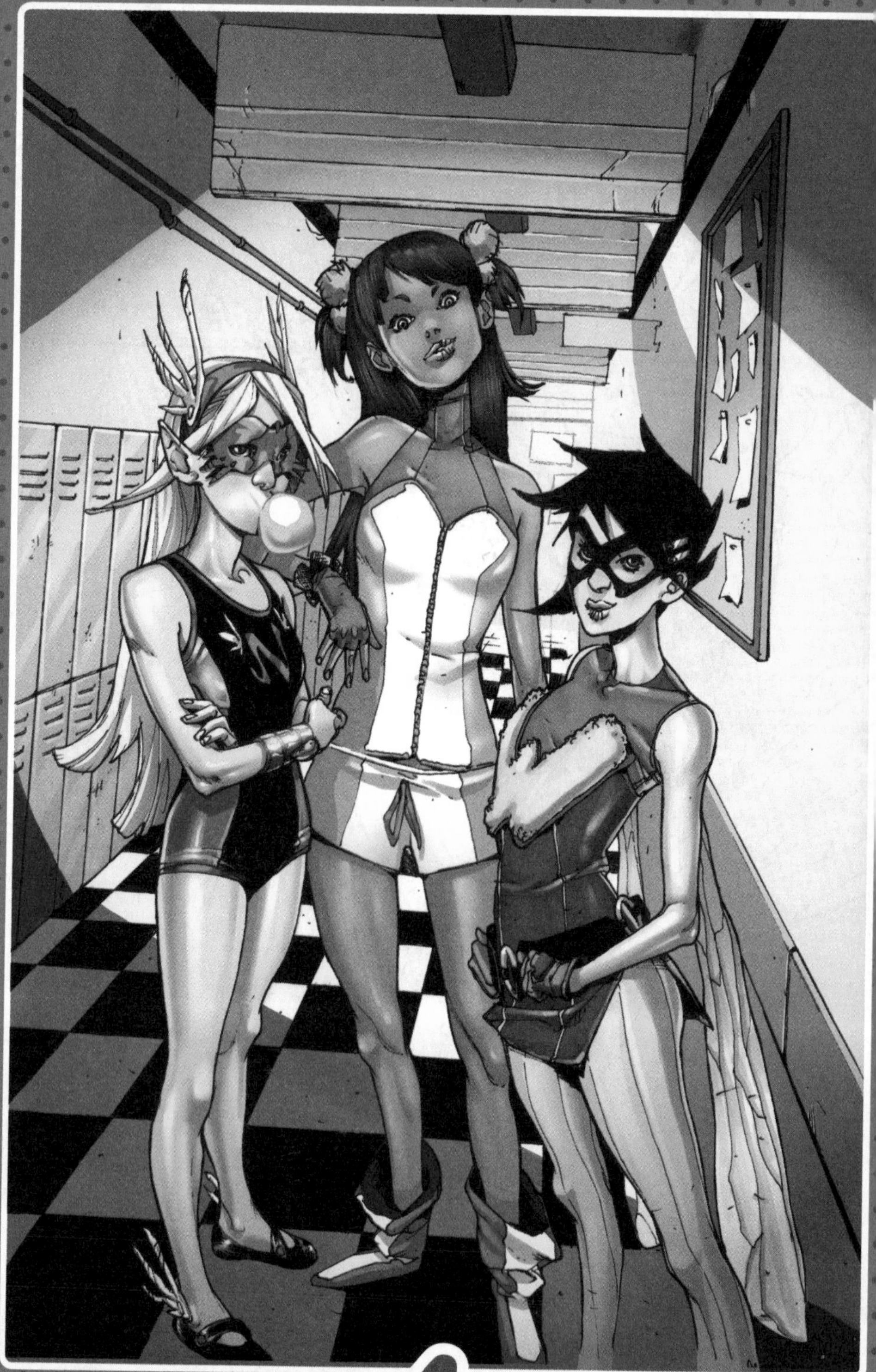

4

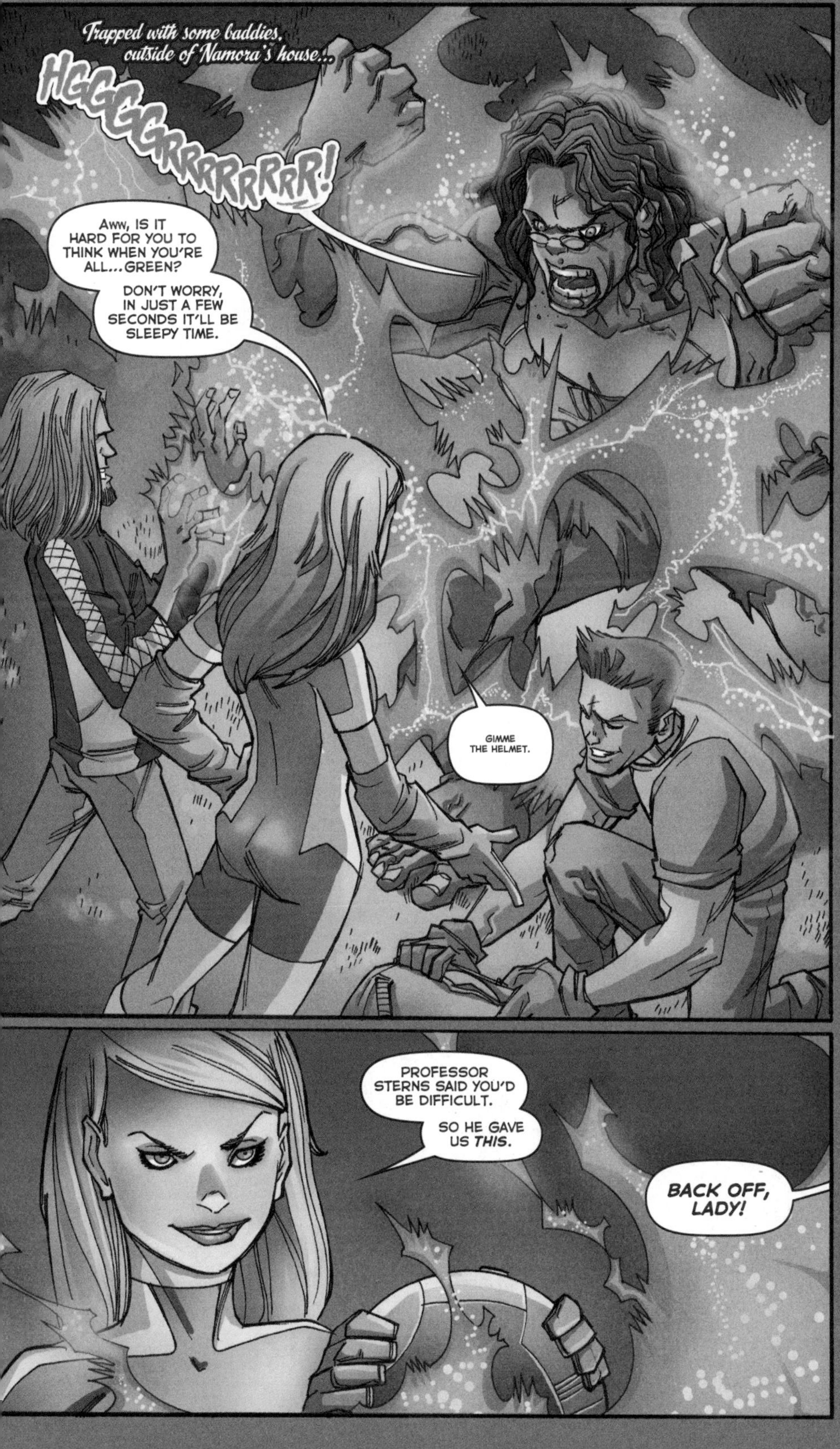
Trapped with some baddies, outside of Namora's house...
HGGGGRRRRRRRRR!
AWW, IS IT HARD FOR YOU TO THINK WHEN YOU'RE ALL...GREEN?
DON'T WORRY, IN JUST A FEW SECONDS IT'LL BE SLEEPY TIME.
GIMME THE HELMET.
PROFESSOR STERNS SAID YOU'D BE DIFFICULT.
SO HE GAVE US THIS.
BACK OFF, LADY!

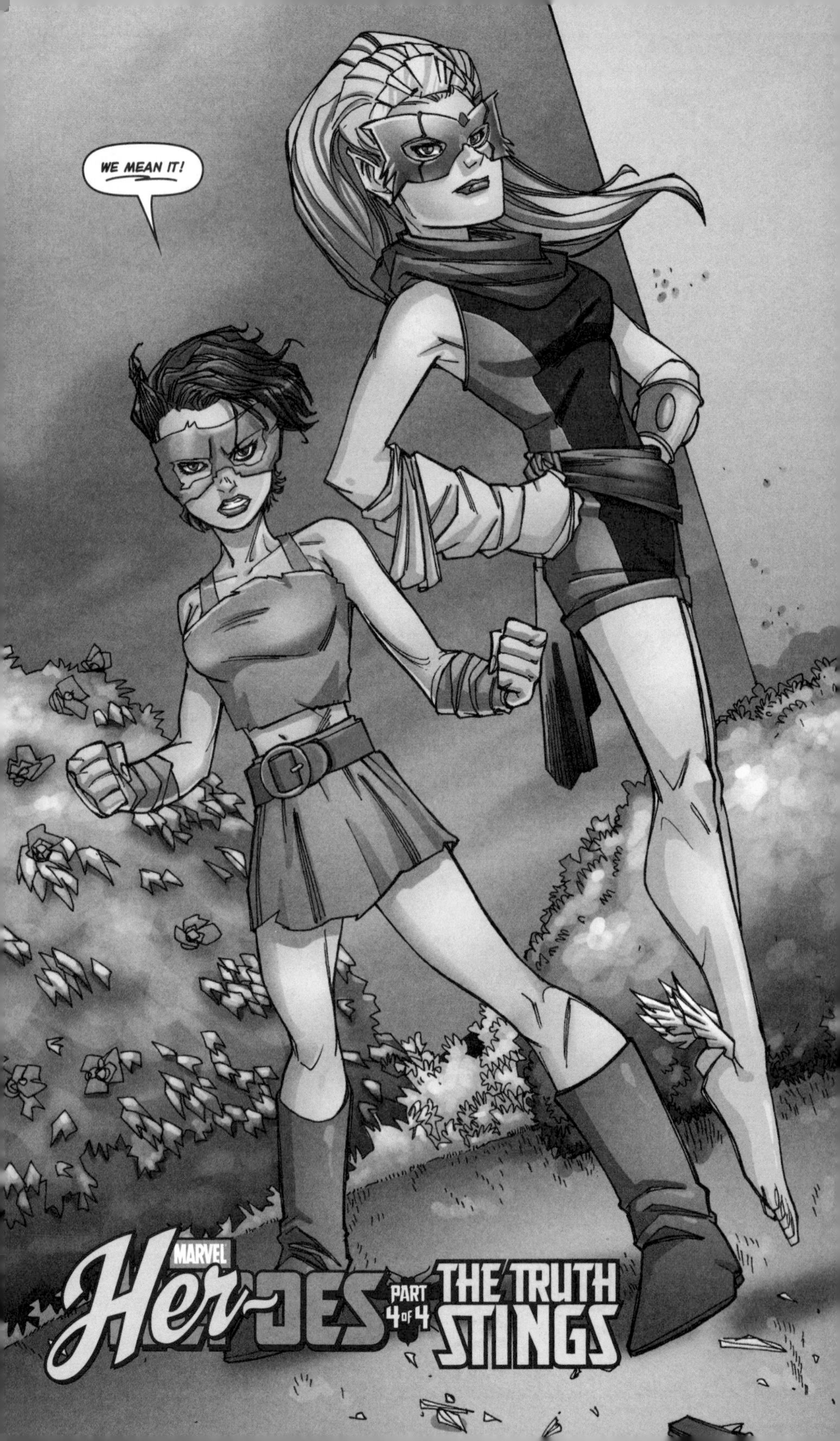
WE MEAN IT!
MARVEL
Her-oes
PART 4 of 4
THE TRUTH STINGS

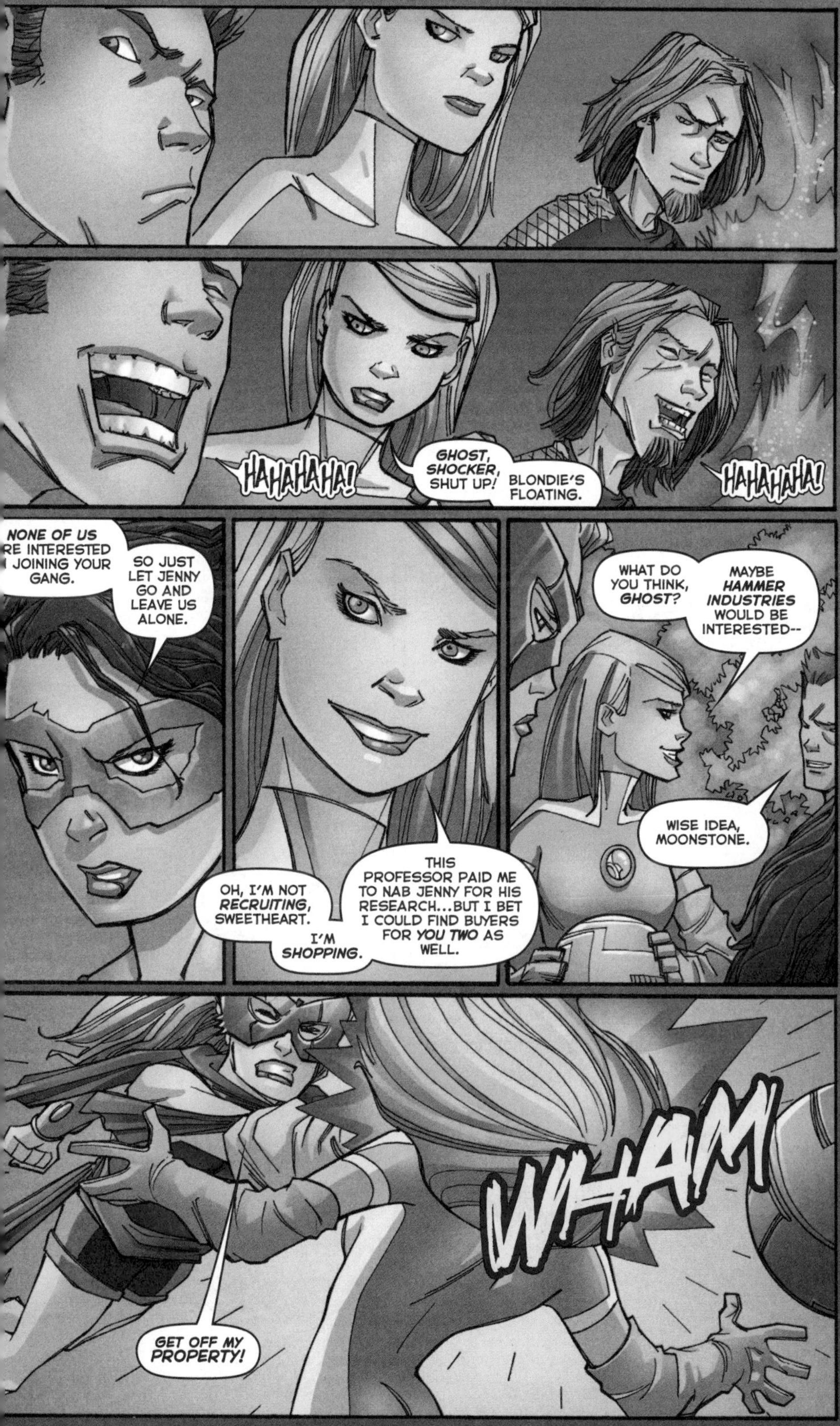
HAHAHAHA!
GHOST, SHOCKER, SHUT UP!
BLONDIE'S FLOATING.
HAHAHAHA!
NONE OF US RE INTERESTED I JOINING YOUR GANG.
SO JUST LET JENNY GO AND LEAVE US ALONE.
OH, I'M NOT RECRUITING, SWEETHEART.
I'M SHOPPING.
THIS PROFESSOR PAID ME TO NAB JENNY FOR HIS RESEARCH...BUT I BET I COULD FIND BUYERS FOR YOU TWO AS WELL.
WHAT DO YOU THINK, GHOST?
MAYBE HAMMER INDUSTRIES WOULD BE INTERESTED--
WISE IDEA, MOONSTONE.
WHAM
GET OFF MY PROPERTY!

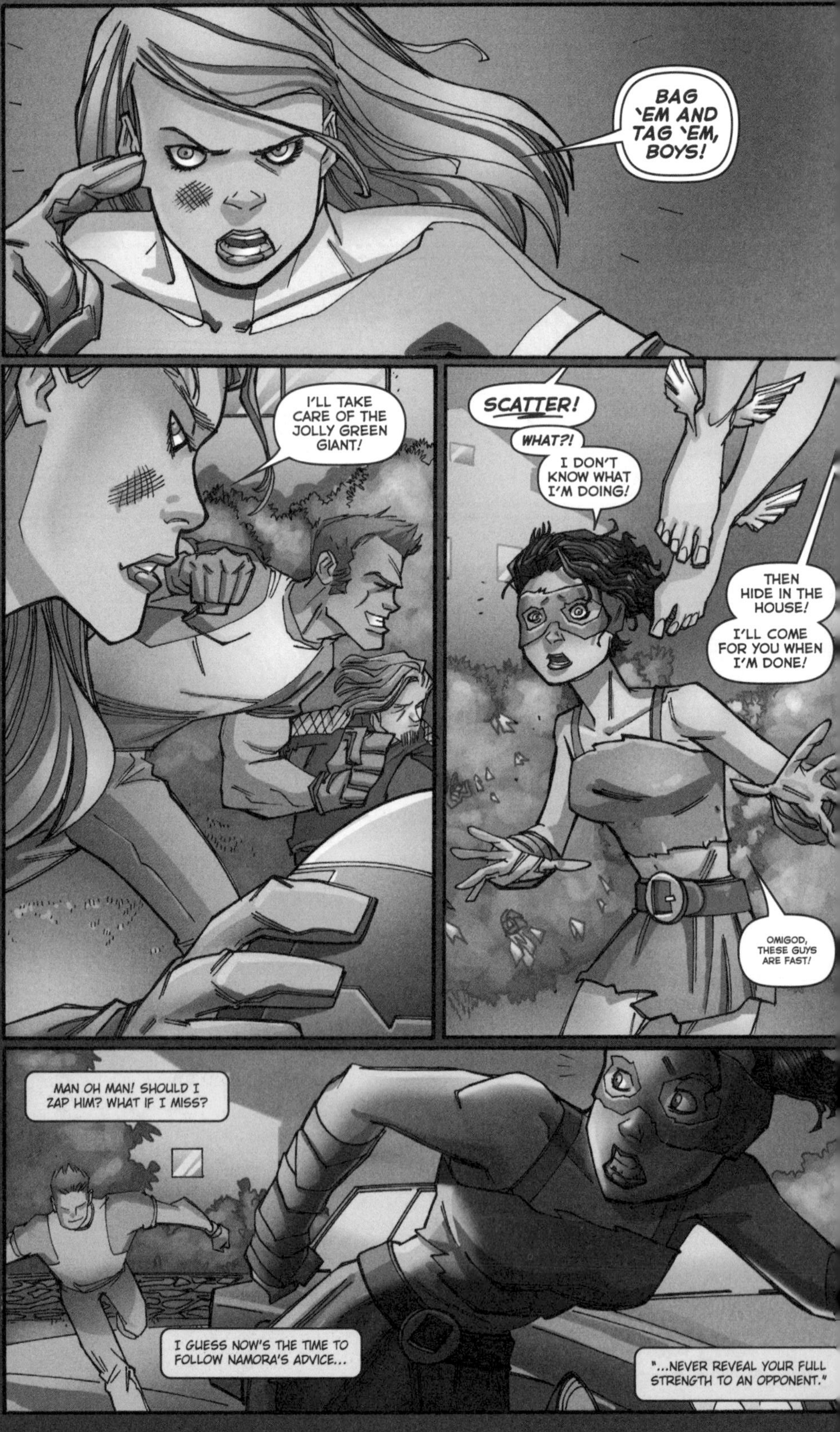
BAG 'EM AND TAG 'EM, BOYS!
I'LL TAKE CARE OF THE JOLLY GREEN GIANT!
SCATTER!
WHAT?!
I DON'T KNOW WHAT I'M DOING!
THEN HIDE IN THE HOUSE!
I'LL COME FOR YOU WHEN I'M DONE!
OMIGOD, THESE GUYS ARE FAST!
MAN OH MAN! SHOULD I ZAP HIM? WHAT IF I MISS?
I GUESS NOW'S THE TIME TO FOLLOW NAMORA'S ADVICE...
"...NEVER REVEAL YOUR FULL STRENGTH TO AN OPPONENT."

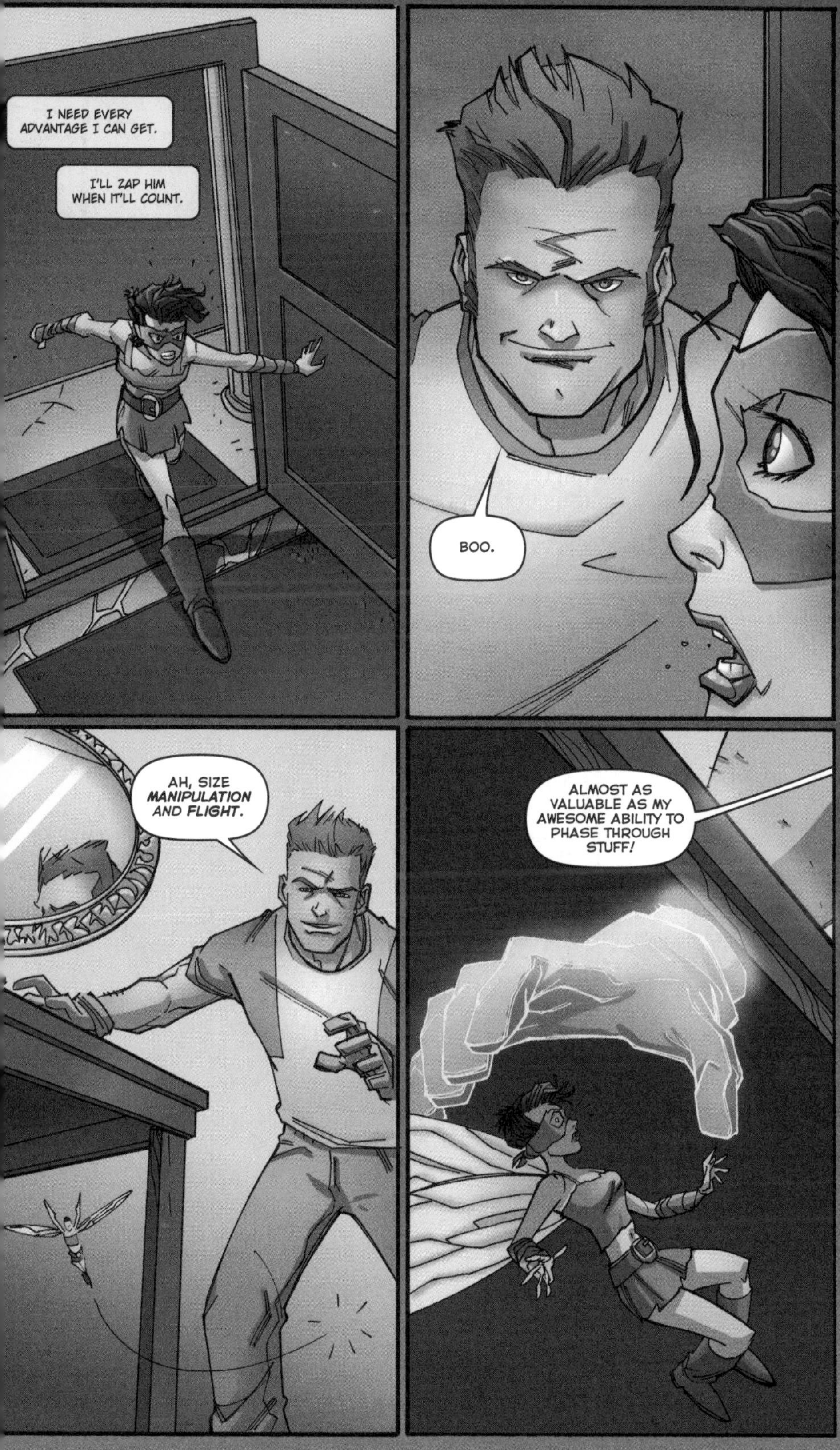
I NEED EVERY ADVANTAGE I CAN GET.
I'LL ZAP HIM WHEN IT'LL COUNT.
BOO.
AH, SIZE *MANIPULATION* AND *FLIGHT*.
ALMOST AS VALUABLE AS MY AWESOME ABILITY TO PHASE THROUGH STUFF!

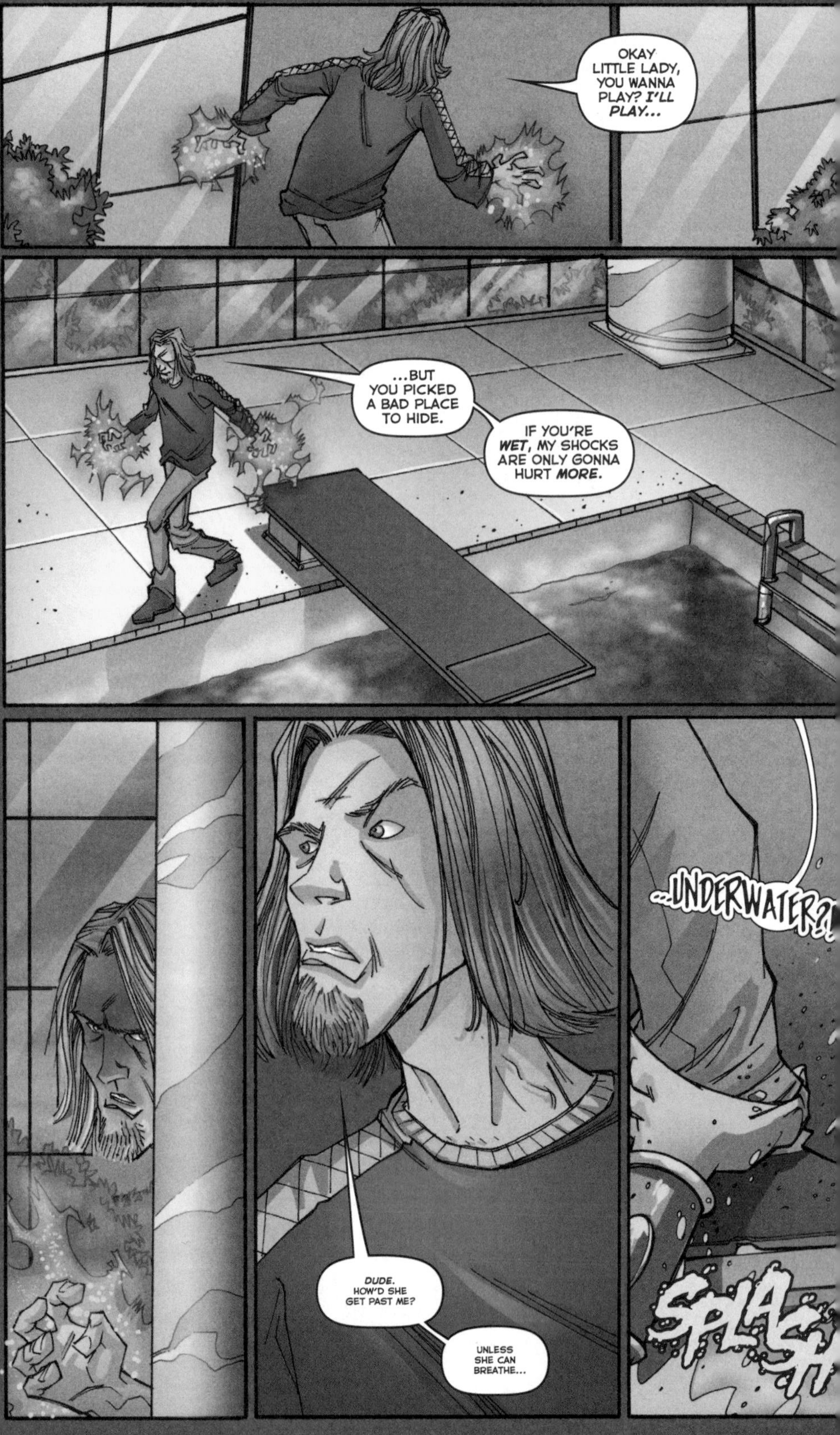
OKAY LITTLE LADY, YOU WANNA PLAY? I'LL PLAY...
...BUT YOU PICKED A BAD PLACE TO HIDE.
IF YOU'RE WET, MY SHOCKS ARE ONLY GONNA HURT MORE.
DUDE. HOW'D SHE GET PAST ME?
UNLESS SHE CAN BREATHE...
...UNDERWATER?!
SPLASH

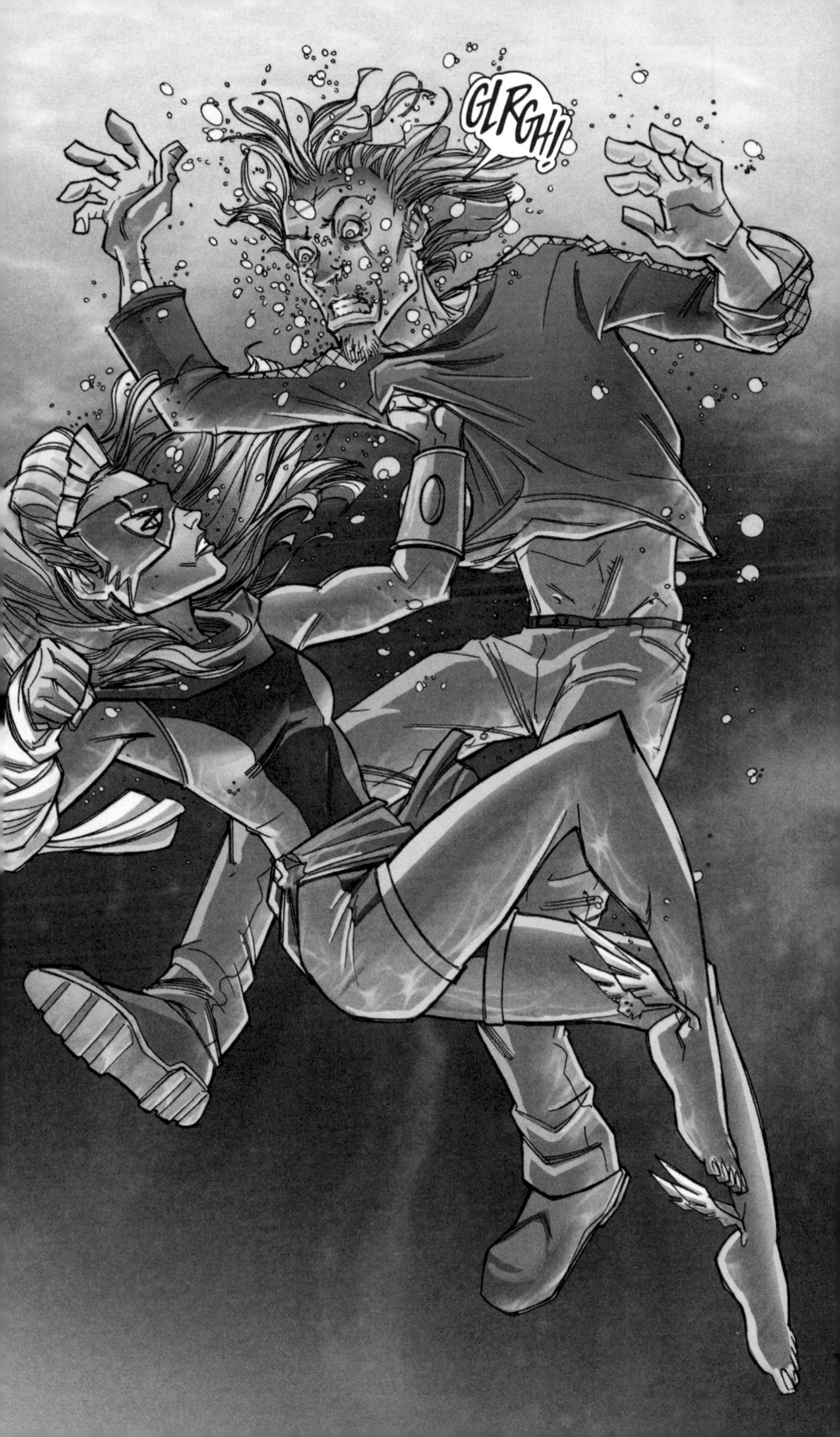
GLRGH!

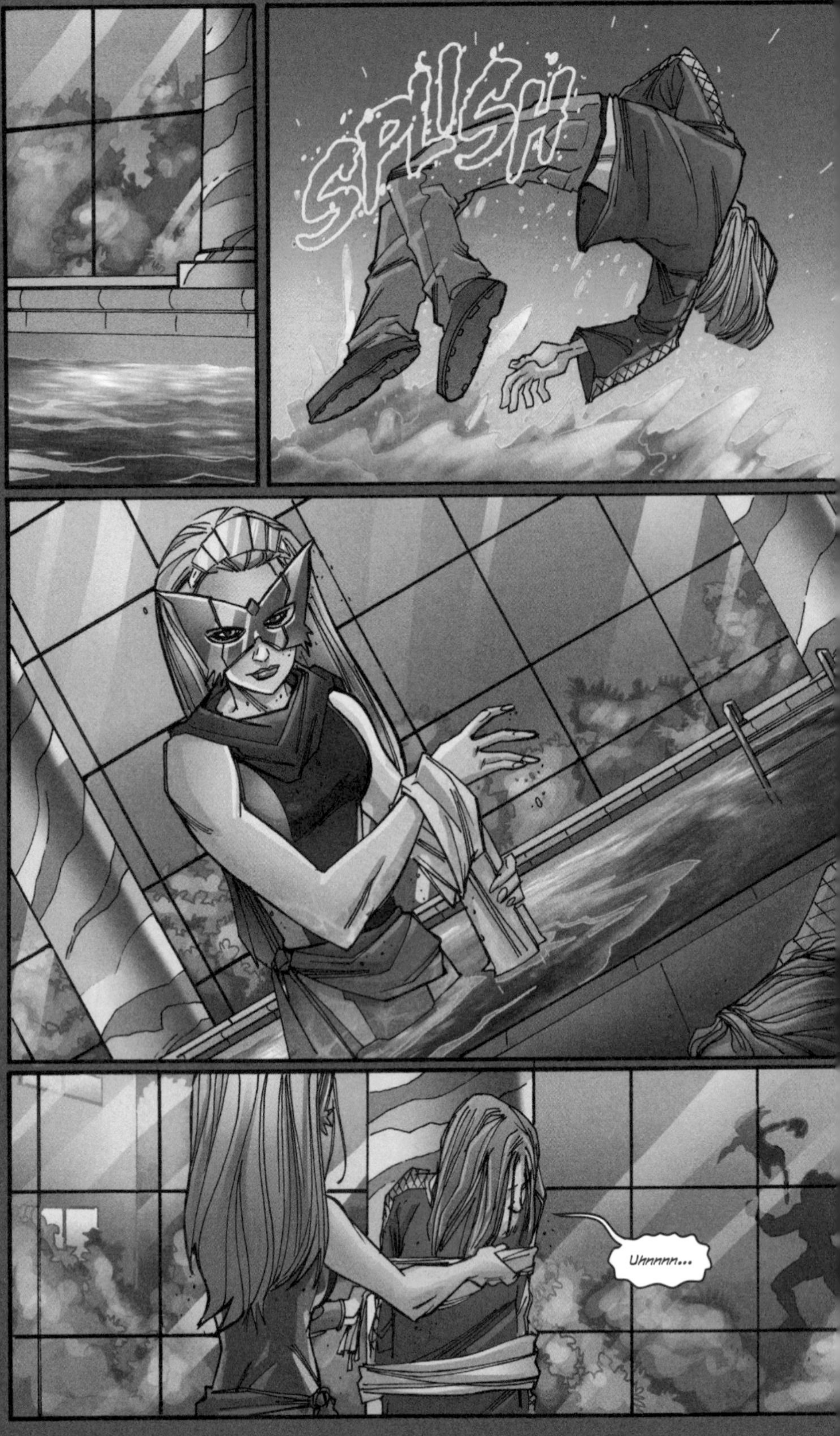
SPLISH
Uhnnnn...

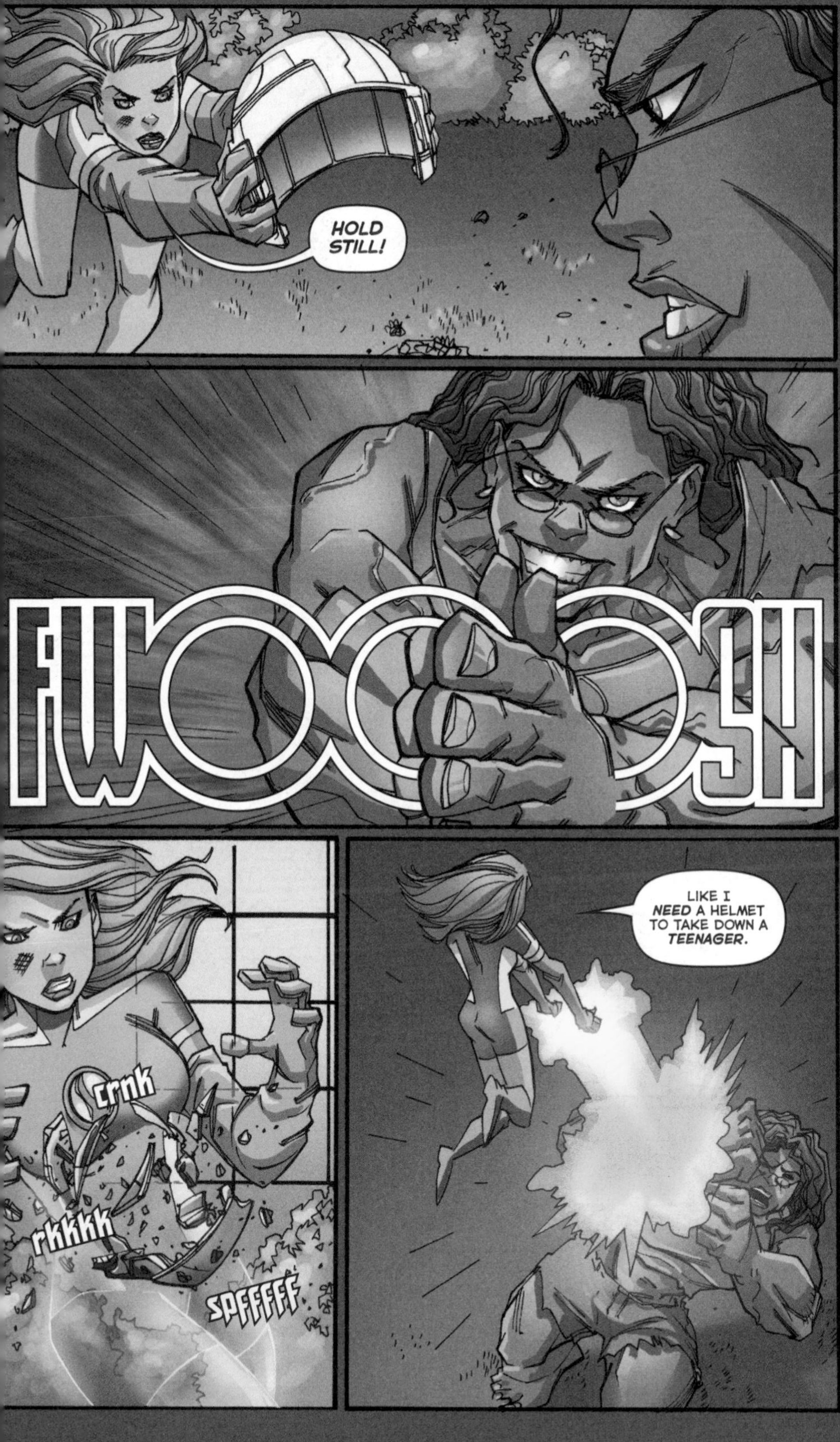
HOLD STILL!
FWOOOSH
crnk
rkkkk
spffffff
LIKE I *NEED* A HELMET TO TAKE DOWN A *TEENAGER*.

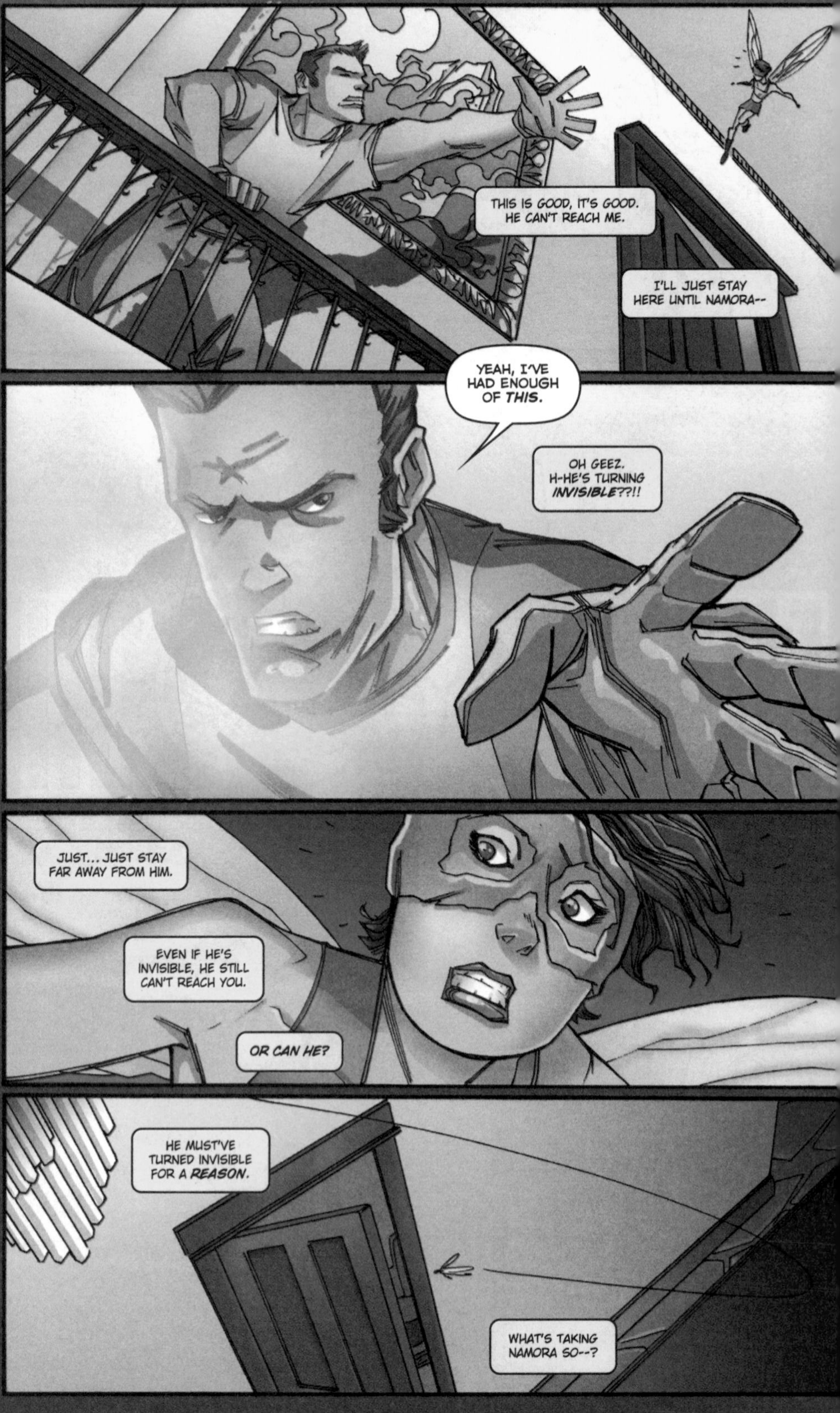
THIS IS GOOD, IT'S GOOD. HE CAN'T REACH ME.
I'LL JUST STAY HERE UNTIL NAMORA--
YEAH, I'VE HAD ENOUGH OF *THIS*.
OH GEEZ. H-HE'S TURNING *INVISIBLE*??!!
JUST... JUST STAY FAR AWAY FROM HIM.
EVEN IF HE'S INVISIBLE, HE STILL CAN'T REACH YOU.
OR CAN HE?
HE MUST'VE TURNED INVISIBLE FOR A *REASON*.
WHAT'S TAKING NAMORA SO--?

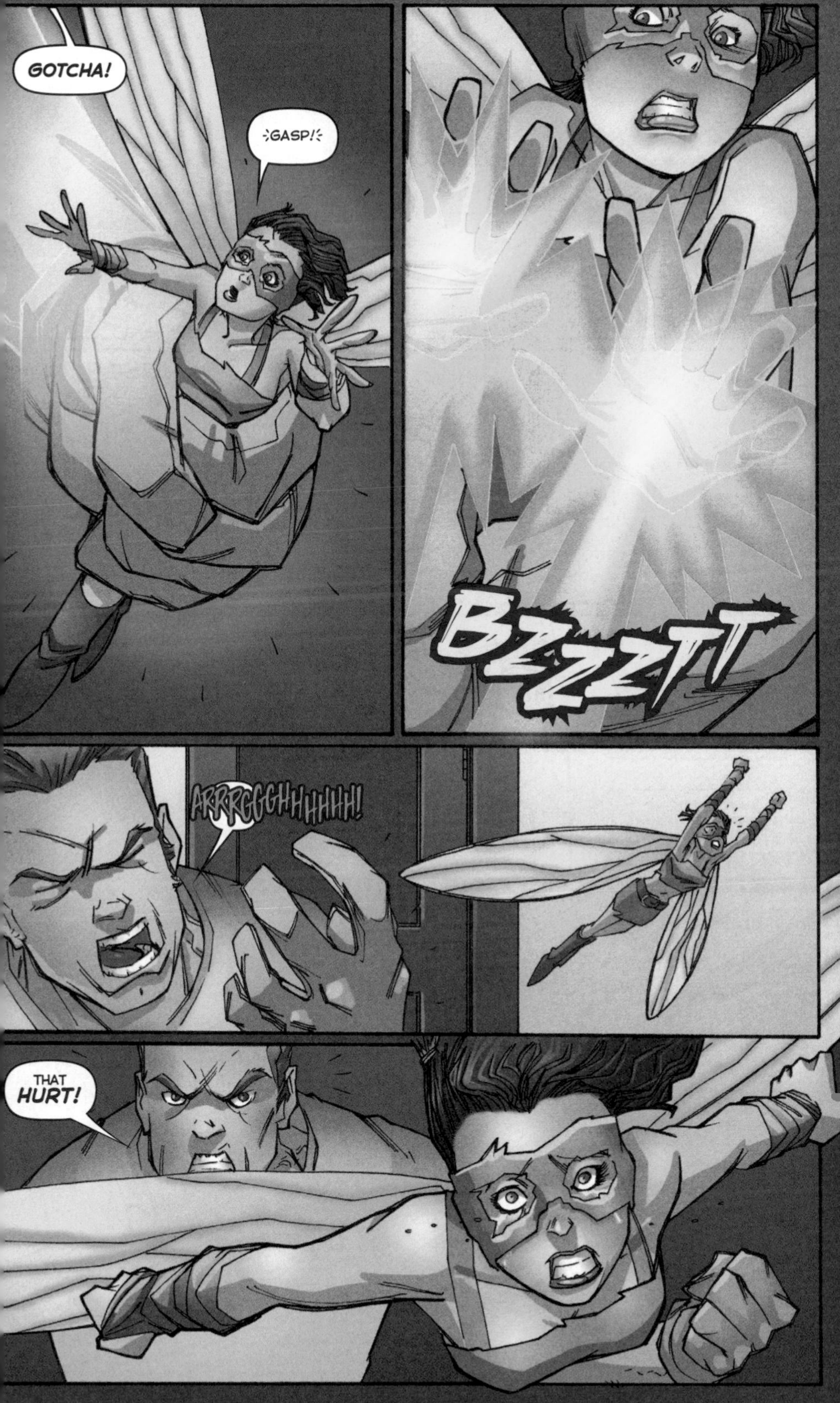
GOTCHA!
GASP!
BZZZTT
ARRRGGGHHHHHH!
THAT HURT!

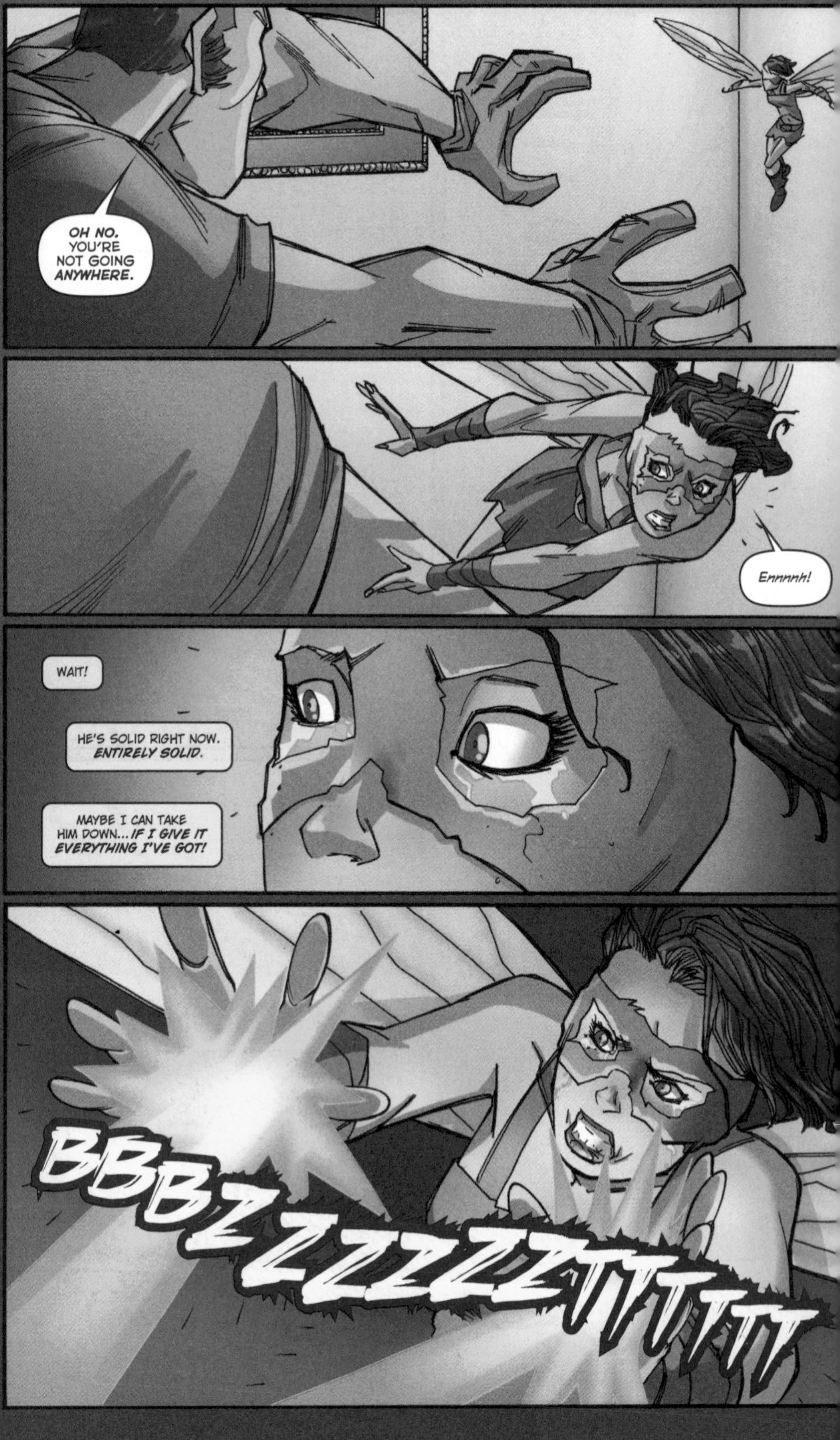
OH NO. YOU'RE NOT GOING ANYWHERE.
Ennnnh!
WAIT!
HE'S SOLID RIGHT NOW. ENTIRELY SOLID.
MAYBE I CAN TAKE HIM DOWN...IF I GIVE IT EVERYTHING I'VE GOT!
BBBZZZZZZTTTTTT

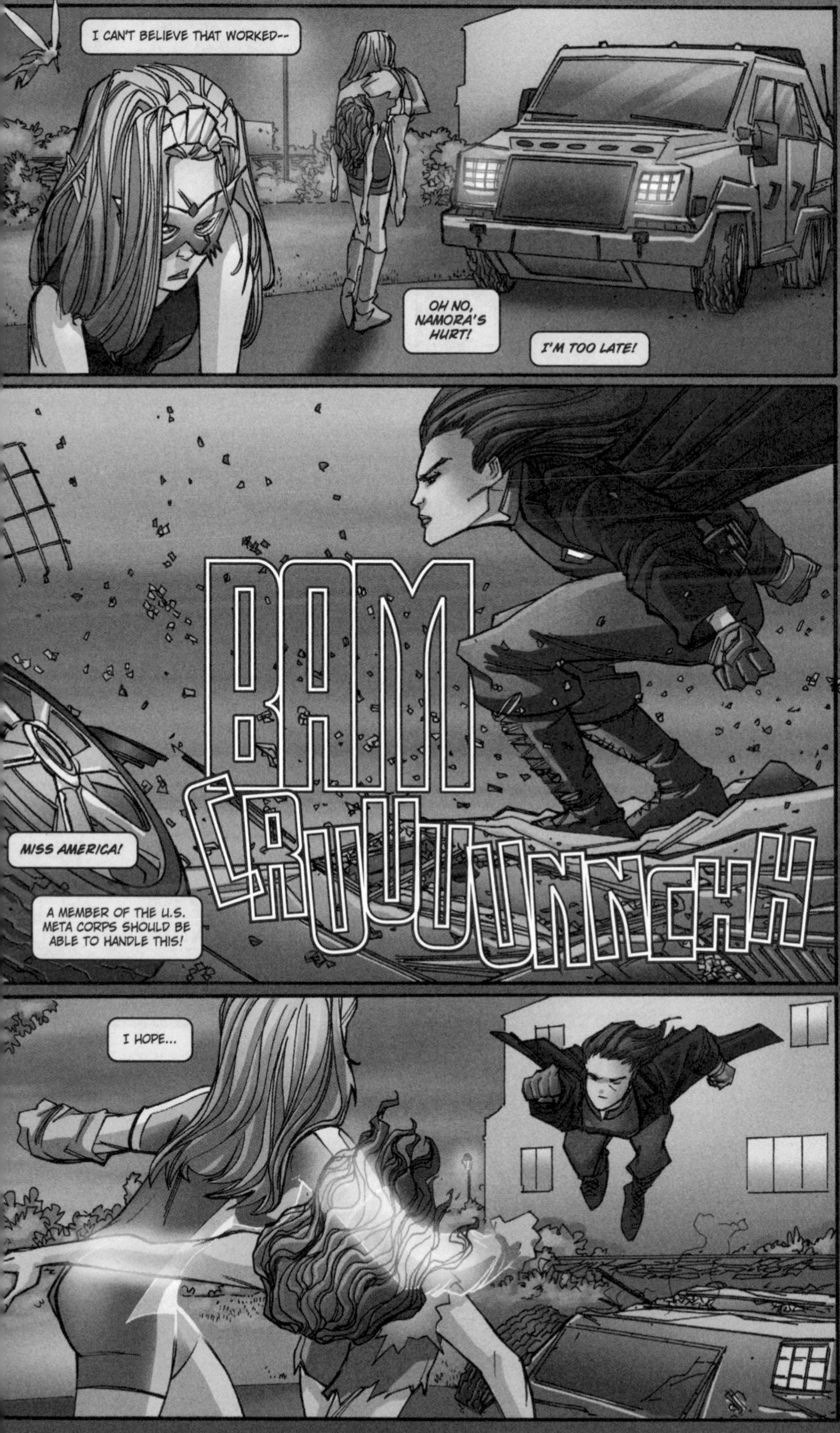
I CAN'T BELIEVE THAT WORKED--
OH NO, NAMORA'S HURT!
I'M TOO LATE!
BAM
CRUUUUNNCHH
MISS AMERICA!
A MEMBER OF THE U.S. META CORPS SHOULD BE ABLE TO HANDLE THIS!
I HOPE...

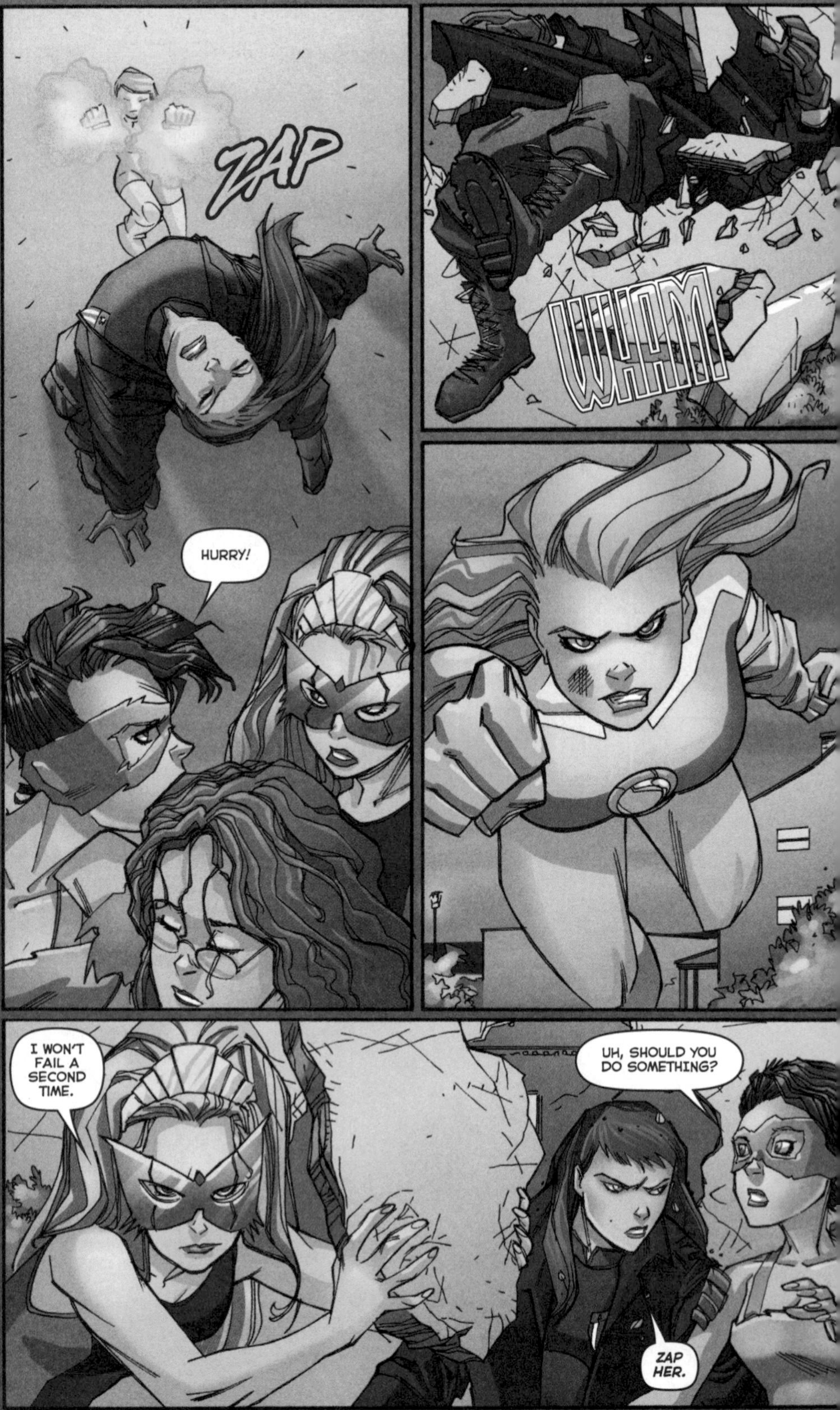
ZAP
WHAM
HURRY!
I WON'T FAIL A SECOND TIME.
UH, SHOULD YOU DO SOMETHING?
ZAP HER.

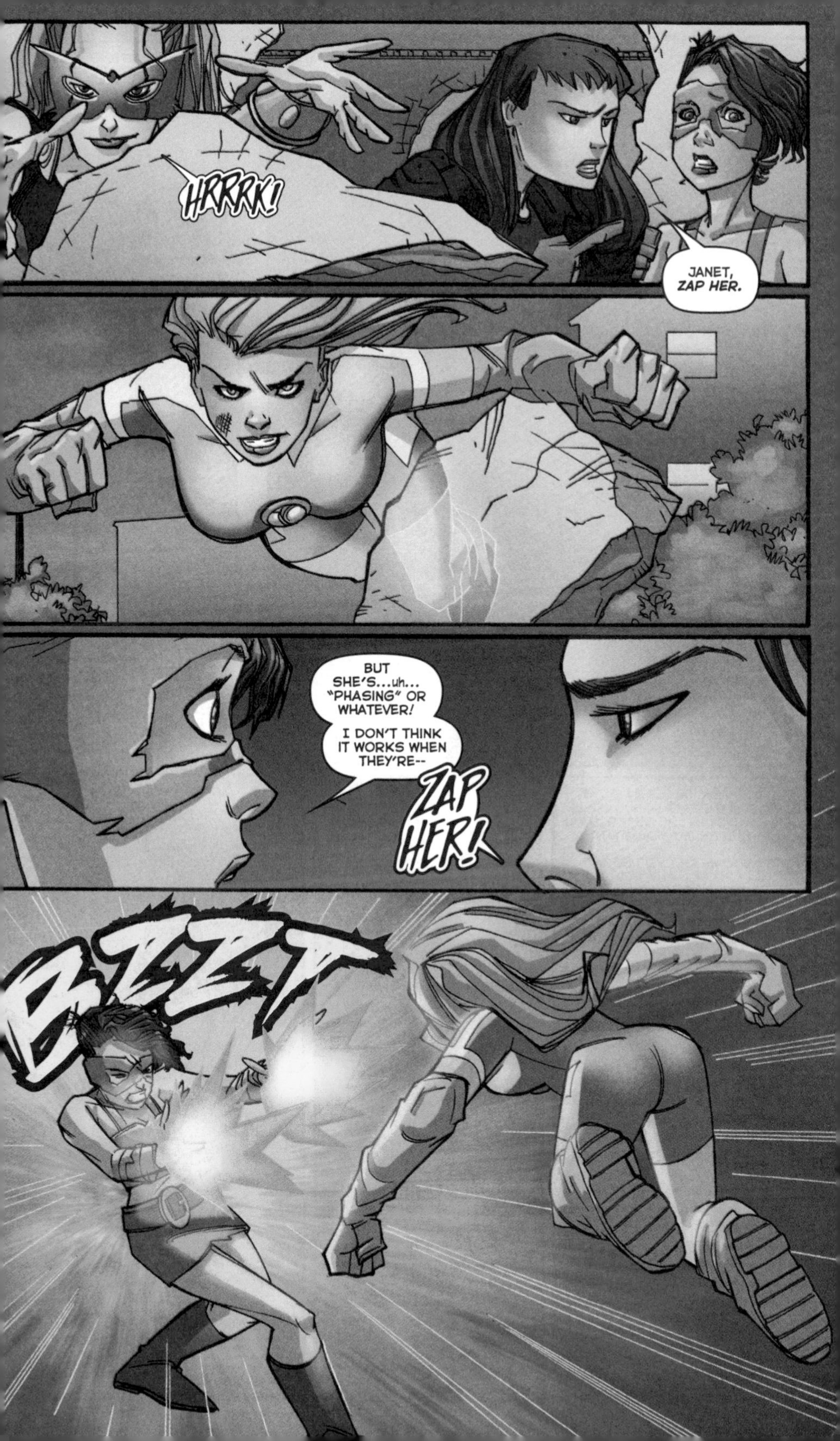
HRRRK!
JANET, ZAP HER.
BUT SHE'S...uh... "PHASING" OR WHATEVER!
I DON'T THINK IT WORKS WHEN THEY'RE--
ZAP HER!
BZZZT

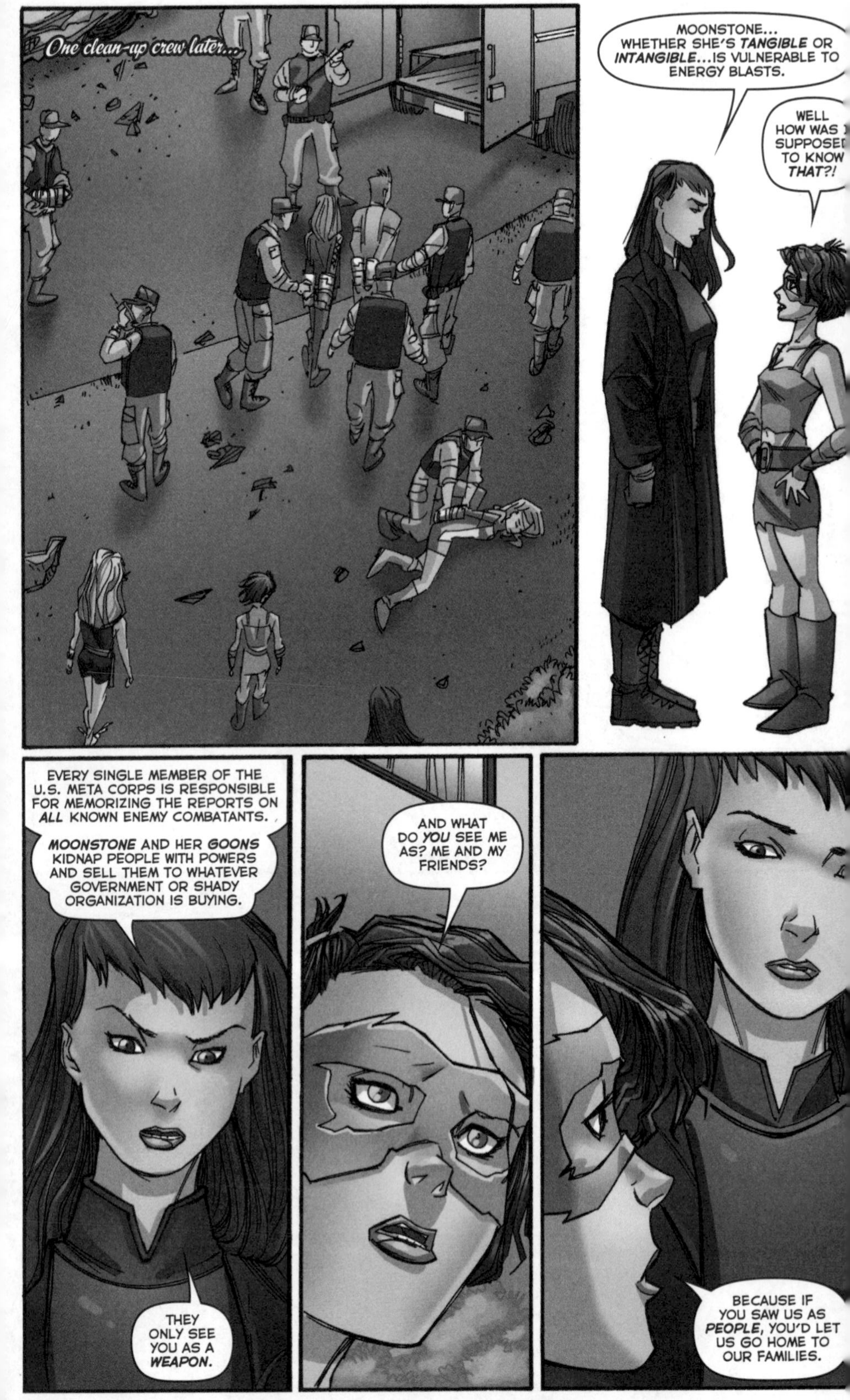
One clean-up crew later...
MOONSTONE... WHETHER SHE'S TANGIBLE OR INTANGIBLE...IS VULNERABLE TO ENERGY BLASTS.
WELL HOW WAS I SUPPOSED TO KNOW THAT?!
EVERY SINGLE MEMBER OF THE U.S. META CORPS IS RESPONSIBLE FOR MEMORIZING THE REPORTS ON ALL KNOWN ENEMY COMBATANTS.
MOONSTONE AND HER GOONS KIDNAP PEOPLE WITH POWERS AND SELL THEM TO WHATEVER GOVERNMENT OR SHADY ORGANIZATION IS BUYING.
THEY ONLY SEE YOU AS A WEAPON.
AND WHAT DO YOU SEE ME AS? ME AND MY FRIENDS?
BECAUSE IF YOU SAW US AS PEOPLE, YOU'D LET US GO HOME TO OUR FAMILIES.

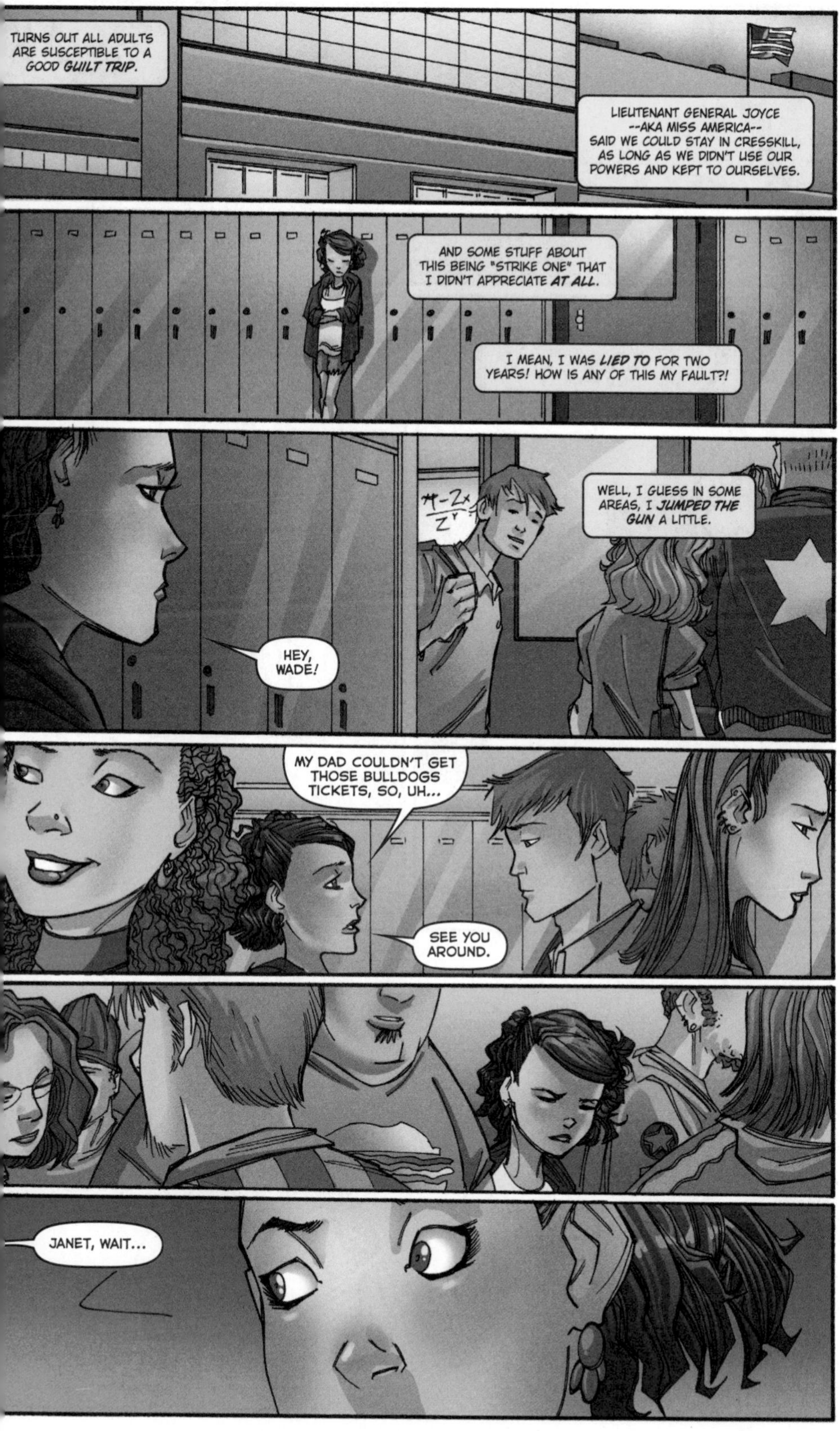
TURNS OUT ALL ADULTS ARE SUSCEPTIBLE TO A GOOD GUILT TRIP.
LIEUTENANT GENERAL JOYCE --AKA MISS AMERICA-- SAID WE COULD STAY IN CRESSKILL, AS LONG AS WE DIDN'T USE OUR POWERS AND KEPT TO OURSELVES.
AND SOME STUFF ABOUT THIS BEING "STRIKE ONE" THAT I DIDN'T APPRECIATE AT ALL.
I MEAN, I WAS LIED TO FOR TWO YEARS! HOW IS ANY OF THIS MY FAULT?!
WELL, I GUESS IN SOME AREAS, I JUMPED THE GUN A LITTLE.
HEY, WADE!
MY DAD COULDN'T GET THOSE BULLDOGS TICKETS, SO, UH...
SEE YOU AROUND.
JANET, WAIT...

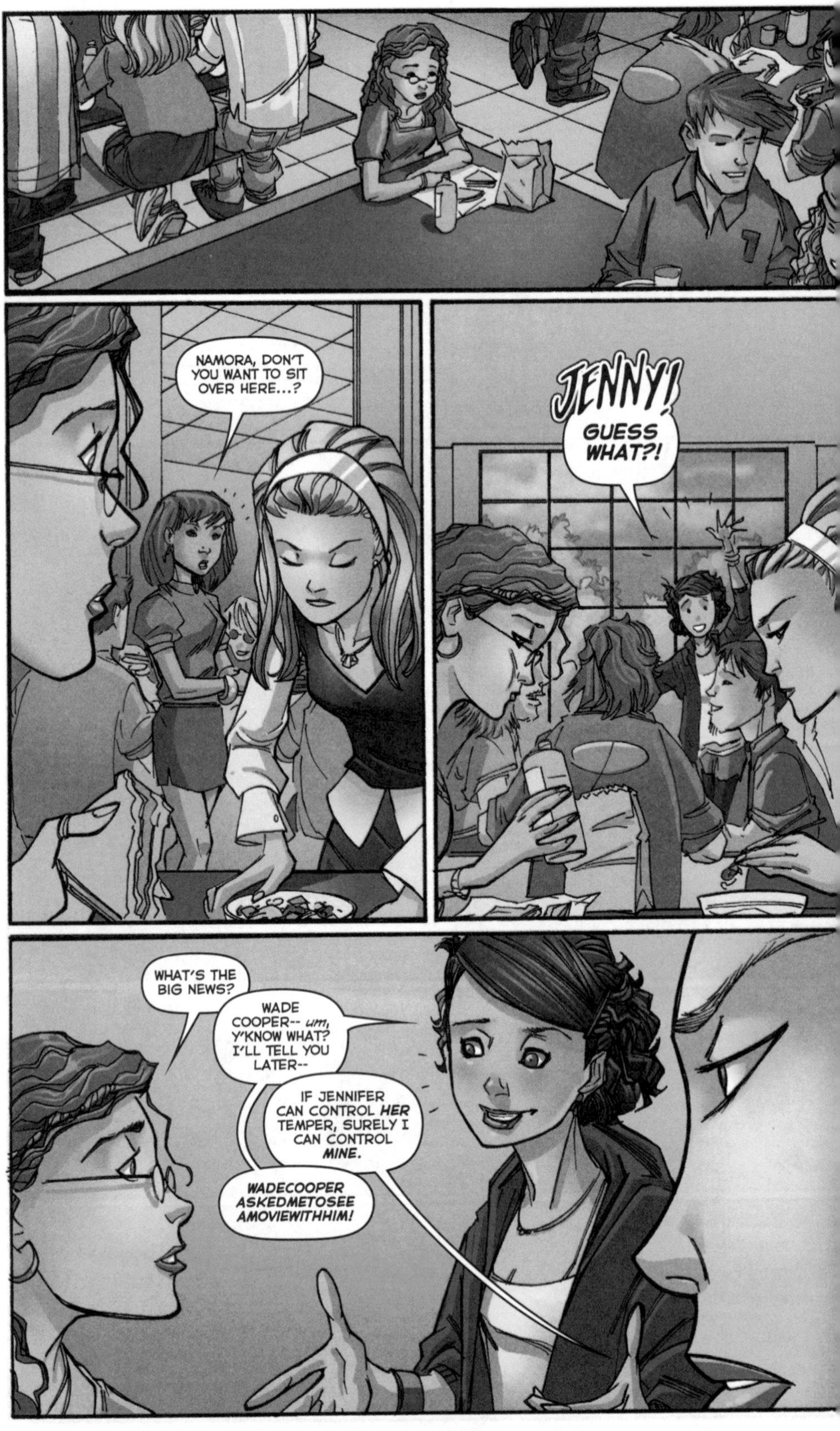
NAMORA, DON'T YOU WANT TO SIT OVER HERE...?
JENNY!
GUESS WHAT?!
WHAT'S THE BIG NEWS?
WADE COOPER-- *um,* Y'KNOW WHAT? I'LL TELL YOU LATER--
IF JENNIFER CAN CONTROL *HER* TEMPER, SURELY I CAN CONTROL *MINE.*
WADECOOPER ASKEDMETOSEE AMOVIEWITHHIM!

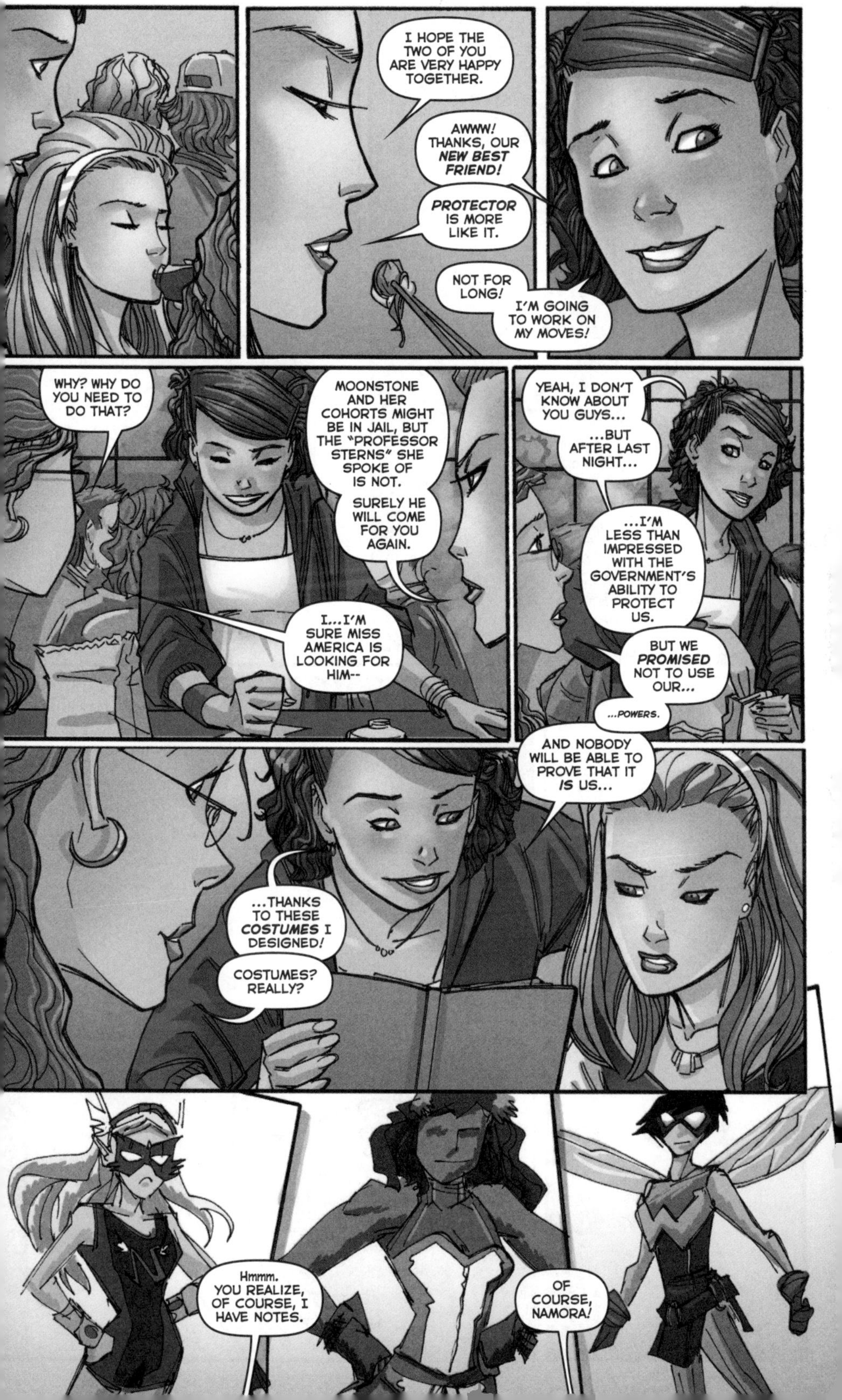
I HOPE THE TWO OF YOU ARE VERY HAPPY TOGETHER.
AWWW! THANKS, OUR NEW BEST FRIEND!
PROTECTOR IS MORE LIKE IT.
NOT FOR LONG!
I'M GOING TO WORK ON MY MOVES!
WHY? WHY DO YOU NEED TO DO THAT?
MOONSTONE AND HER COHORTS MIGHT BE IN JAIL, BUT THE "PROFESSOR STERNS" SHE SPOKE OF IS NOT.
SURELY HE WILL COME FOR YOU AGAIN.
I...I'M SURE MISS AMERICA IS LOOKING FOR HIM--
YEAH, I DON'T KNOW ABOUT YOU GUYS...
...BUT AFTER LAST NIGHT...
...I'M LESS THAN IMPRESSED WITH THE GOVERNMENT'S ABILITY TO PROTECT US.
BUT WE PROMISED NOT TO USE OUR...
...POWERS.
AND NOBODY WILL BE ABLE TO PROVE THAT IT IS US...
...THANKS TO THESE COSTUMES I DESIGNED!
COSTUMES? REALLY?
Hmmm. YOU REALIZE, OF COURSE, I HAVE NOTES.
OF COURSE, NAMORA!

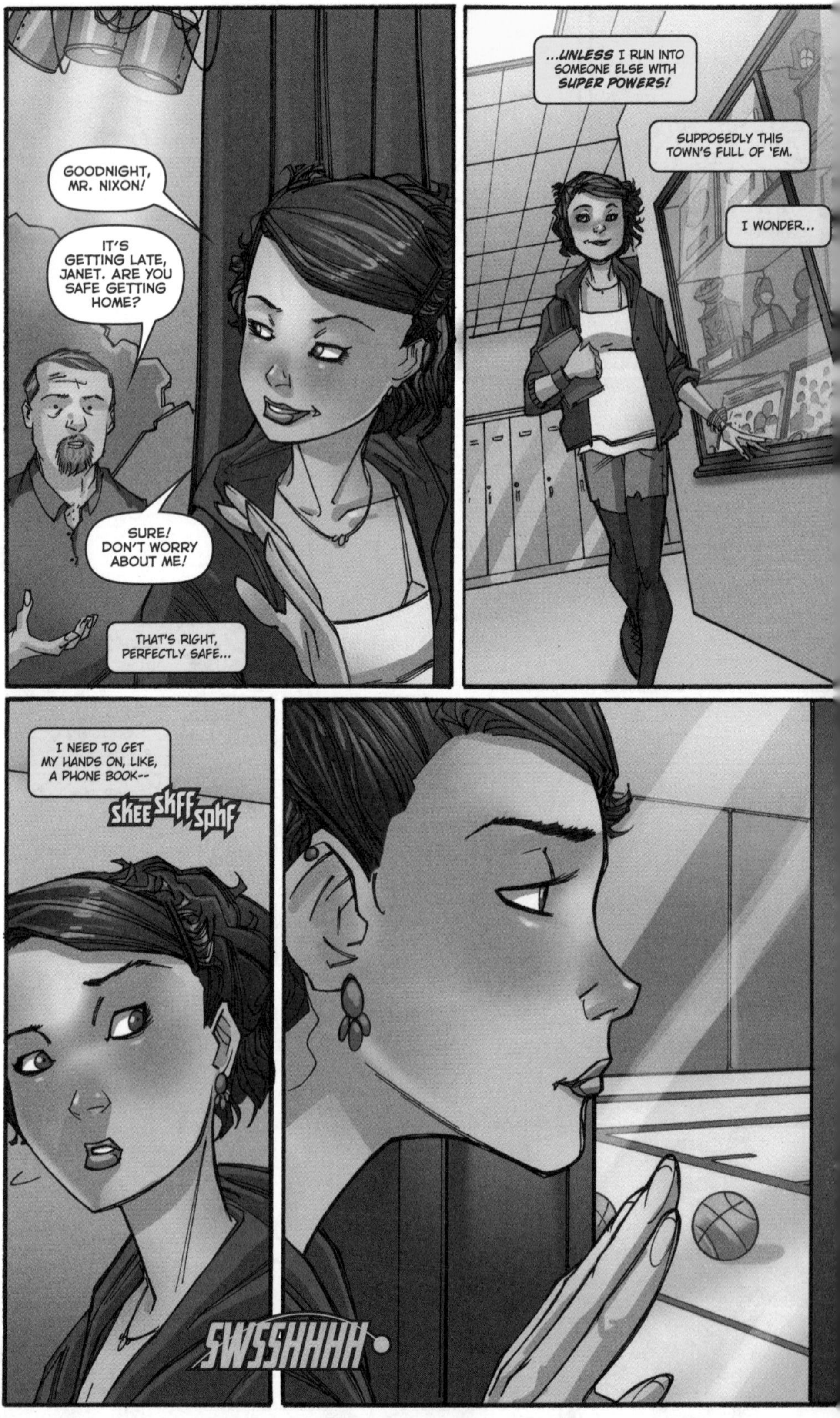
GOODNIGHT, MR. NIXON!
IT'S GETTING LATE, JANET. ARE YOU SAFE GETTING HOME?
SURE! DON'T WORRY ABOUT ME!
THAT'S RIGHT, PERFECTLY SAFE...
...UNLESS I RUN INTO SOMEONE ELSE WITH SUPER POWERS!
SUPPOSEDLY THIS TOWN'S FULL OF 'EM.
I WONDER...
I NEED TO GET MY HANDS ON, LIKE, A PHONE BOOK--
SKEE SKFF SPHF
SWSSHHHH

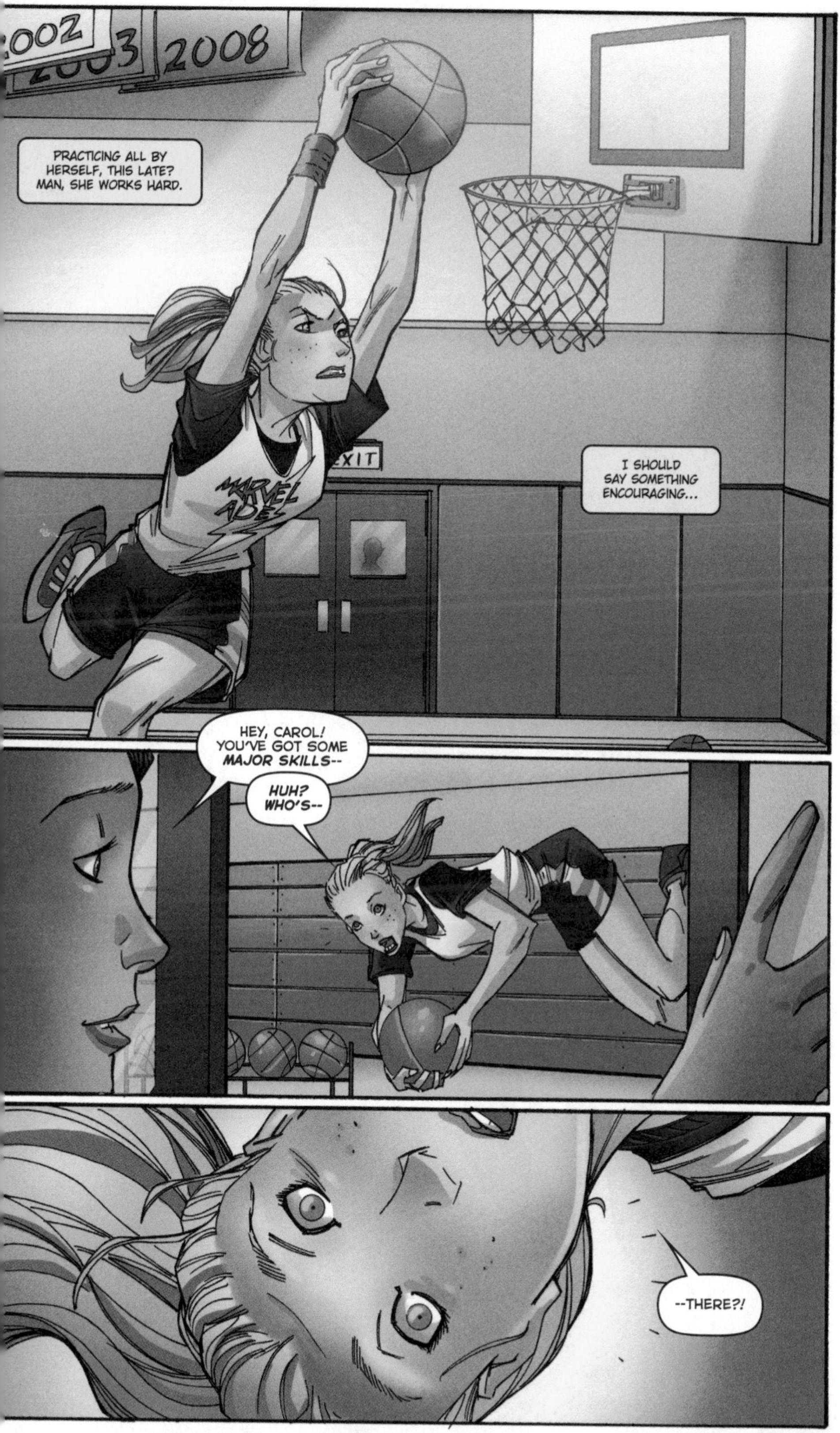
2002
2003
2008
PRACTICING ALL BY HERSELF, THIS LATE? MAN, SHE WORKS HARD.
EXIT
I SHOULD SAY SOMETHING ENCOURAGING...
HEY, CAROL! YOU'VE GOT SOME MAJOR SKILLS--
HUH? WHO'S--
--THERE?!

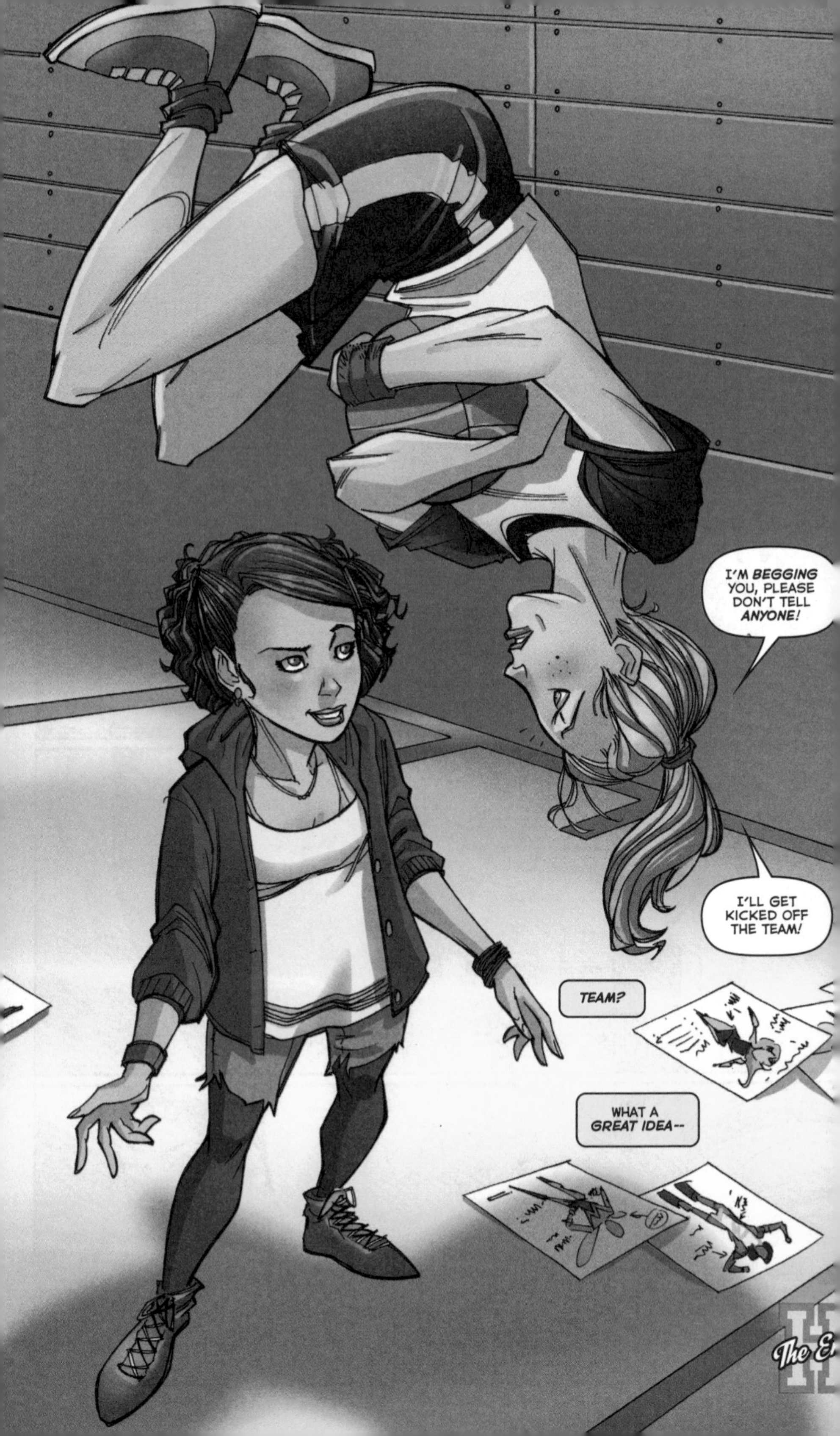
I'M *BEGGING* YOU, PLEASE DON'T TELL *ANYONE!*
I'LL GET KICKED OFF THE TEAM!
TEAM?
WHAT A *GREAT IDEA--*

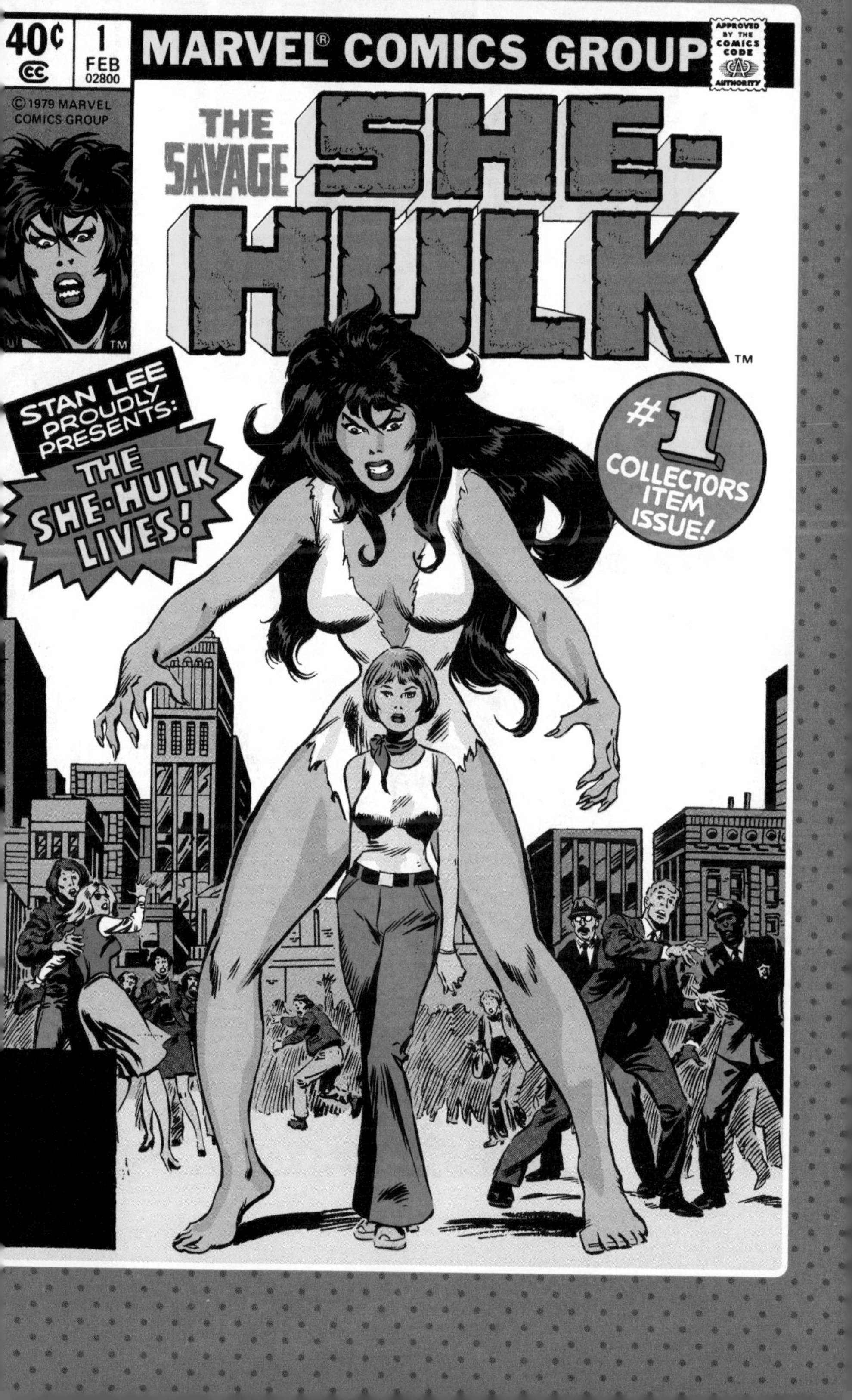
40¢
CC
1
FEB
02800
MARVEL® COMICS GROUP
APPROVED BY THE COMICS CODE AUTHORITY
© 1979 MARVEL COMICS GROUP
TM
THE SAVAGE SHE-HULK
TM
STAN LEE PROUDLY PRESENTS:
THE SHE-HULK LIVES!
#1 COLLECTORS ITEM ISSUE!

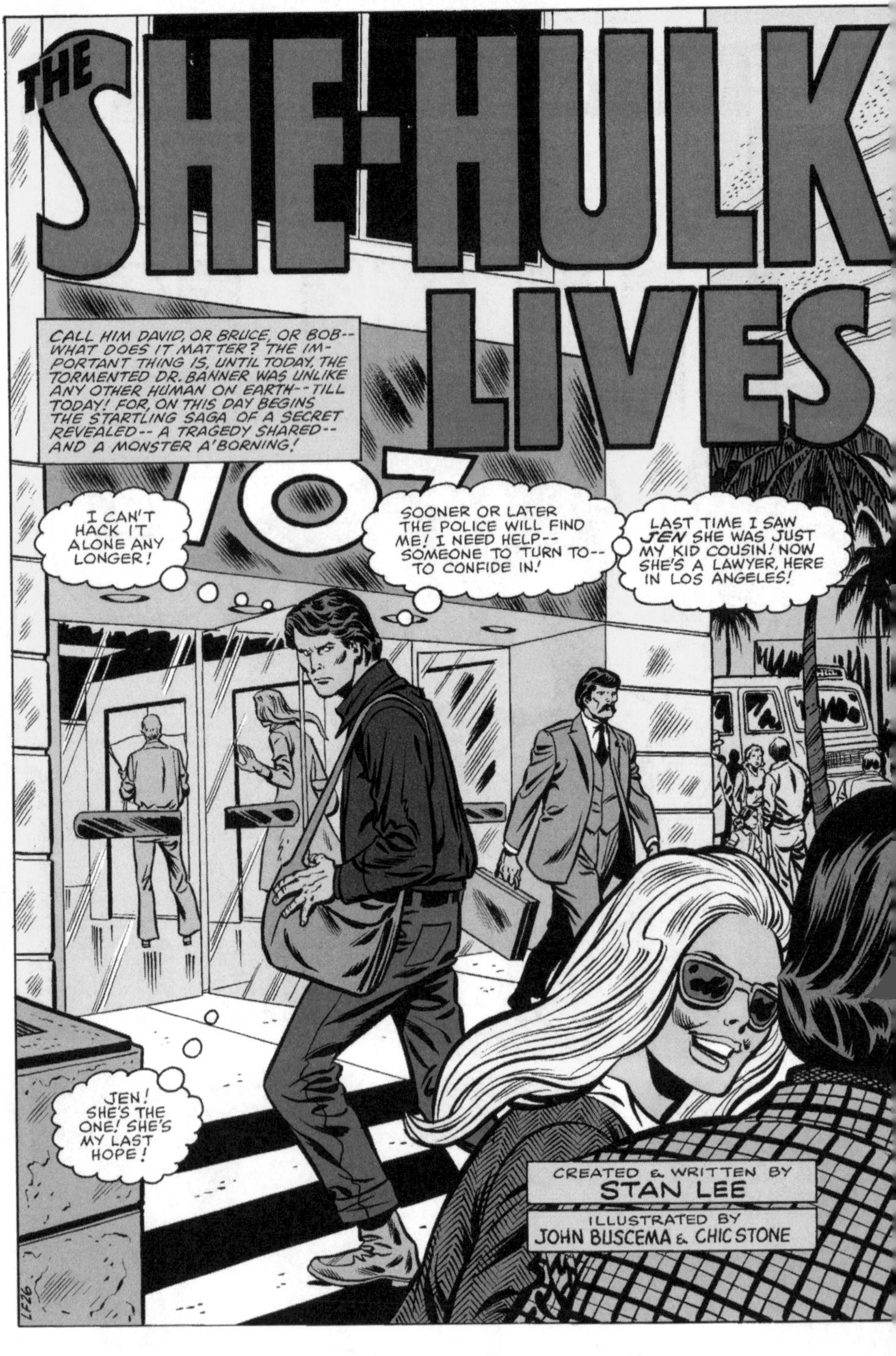
THE SHE-HULK LIVES
CALL HIM DAVID, OR BRUCE, OR BOB-- WHAT DOES IT MATTER? THE IMPORTANT THING IS, UNTIL TODAY, THE TORMENTED DR. BANNER WAS UNLIKE ANY OTHER HUMAN ON EARTH--TILL TODAY! FOR, ON THIS DAY BEGINS THE STARTLING SAGA OF A SECRET REVEALED-- A TRAGEDY SHARED-- AND A MONSTER A'BORNING!
I CAN'T HACK IT ALONE ANY LONGER!
SOONER OR LATER THE POLICE WILL FIND ME! I NEED HELP-- SOMEONE TO TURN TO-- TO CONFIDE IN!
LAST TIME I SAW JEN SHE WAS JUST MY KID COUSIN! NOW SHE'S A LAWYER, HERE IN LOS ANGELES!
JEN! SHE'S THE ONE! SHE'S MY LAST HOPE!
CREATED & WRITTEN BY STAN LEE
ILLUSTRATED BY JOHN BUSCEMA & CHIC STONE
LF26

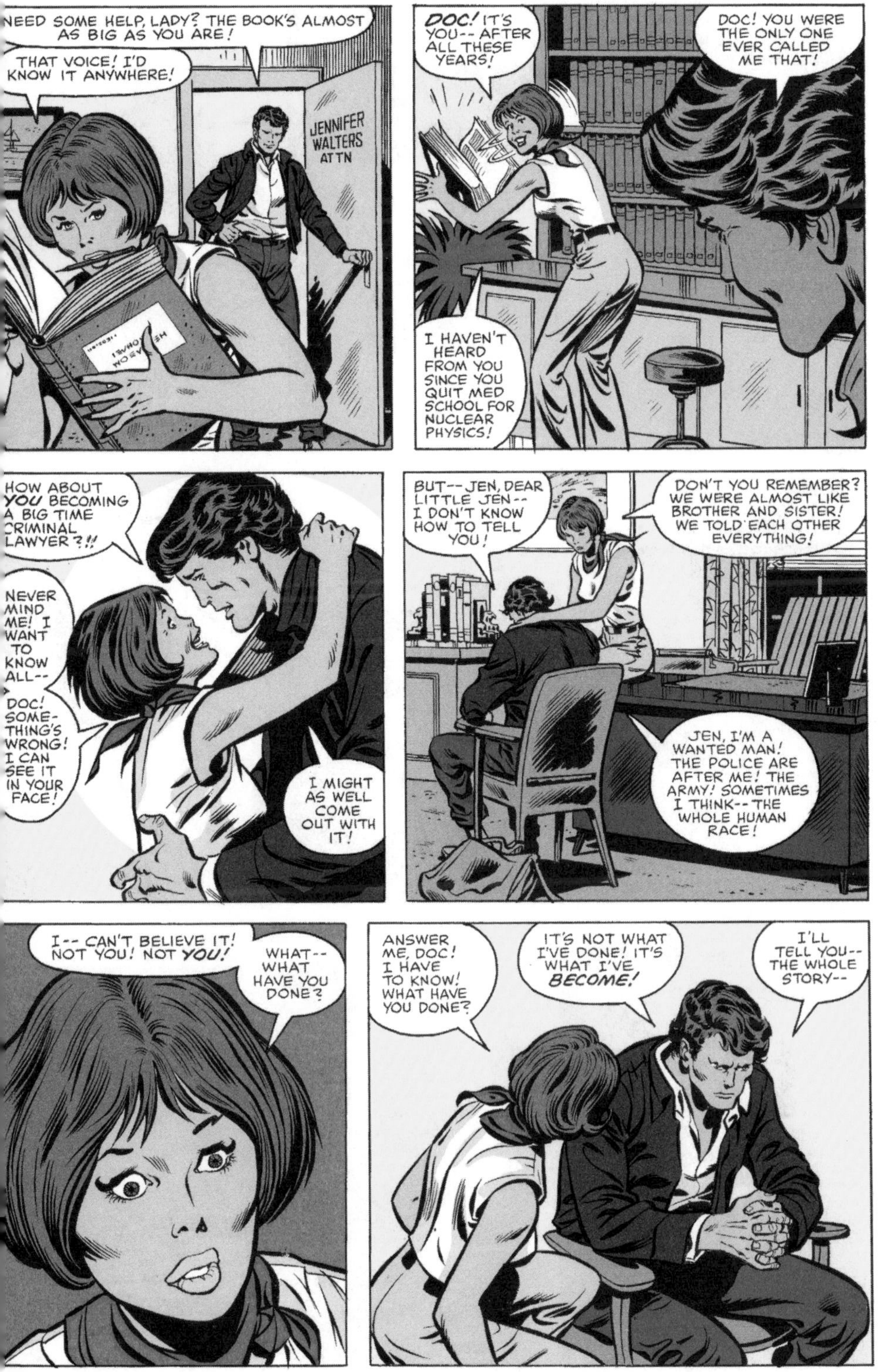
NEED SOME HELP, LADY? THE BOOK'S ALMOST AS BIG AS YOU ARE!
THAT VOICE! I'D KNOW IT ANYWHERE!
JENNIFER WALTERS ATTN
DOC! IT'S YOU-- AFTER ALL THESE YEARS!
DOC! YOU WERE THE ONLY ONE EVER CALLED ME THAT!
I HAVEN'T HEARD FROM YOU SINCE YOU QUIT MED SCHOOL FOR NUCLEAR PHYSICS!
HOW ABOUT YOU BECOMING A BIG TIME CRIMINAL LAWYER ?!!
NEVER MIND ME! I WANT TO KNOW ALL--
DOC! SOME-THING'S WRONG! I CAN SEE IT IN YOUR FACE!
I MIGHT AS WELL COME OUT WITH IT!
BUT-- JEN, DEAR LITTLE JEN-- I DON'T KNOW HOW TO TELL YOU!
DON'T YOU REMEMBER? WE WERE ALMOST LIKE BROTHER AND SISTER! WE TOLD EACH OTHER EVERYTHING!
JEN, I'M A WANTED MAN! THE POLICE ARE AFTER ME! THE ARMY! SOMETIMES I THINK-- THE WHOLE HUMAN RACE!
I-- CAN'T BELIEVE IT! NOT YOU! NOT YOU!
WHAT-- WHAT HAVE YOU DONE?
ANSWER ME, DOC! I HAVE TO KNOW! WHAT HAVE YOU DONE?
IT'S NOT WHAT I'VE DONE! IT'S WHAT I'VE BECOME!
I'LL TELL YOU-- THE WHOLE STORY--

"IT BEGAN A FEW YEARS AGO! AFTER LEAVING MED SCHOOL, I DEVOTED MYSELF TO WORKING ON THE AWESOME *G-BOMB*!"

SIX SECONDS TO COUNT-DOWN!

GAMMA RAYS! THE MOST MYS-TERIOUS POWER ON EARTH! IF I CAN HARNESS THEM--

YOU'RE A *FOOL*, BANNER!

IT'S TOO DANGEROUS! YOU'RE UNLEASHING FORCES NO MAN CAN CONTROL!

"I HAD NEVER LIKED IGOR, NOR TRUSTED HIM! BUT, BEFORE I COULD REPLY--

NO! THERE'S SOMEBODY OUT THERE!

"IT WAS A TEENAGER! LOST IN A WORLD OF HIS OWN, OBLIVIOUS TO THE WARNING SIGNS, HE WAS HEADING FOR CERTAIN *DEATH!*

"ORDERING IGOR TO *STOP* THE COUNTDOWN, I RACED TO THE SITE--!

YOU FOOL! YOU'RE IN *DANGER!*

"IGOR *BETRAYED* ME! THE COUNTDOWN *CONTINUED*, UNTIL--

KLKK

"I JUST HAD TIME TO TOSS THE BOY INTO A PROTECTIVE TRENCH-- BUT I CAUGHT THE BLAST MYSELF!

"IT WAS *THAT* BLAST THAT TURNED ME INTO THE RAMPAGING MONSTER THE WHOLE WORLD FEARS-- AND HATES--"

"--THE *INCREDIBLE HULK!*"

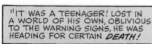

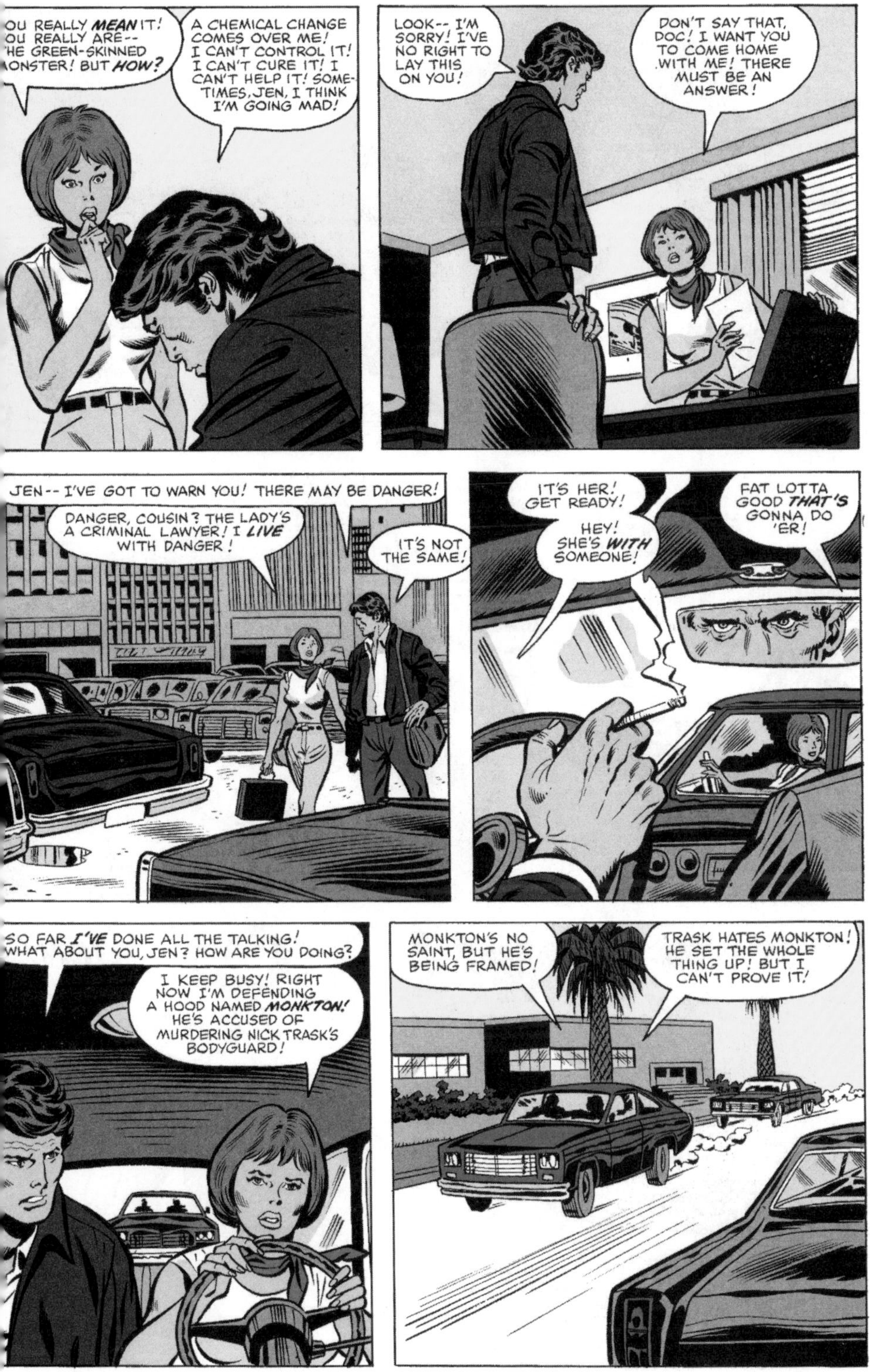
OU REALLY MEAN IT! OU REALLY ARE-- HE GREEN-SKINNED ONSTER! BUT HOW?
A CHEMICAL CHANGE COMES OVER ME! I CAN'T CONTROL IT! I CAN'T CURE IT! I CAN'T HELP IT! SOMETIMES, JEN, I THINK I'M GOING MAD!
LOOK-- I'M SORRY! I'VE NO RIGHT TO LAY THIS ON YOU!
DON'T SAY THAT, DOC! I WANT YOU TO COME HOME WITH ME! THERE MUST BE AN ANSWER!
JEN-- I'VE GOT TO WARN YOU! THERE MAY BE DANGER!
DANGER, COUSIN? THE LADY'S A CRIMINAL LAWYER! I LIVE WITH DANGER!
IT'S NOT THE SAME!
IT'S HER! GET READY!
HEY! SHE'S WITH SOMEONE!
FAT LOTTA GOOD THAT'S GONNA DO 'ER!
SO FAR I'VE DONE ALL THE TALKING! WHAT ABOUT YOU, JEN? HOW ARE YOU DOING?
I KEEP BUSY! RIGHT NOW I'M DEFENDING A HOOD NAMED MONKTON! HE'S ACCUSED OF MURDERING NICK TRASK'S BODYGUARD!
MONKTON'S NO SAINT, BUT HE'S BEING FRAMED!
TRASK HATES MONKTON! HE SET THE WHOLE THING UP! BUT I CAN'T PROVE IT!

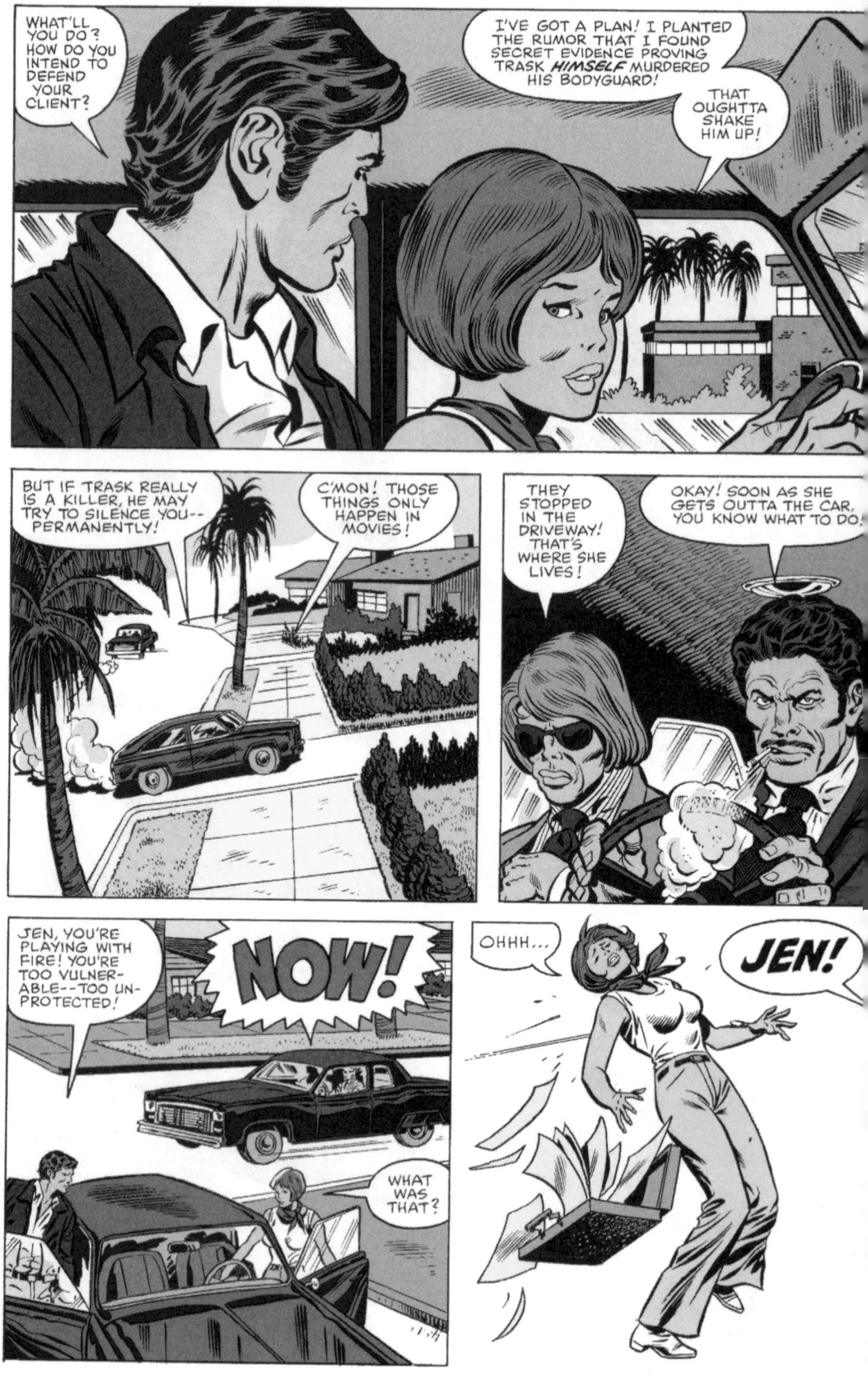

WHAT'LL YOU DO? HOW DO YOU INTEND TO DEFEND YOUR CLIENT?
I'VE GOT A PLAN! I PLANTED THE RUMOR THAT I FOUND SECRET EVIDENCE PROVING TRASK HIMSELF MURDERED HIS BODYGUARD!
THAT OUGHTTA SHAKE HIM UP!
BUT IF TRASK REALLY IS A KILLER, HE MAY TRY TO SILENCE YOU-- PERMANENTLY!
C'MON! THOSE THINGS ONLY HAPPEN IN MOVIES!
THEY STOPPED IN THE DRIVEWAY! THAT'S WHERE SHE LIVES!
OKAY! SOON AS SHE GETS OUTTA THE CAR, YOU KNOW WHAT TO DO!
JEN, YOU'RE PLAYING WITH FIRE! YOU'RE TOO VULNERABLE--TOO UNPROTECTED!
NOW!
WHAT WAS THAT?
OHHH...
JEN!

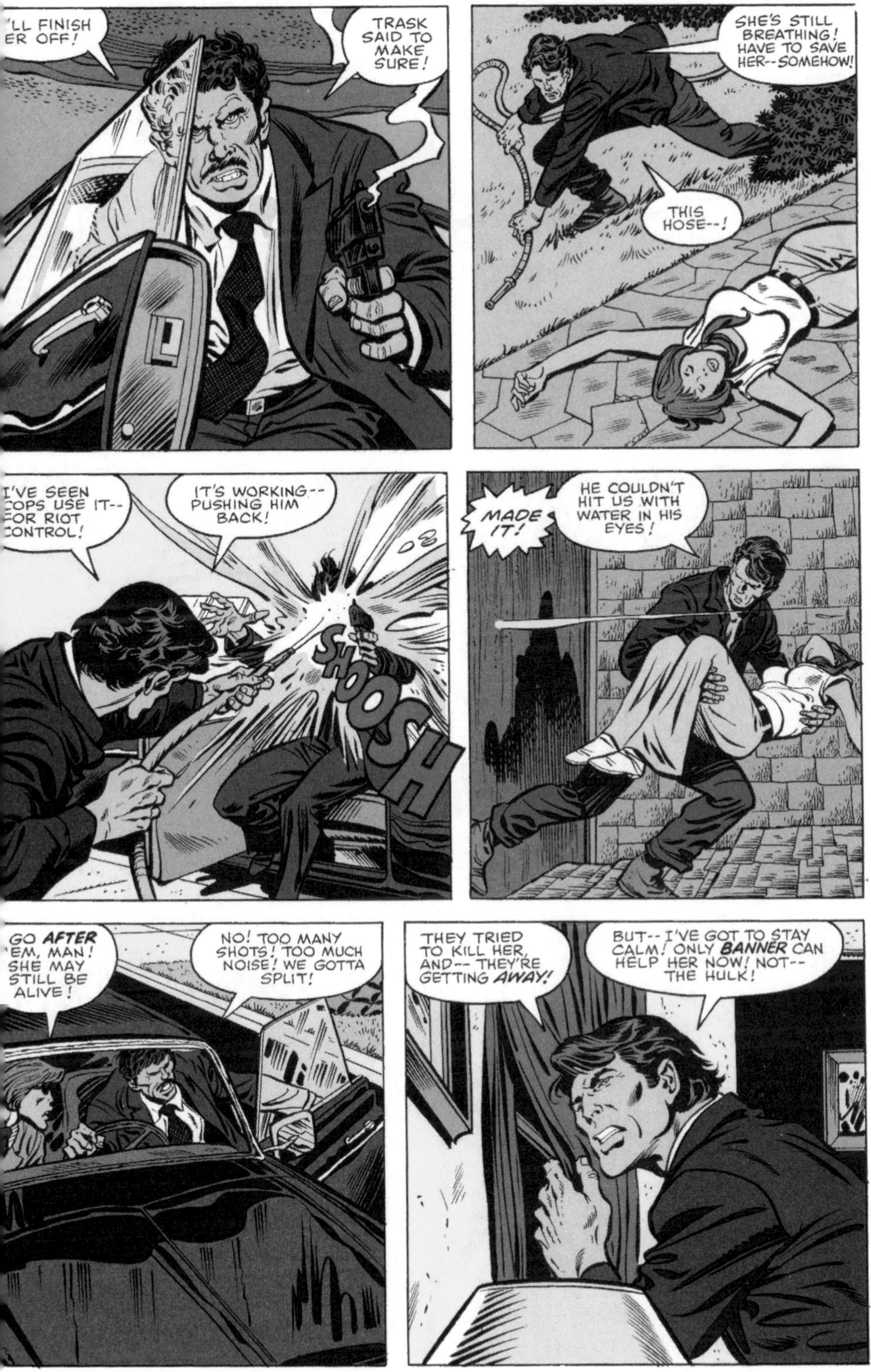
'LL FINISH
ER OFF!
TRASK SAID TO MAKE SURE!
SHE'S STILL BREATHING! HAVE TO SAVE HER--SOMEHOW!
THIS HOSE--!
I'VE SEEN COPS USE IT-- FOR RIOT CONTROL!
IT'S WORKING-- PUSHING HIM BACK!
SHOOSH
MADE IT!
HE COULDN'T HIT US WITH WATER IN HIS EYES!
GO AFTER 'EM, MAN! SHE MAY STILL BE ALIVE!
NO! TOO MANY SHOTS! TOO MUCH NOISE! WE GOTTA SPLIT!
THEY TRIED TO KILL HER, AND-- THEY'RE GETTING AWAY!
BUT-- I'VE GOT TO STAY CALM! ONLY BANNER CAN HELP HER NOW! NOT-- THE HULK!

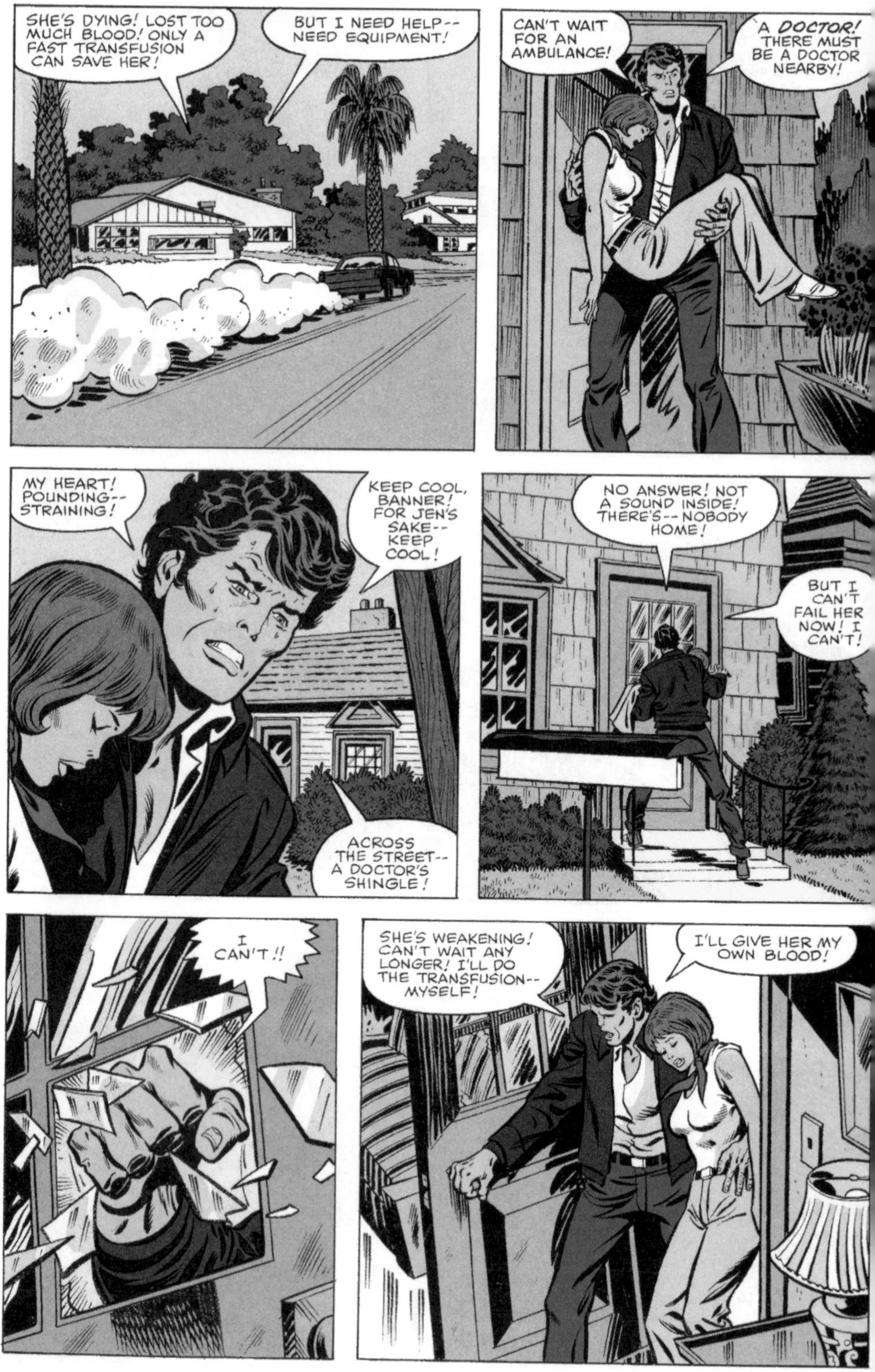
SHE'S DYING! LOST TOO MUCH BLOOD! ONLY A FAST TRANSFUSION CAN SAVE HER!
BUT I NEED HELP-- NEED EQUIPMENT!
CAN'T WAIT FOR AN AMBULANCE!
A DOCTOR! THERE MUST BE A DOCTOR NEARBY!
MY HEART! POUNDING-- STRAINING!
KEEP COOL, BANNER! FOR JEN'S SAKE-- KEEP COOL!
ACROSS THE STREET-- A DOCTOR'S SHINGLE!
NO ANSWER! NOT A SOUND INSIDE! THERE'S-- NOBODY HOME!
BUT I CAN'T FAIL HER NOW! I CAN'T!
I CAN'T!!
SHE'S WEAKENING! CAN'T WAIT ANY LONGER! I'LL DO THE TRANSFUSION-- MYSELF!
I'LL GIVE HER MY OWN BLOOD!

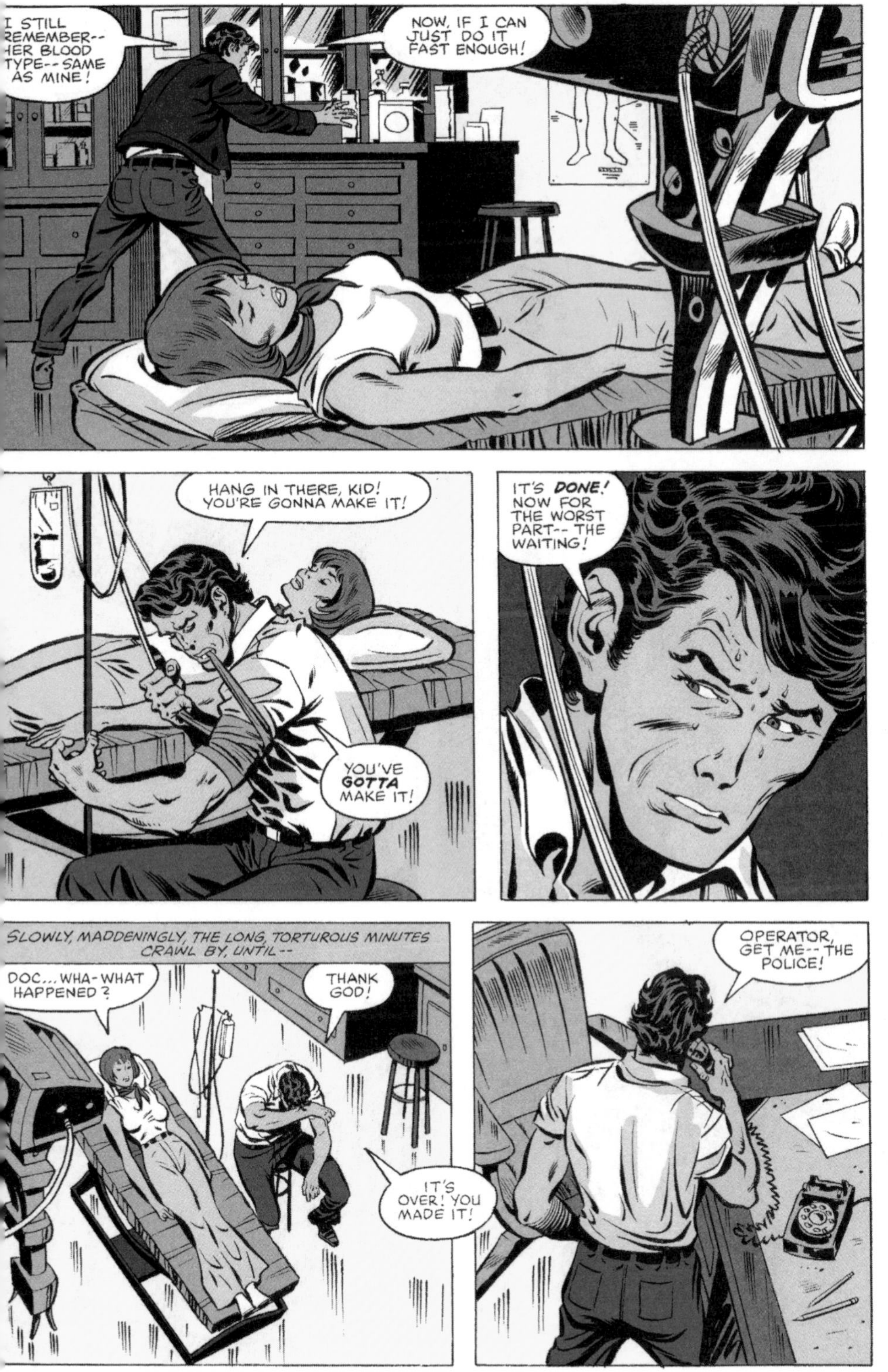
I STILL REMEMBER-- HER BLOOD TYPE-- SAME AS MINE!
NOW, IF I CAN JUST DO IT FAST ENOUGH!
HANG IN THERE, KID! YOU'RE GONNA MAKE IT!
YOU'VE GOTTA MAKE IT!
IT'S DONE! NOW FOR THE WORST PART-- THE WAITING!
SLOWLY, MADDENINGLY, THE LONG, TORTUROUS MINUTES CRAWL BY, UNTIL--
DOC... WHA-WHAT HAPPENED?
THANK GOD!
IT'S OVER! YOU MADE IT!
OPERATOR, GET ME-- THE POLICE!

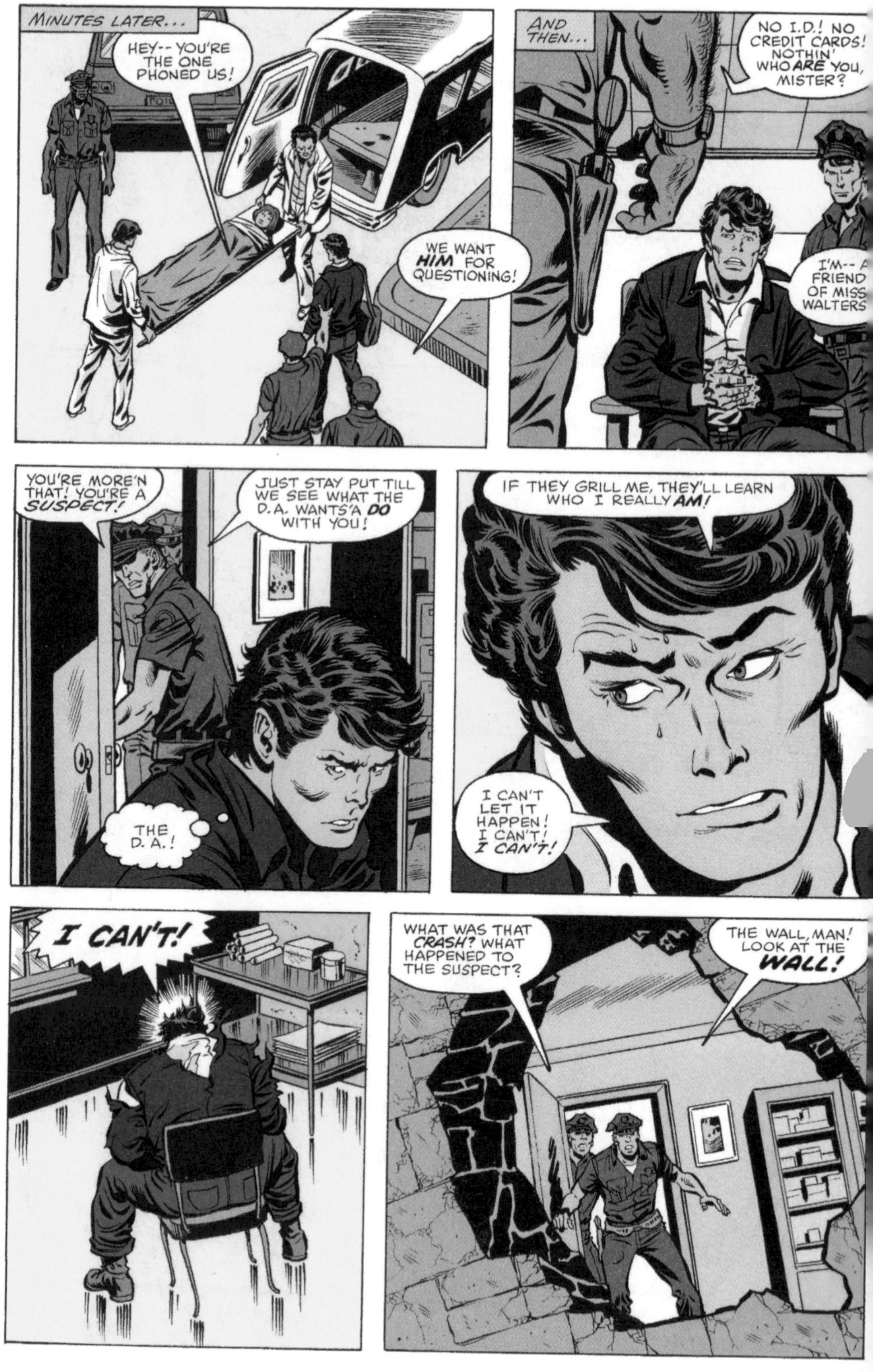
MINUTES LATER...
HEY-- YOU'RE THE ONE PHONED US!
WE WANT HIM FOR QUESTIONING!
AND THEN...
NO I.D.! NO CREDIT CARDS! NOTHIN' WHO ARE YOU, MISTER?
I'M-- A FRIEND OF MISS WALTERS
YOU'RE MORE'N THAT! YOU'RE A SUSPECT!
JUST STAY PUT TILL WE SEE WHAT THE D.A. WANTS'A DO WITH YOU!
THE D. A.!
IF THEY GRILL ME, THEY'LL LEARN WHO I REALLY AM!
I CAN'T LET IT HAPPEN! I CAN'T! I CAN'T!
I CAN'T!
WHAT WAS THAT CRASH? WHAT HAPPENED TO THE SUSPECT?
THE WALL, MAN! LOOK AT THE WALL!

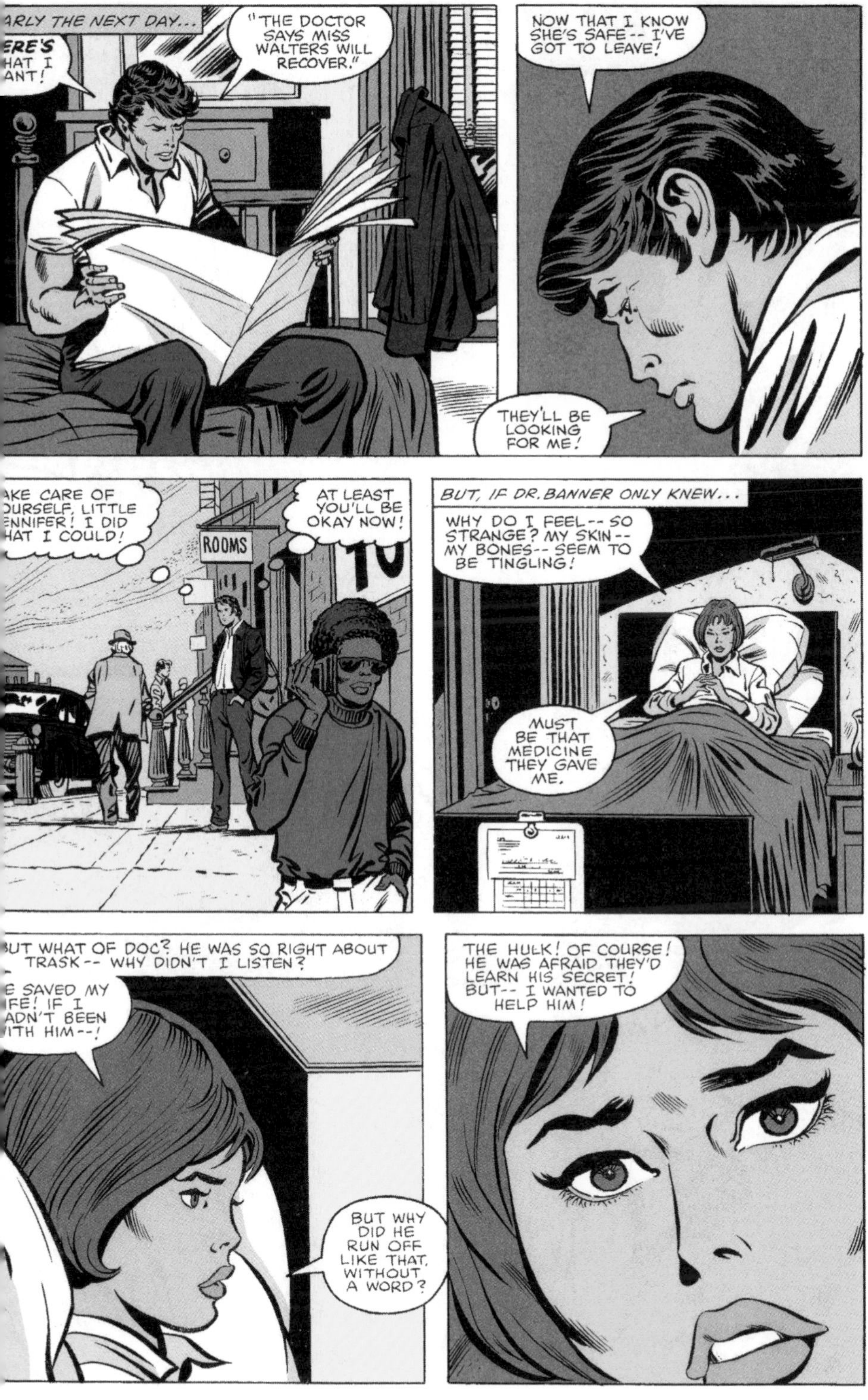
ARLY THE NEXT DAY...
ERE'S HAT I ANT!
"THE DOCTOR SAYS MISS WALTERS WILL RECOVER."
NOW THAT I KNOW SHE'S SAFE -- I'VE GOT TO LEAVE!
THEY'LL BE LOOKING FOR ME!
AKE CARE OF OURSELF, LITTLE ENNIFER! I DID HAT I COULD!
AT LEAST YOU'LL BE OKAY NOW!
ROOMS
BUT, IF DR. BANNER ONLY KNEW...
WHY DO I FEEL -- SO STRANGE? MY SKIN -- MY BONES -- SEEM TO BE TINGLING!
MUST BE THAT MEDICINE THEY GAVE ME.
BUT WHAT OF DOC? HE WAS SO RIGHT ABOUT TRASK -- WHY DIDN'T I LISTEN?
E SAVED MY IFE! IF I ADN'T BEEN ITH HIM --!
BUT WHY DID HE RUN OFF LIKE THAT, WITHOUT A WORD?
THE HULK! OF COURSE! HE WAS AFRAID THEY'D LEARN HIS SECRET! BUT -- I WANTED TO HELP HIM!

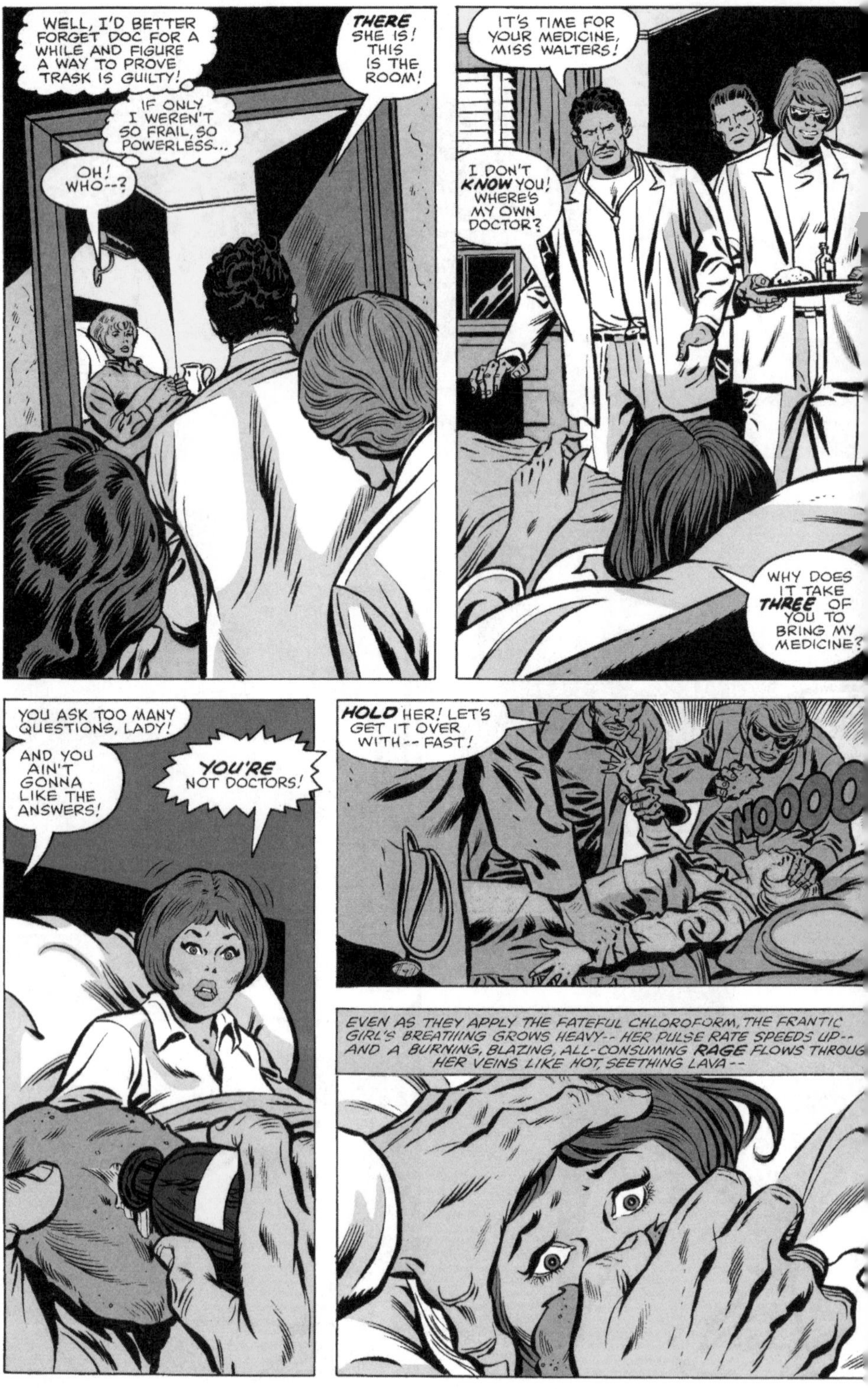

WELL, I'D BETTER FORGET DOC FOR A WHILE AND FIGURE A WAY TO PROVE TRASK IS GUILTY!
IF ONLY I WEREN'T SO FRAIL, SO POWERLESS...
OH! WHO--?
THERE SHE IS! THIS IS THE ROOM!
IT'S TIME FOR YOUR MEDICINE, MISS WALTERS!
I DON'T KNOW YOU! WHERE'S MY OWN DOCTOR?
WHY DOES IT TAKE THREE OF YOU TO BRING MY MEDICINE?
YOU ASK TOO MANY QUESTIONS, LADY!
AND YOU AIN'T GONNA LIKE THE ANSWERS!
YOU'RE NOT DOCTORS!
HOLD HER! LET'S GET IT OVER WITH--FAST!
NOOOO
EVEN AS THEY APPLY THE FATEFUL CHLOROFORM, THE FRANTIC GIRL'S BREATHIING GROWS HEAVY-- HER PULSE RATE SPEEDS UP-- AND A BURNING, BLAZING, ALL-CONSUMING RAGE FLOWS THROUG HER VEINS LIKE HOT, SEETHING LAVA--

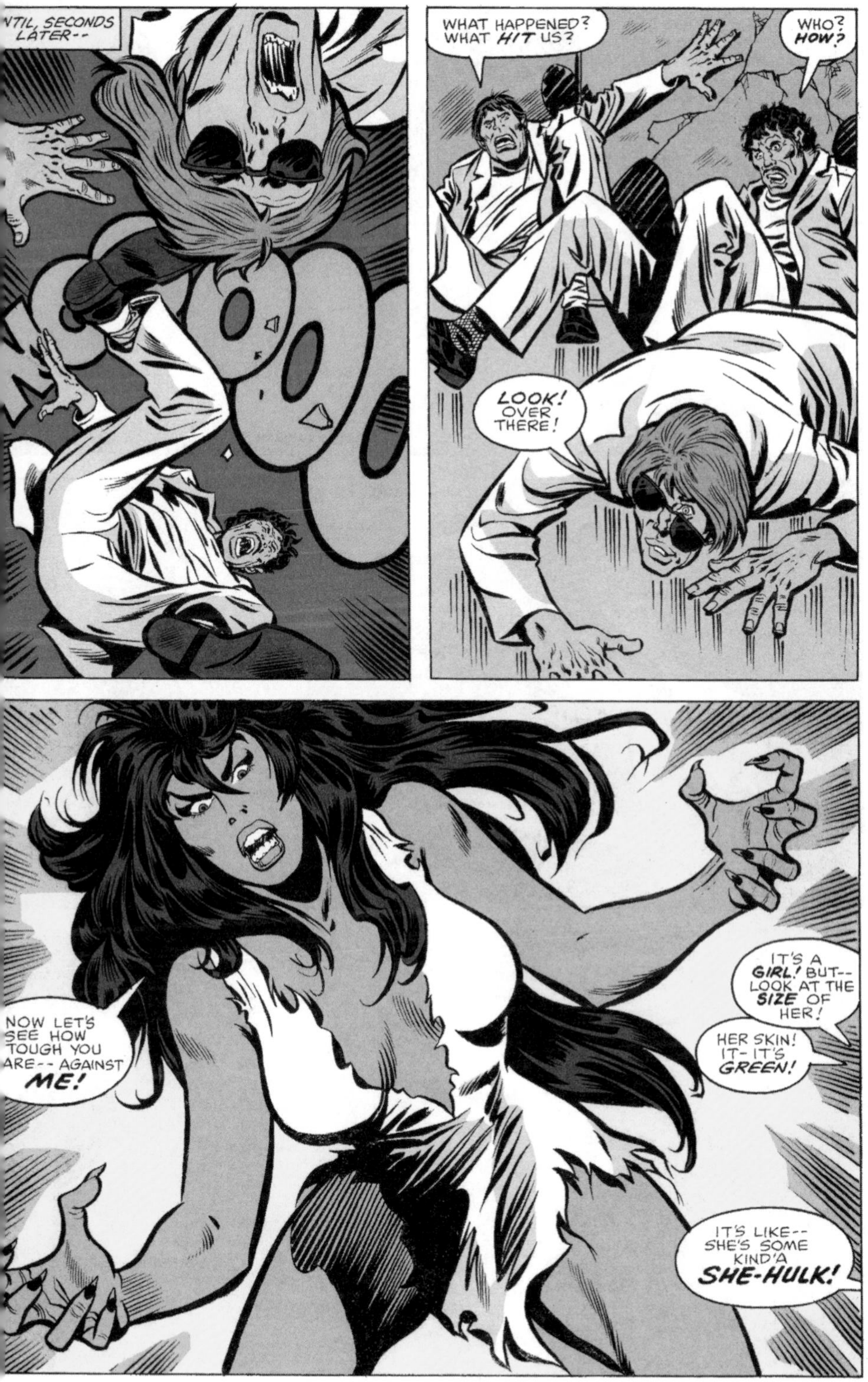
NTIL, SECONDS LATER--
WHAT HAPPENED? WHAT HIT US?
WHO? HOW?
LOOK! OVER THERE!
NOW LET'S SEE HOW TOUGH YOU ARE-- AGAINST ME!
IT'S A GIRL! BUT-- LOOK AT THE SIZE OF HER!
HER SKIN! IT- IT'S GREEN!
IT'S LIKE-- SHE'S SOME KIND'A SHE-HULK!

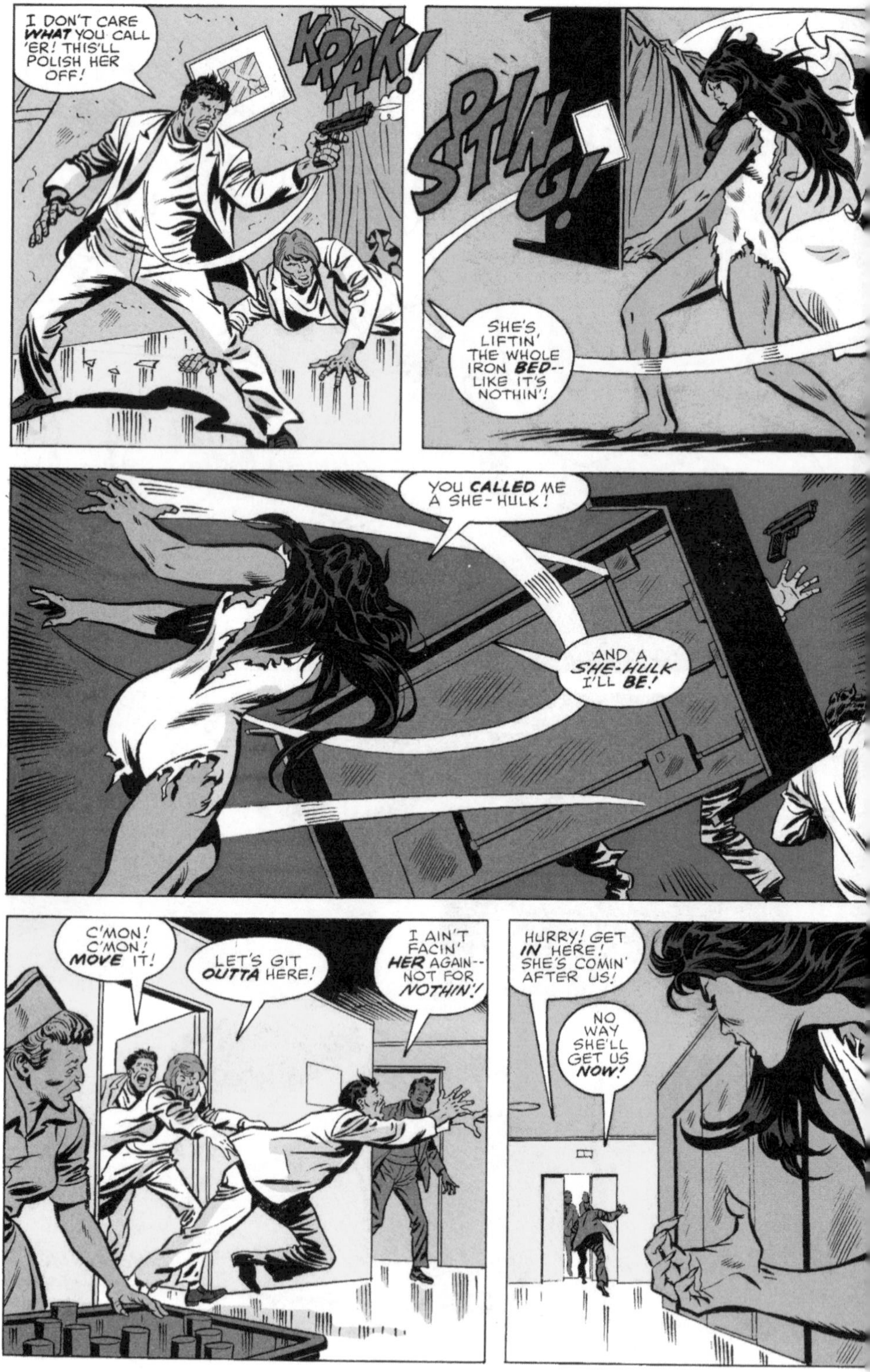
I DON'T CARE WHAT YOU CALL 'ER! THIS'LL POLISH HER OFF!
KRAK!
SPTING!
SHE'S LIFTIN' THE WHOLE IRON BED-- LIKE IT'S NOTHIN'!
YOU CALLED ME A SHE-HULK!
AND A SHE-HULK I'LL BE!
C'MON! C'MON! MOVE IT!
LET'S GIT OUTTA HERE!
I AIN'T FACIN' HER AGAIN-- NOT FOR NOTHIN'!
HURRY! GET IN HERE! SHE'S COMIN' AFTER US!
NO WAY SHE'LL GET US NOW!

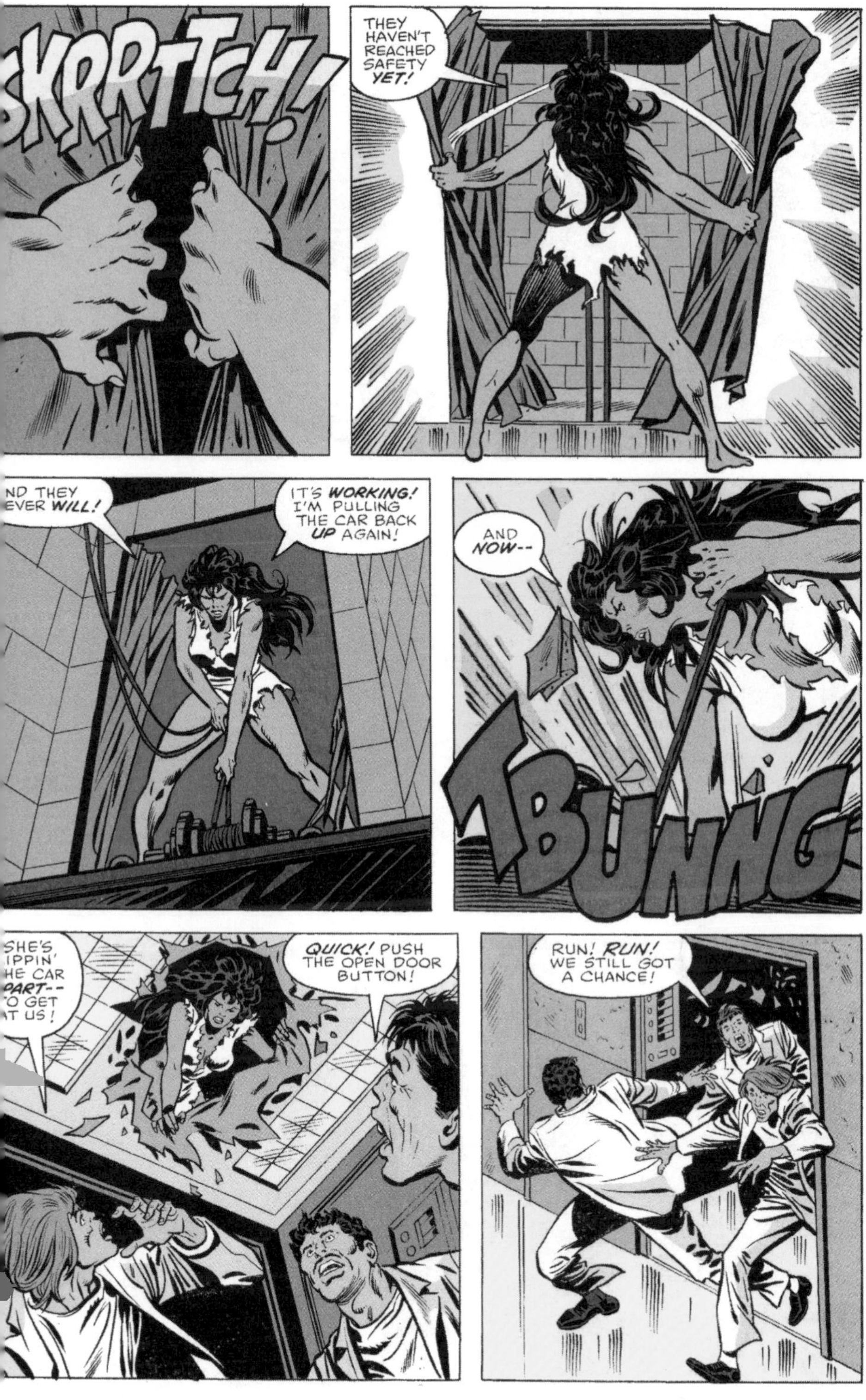
SKRRTCH!
THEY HAVEN'T REACHED SAFETY YET!
ND THEY EVER WILL!
IT'S WORKING! I'M PULLING THE CAR BACK UP AGAIN!
AND NOW--
TBUNNG
SHE'S IPPIN' HE CAR PART-- O GET T US!
QUICK! PUSH THE OPEN DOOR BUTTON!
RUN! RUN! WE STILL GOT A CHANCE!

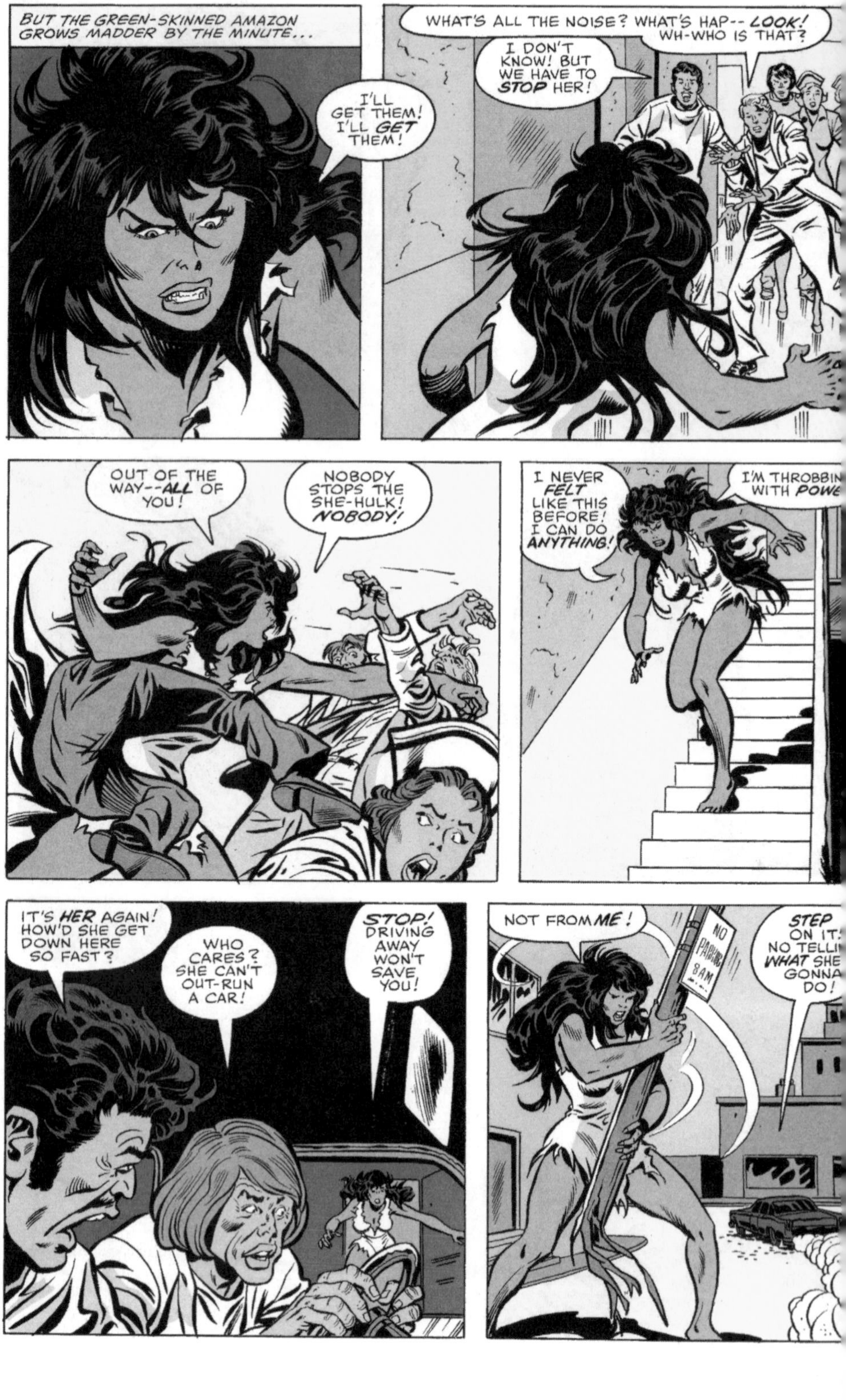
BUT THE GREEN-SKINNED AMAZON GROWS MADDER BY THE MINUTE...
I'LL GET THEM! I'LL GET THEM!
WHAT'S ALL THE NOISE? WHAT'S HAP-- LOOK! WH-WHO IS THAT?
I DON'T KNOW! BUT WE HAVE TO STOP HER!
OUT OF THE WAY--ALL OF YOU!
NOBODY STOPS THE SHE-HULK! NOBODY!
I NEVER FELT LIKE THIS BEFORE! I CAN DO ANYTHING!
I'M THROBBIN WITH POWE
IT'S HER AGAIN! HOW'D SHE GET DOWN HERE SO FAST?
WHO CARES? SHE CAN'T OUT-RUN A CAR!
STOP! DRIVING AWAY WON'T SAVE YOU!
NOT FROM ME!
NO PARKING 8AM
STEP ON IT! NO TELLI WHAT SHE GONNA DO!

HAVE THE STRENGTH NOW-- THE POWER!

I CAN DO ANYTHING!

ANYTHING!

WHAT HAPPENED? WHAT HIT US?

OH, NO! NO! YOU WOULDN'T BELIEVE IT!

SKINNG

COME OUT, LITTLE MAN! YOU'VE GOT SOME TALKING TO DO!

ANYTHING! ANYTHING! D-DON'T HURT ME-- PLEASE!

IT WAS TRASK! HE PAID US TO KILL THE WALTERS DAME!

HE WAS AFRAID SHE'D PROVE HE FRAMED MONKTON FOR MURDER!

THE MURDER THAT TRASK HIMSELF COMMITTED?

YEAH! RIGHT! I SWEAR IT!

YOU HEARD THAT! THEY'RE YOURS!

COME BACK! YOU WANT ME-- CATCH ME!

WAIT, JOE! I NEED YOU HERE! THERE'S NO LAW AGAINST GREEN SKIN!

MY ANGER'S FADING-- AND SO IS MY STRENGTH!

MUST GET BACK-- FAST!

I'LL USE THE FIRE STAIRS! NO ONE MUST SEE ME!

JUST ONE MORE FLIGHT!

I'M IN LUCK! THE HALL'S EMPTY!

I'LL HAVE T TAKE THE C NEXT-DOOR

BUT-- MY ROOM WAS WRECKED!

MISS WALTERS! WHAT ARE YOU DOING IN HERE?

I WAS FRIGHTENED! ALL THAT YELLING-- AND FIGHTING!

YOU POOR DEAR! LUCKY YOU WEREN'T HURT!

YES-- LUCKY!

THAT FEMALE SAVAGE WAS JUST HORRIBLE!

BUT DON'T WORRY-- IT'S OVER NOW!

HOW WRONG SHE IS! IT ISN'T OVER! IT'S JUST BEGINNING!

THE BLOOD TRANSFUSION MUST HAVE CAUSED IT! I'VE BECOME A GAMMA-RAY MONSTER-- LIKE POOR DOC!

BUT I'LL LEARN TO LIVE WITH IT! FROM NOW ON, WHATEVER JENNIFER WALTERS CAN'T HANDLE-- THE SHE-HULK WILL DO!

AND SO THE SAG. STARTS

NEXT ISSUE: DEATHRACE! 'NUF SAI